The Guide to Period Styles for Interiors

The Guide to Period Styles for Interiors:
From the 17th Century to the Present

Second Edition

Judith Gura

FAIRCHILD BOOKS

NEW YORK · LONDON · OXFORD · NEW DELHI · SYDNEY

FAIRCHILD BOOKS
Bloomsbury Publishing Inc
1385 Broadway, New York, NY 10018, USA
50 Bedford Square, London, WC1B 3DP, UK
29 Earlsfort Terrace, Dublin 2, Ireland

BLOOMSBURY, FAIRCHILD BOOKS and the Fairchild Books
logo are trademarks of Bloomsbury Publishing Plc

First published in the United States of America 2005
This edition published 2016
Reprinted 2020 (twice), 2021

Library of Congress Cataloging-in-Publication Data
Gura, Judith.
[Abrams guide to period styles for interiors]
The guide to period styles for interiors : from the 17th century to the
present / Judith Gura.—Second Edition.
pages cm
Includes bibliographical references and index.
ISBN 978-1-6289-2471-8 (alk. paper)
1. Interior decoration—History. I. Title.
NK1860.G87 2015
747—dc23
2015005290

ISBN: PB: 978-1-6289-2471-8
ePDF: 978-1-6289-2510-4
ePUB: 978-1-6289-2508-1

Typeset by Lachina
Printed and bound in Great Britain

To find out more about our authors and books visit
www.fairchildbooks.com and sign up for our newsletter.

To Jolie: future superstar.

Contents

Part III

19th Century: Revival and Reform   159

Part IV

20th Century: Modernism and After   257

Part V

21st century: the future is here **401**

Preface to the Second Edition

"What style is that?" is the question that prompted the first edition of this book, which was published eight years ago. It remains a key question for anyone who is interested in design, whether for professional study or general interest. By examining interiors and furnishings in their proper context, we gain a deeper understanding of the world we live in today. A new edition, therefore, seemed appropriate.

But this is not so much a new edition as a new book altogether. All of the sections have been revised, expanded, and updated; an entirely new chapter about 21st-century design has been added, along with sections on office interiors and design from the Far East. The format has been reorganized, the bibliography and glossary have been updated, and a useful chronology of styles and dates—especially valuable for students—has been added.

Most of the images are new, and there are more of them to illustrate the most important forms and ornament for each style. As in the previous edition, each section also features an image of a typical interior, as well as close-up photos of textile patterns and a list of bullet points to help identify the style.

One caution merits repeating: although the illustrations capture the essence of each style, they cannot include its every interpretation. In real life, interiors and furnishings were—and are—as varied and individual as those who create them and those for whom they are created. The in-depth study of interiors and furnishings through these four-plus centuries of history is a fascinating journey, to which this book will serve as an introduction.

Acknowledgments

Putting together a new and revised edition of this book, with a new publisher, a redesigned format, and scores of new photographs was only possible with help a number of people, and I am grateful to all of them.

In acquiring images, Erin Gillis was indispensable to the project: a skillful researcher, she was also superbly organized and meticulous at detail and follow-through.

My thanks to those who were generous with their time and their image files. From auction houses: Alex Heminway, Georgia Trotter, and Alex Gordon-Brown at Phillips; David Rago and Anthony Barnes at Rago; Darrell Rocha and Shannon Demers at Sotheby's New York, Katherine Marshall at Sotheby's London, and Chloé Brezét at Sotheby's Paris; Richard Wright and Todd Simeone at Wright. From dealers: Katelyn Remington at Associated Artists, Martin Levy and Sara Sowerby at Blairman, Alex Maas at Box House Antiques, Eric Baumgartner at Hirschl and Adler, Daniel Bruce at Hyde Park Antiques, Frank Levy at Bernard and S. Dean Levy, Tony Virardi at Macklowe Gallery, Benoist Droit and Julia Hartshorn at Maison Gerard, Katie Hollyoak at Mallett, Robert Aibel at Moderne Gallery, Frank Partridge, Christopher Johnstone at Ronald Phillips, Paul Reeves, Jaime at Pook and Pook, and Martine Baverel at Galerie Vallois. From textile firms: Beverly Phillips at Bradbury & Bradbury, Sarah Heinemann at Kravet, Ssrah Sheth and Elizabeth Nettinger at Maharam, Terry Wendell at Prelle, Andrea Rubelli at Rubelli, Solveig Ek at Unika Vaev, Elle Ferrier at Walker Greenbank. And special thanks to Oren Silverstein, Peter Rohowsky, and Andrew Gutterson for their patience with my searches, and my limited budget.

From start to finish, the Fairchild/Bloomsbury people were enthusiastic about the project, and a pleasure to work with. Thanks to Priscilla McGeehon and Stephen Pinto, who thought the book was worth a second edition, to Joe Miranda for good advice and thoughtful editing, to Edie Weinberg for making sure the illustrations pulled together, and to the designers who made the pages visually appealing.

And thanks always to my husband Martin, for unflagging patience, ongoing support, and a fine critical eye.

Introduction

The Evolution of Period Styles

People have been making interiors and furnishings for many centuries, but the concept of designing—a conscious effort to make them more attractive—only began 400 or so years ago. Those years encompass the great period styles.

Design, even at its most avant-garde, is seldom entirely new. Styles evolve in a historical continuum, each reflecting the one preceding and incubating the one to follow. And each revival of style is a reinvention rather than a reproduction, inadvertently or arbitrarily tweaking the original to suit its new environment. This grafting of new (or newish) onto old is, to some degree, predictable. It can be brought on by political pressures and cultural change, by new production methods and materials, by expanding trade, by the foibles of fashion, and by the skills and preferences of those who design and those for whom designs are made. Except for political upheavals, these changes take time to develop, as do the changes in style.

The fact that a style is new may not mean that it has improved on its predecessor; change does not necessarily equate with progress. Nevertheless, the permutations of style throughout these centuries reveal a pattern, if not of specific progress, then at least of gradual development toward a more complex and technologically advanced society in which design and designers are woven into the fabric of modern society.

The term "design" originated during the Renaissance, derived from the Italian word *disegno*, meaning drawing. It was an era of capitalism, prosperity, and the beginning of patronage of the arts, stimulating interest in domestic architecture and design. Renaissance style was actually the first period of Neoclassicism—the return to design elements from the ancient worlds of Greece and Rome. The classical orders were revived, objects like the tripod table and the curule chair were updated, and furniture craftsmen began to be regarded as artists.

With the dawn of the 17th century, changing fashions and a taste for luxury ushered in the flamboyant Baroque period, which manipulated the same classical forms into an exuberant, pompous, and materialistic style. Taking root in Italy, it reached its apogee in France under Louis XIV, spreading from there to England

and other countries and dominating Europe for more than a century. In that time, European designers created interiors and objects that are known to most of the current generation only through published images and museum exhibitions. The few surviving objects are prized by those who are fortunate enough to own them and copied by countless others. Over the ensuing years, successive reinterpretations of these defining styles merged national and international characteristics in translations that, mirroring the changes in society, reflected the slow and sometimes controversial transition toward modernity.

The 18th century was dominated in its first half by the Rococo, which brought a new lightness and domesticity to interiors, and in its second half by the most sophisticated and influential renderings of Neoclassicism among its many incarnations. The styles of this century, each capturing public fancy for a relatively brief but glorious reign, included the modest Queen Anne and the more frivolous Louis XV, the refined classical inspiration of Louis XVI and Robert Adam interiors, and the furniture of Chippendale, Hepplewhite, and Sheraton in Georgian England, as well as individualistic American variants of English designs. The styles of the 18th century are the most familiar, most easily recognized, and most frequently copied of any before the advent of Modernism.

The 19th century saw the growth of a new social order: an age of industrialization, urbanization, and conflict between a liberal new middle class and a conservative elite. In design, it was a time of both unprecedented options and cataclysmic change. On the one hand, the Industrial Revolution had made more goods available, in greater variety and at affordable prices, to a broader market than ever before. On the other hand, much had been lost in the rush to machine production, and there was a yearning to recapture the humanity and individuality of handcrafted objects.

For the first time, historic styles were not simply used as inspiration but were enthusiastically copied and exaggerated. The result was an era of revivals rather than new design ideas. Disseminated by improved transportation, exhibitions, and the first decorating guides, revival styles crossed national as well as historical boundaries, influencing architecture as well as furniture and interior design. This period marked the ascendance of the new middle class, who signaled their status in society as had the aristocracy of earlier times—by filling their homes with the finest, and most fashionable, objects they could acquire.

The 19th century also brought changes in technology that transformed the environments in which people lived and worked. In architecture and building, there were the development of cast iron, sheet glass, steel, and reinforced concrete; the engineering of bridges and railroads; the invention of the elevator; and the harnessing of electricity. In fabrics, wallpaper and carpeting, power looms, roller-printing, and jacquard weaving made available to a mass market products that were previously affordable only to the few.

By the end of the 19th century, the design of a room was dictated more by individual preference than by the structure that housed it, or even by prevailing fashion. There was, in fact, no prevailing fashion. With so many options, it was no longer possible for a single style to dominate a given period, as it had throughout history. That freedom of choice, more than any aesthetic, is the legacy of 19th-century design.

Design periods in the 20th century did not move in such clear transitions as those that preceded. Modernism, in its varied and not always successful interpretations, sought to break new ground to meet the challenges of a changed, and still changing, world. Discarding the past in its search for the future, modernism moved in several and sometimes overlapping directions, not all of them consistent in either philosophy or aesthetic. The 20th century brought a greater diversity of styles than ever before, but there was an important difference in the objects: although no two Chippendale chairs are exactly alike—even if they were made from the same drawing—a pair of Mies van der Rohe Barcelona chairs are identical factory-made products, as are virtually all modern designs. The handcrafted object is no longer the norm.

Moreover, although there were centers of style and arbiters of taste, none of these places or people mandated styles as did the monarchies or aristocracies of earlier periods. Fashion leadership had passed from the elite to a larger and more democratic community. The rise of periodicals and design magazines initiated still another influential group—the media professionals who were critics and dictators of design, rather than its users or practitioners.

Perhaps the most significant change in the modern era has been the break-down of the relationship between interior and exterior. Although some interiors are dictated by the architectural structure, most are independent of them. For the first time in history, people live in homes they did not build, in a style that is no longer current, and that they may not even like. They can choose to furnish the interiors in the most modern fashion, or, just as appropriately, may reprise a traditional aesthetic. Modern architecture itself may encourage these options, because the relative neutrality of the spaces does not impose modernity on its occupants. Even the most admired styles of the 20th century, like those of the 19th, have coexisted with other equally acceptable possibilities. They have tended to polarize designers and their clients toward either the architectural or the decorative, in an ongoing competition between restraint and extroversion.

All of the styles of the modern era, however, have several things in common: (1) acceptance (if not always full embrace) of machines and mass production, (2) acceptance of functionalism as a defining element of design, and (3) aversion to excesses in ornament. This commonality lends coherence to the styles of the 20th century and their coalescence under the general heading of Modernism.

Despite the introduction of new styles throughout the last century and into the present one, reprises of classical and 18th-century design have continued along a parallel track to the various forms of Modernism, but rejecting its per-ceived severity and commitment to restraint. Furnished with period antiques or reproductions, these interiors break with tradition in using an unconventional vocabulary of color, a random mix of pattern, and an idiosyncratic mélange of accessories and ornament. In many cases, historic authenticity is second to visual effect, but the great styles of history are kept alive through these interiors.

The 21st century has brought new directions in design and a diversity of styles rather than any single dominant aesthetic. The most pervasive influence of current design is the concern for sustainable, ecologically sensitive design, both in terms of materials and processes. Equally important are the technological inno-vations that have changed the way buildings and objects are conceived; designing with computers enables forms that cannot be drawn by hand and engineering of structures that were once impossible to build. Materials developed in the laboratory are challenging designers to create objects never before imagined, some of which cross the barriers that once separated art, craft, and design. A global community of design, and a global market, has removed international barriers, erasing differences in design from one country to another. Developments in lighting and climate control, electronics that allow interior elements to change with push-button speed, and colors that transition with changes in temperature are just a few of the options that will make interiors and furnishings of the 21st century light-years beyond anything anticipated in preceding years.

With so many possible options, the coming decades promise to bring an unprecedented variety of experimental and original design in every conceivable form and any available material. And that, perhaps, will be the defining characteristic of 21st-century style.

Understanding Styles of Any Period

The style of an interior is defined by many elements—the size and shape of the enclosing space, the backgrounds created by color and decoration, the arrangement of the contents, and the contents themselves. All are described, in broad generalizations and specific examples, for the styles in this book.

Of these elements, the most important is the furniture, which has a specific vocabulary of forms and ornament. Chairs, originally a sign of status, are the most distinctive and most accessible furniture form, and the objects most often chosen by designers to showcase their ingenuity. They are almost always the most striking signifiers of changes in style or new manufacturing techniques.

Case furniture, on the other hand, has translated forms borrowed from architecture into an entirely different genre. From simple chest to monumental armoire or bookcase, these pieces are likelier to reveal shifts in the social fabric of the home, in objects designed for particular rooms and specific purposes.

Color, in almost every period of history, has been used to define the mood of an interior. In choosing bright or muddy tones, in playing with saturated hues or soft pastels, the designer decides between drama and subtlety, assertiveness or restraint, elegance or informality. Finally, the element of pattern, or its absence, relates directly to the aesthetics or philosophical tenets of the style, as does the choice of accessories or accent pieces.

Looking at interiors and objects of the past several centuries presents a somewhat skewed picture. Unlike architecture, which is often built with the expectation of surviving into posterity, interiors are meant for current use, rather than for endurance. What survives has been, until relatively recent times, only the most costly and most carefully preserved rooms, which do not reflect the way most people lived. These artifacts of history did, however, determine the prevailing style to which the less privileged aspired. With that in mind, the picture they paint, if limited, is still authentic.

About generalizations: it is sometimes too easy, and often deceptive, to cite national characteristics in design. Nevertheless, they are often valid. Generalizations about French design may note a preoccupation with intricate detail and exquisite workmanship, a heritage of the country's medieval guild system. English design is often cited as both a reflection of its less-temperate climate and the friction between political and religious factions. Of the major period styles, those originating in America are most quixotic, with exceptions to the rules of every design style; this country's mix of émigrés, materials, and skills, and a refusal to follow the standards of the continent across the ocean, make it the most difficult to classify, and often the most interesting to examine.

No single style is presented here as the best, or most desirable, although personal biases may escape between the lines and the adjectives. Guiding the reader to choosing a preferred style is not the point of this book; its point is to show that each era had its own standards and possibilities, and its most successful designs met those standards and exploited those possibilities. All of the styles included are therefore equally worthy of respect and admiration. Hopefully, this book will help to encourage the reader to feel both.

Part I

CHAPTER 1
French Baroque: Louis XIV Style, c. 1643–1715

ABOUT THE PERIOD

The Baroque style was born in Italy, but its ultimate expression was unquestionably French. The style was imported by Catherine de' Medici, Italian bride of King Henry II, but Baroque came into its own during the 72-year reign of Louis XIV (1638–1715, reigned from 1643). It blossomed into the first of the great court styles, which elevated France to the position of fashion leadership that it would hold for more than a century.

The aesthetic education of Louis, who had succeeded his father on the throne when he was only four years old, was nurtured by Cardinal Mazarin (1602–1661), the first minister after the death of Cardinal Richelieu, and the man who virtually ruled France until his death. After that, Louis became his own chief minister and, with the assistance of finance minister Jean-Baptiste Colbert (1619–1683), used the arts as a vehicle to glorify the country he led. Colbert encouraged French industry by restricting imports, and he established the first royal manufactory at the Gobelins manufactories in Paris.

In the golden years of the monarchy, Italian-trained architects and craftsmen traveled to the royal workshops to create extravagant, profusely decorated furniture and objects for Louis' palace at Versailles. Previously a modest hunting lodge built for Louis XIII, Versailles was transformed for his son by architects Louis Le Vau (1612–1670), Jules-Hardouin Mansart (1646–1708), and Charles Le Brun (1619–1690), and landscape designer André Le Nôtre (1613–1700), into a spectacular 6,000-acre estate that became the archetype for royal residences. Its most celebrated interior is the legendary Hall of Mirrors.

Originally a derogatory term, the name Baroque (from the Portuguese word for an irregular pearl) mocked the overwrought aspects of the style—the elaborate decoration that seemed the opposite of the refined Renaissance classicism from which it evolved. Excesses notwithstanding, Baroque was the first real expression of French decorative style. It established a tradition of royal patronage of artists and designers that enriched French decorative arts, and it enhanced the prestige of the court. It is often referred to as Louis XIV style.

The Baroque style captivated much of Europe, where it was adopted for palaces and grand estates, and was particularly influential in Austria and Germany, where it intermingled with the Rococo style that followed.

ABOUT THE STYLE

Magnificent is the word that best describes the Baroque interior. Its majestic scale and sumptuous ornament reflect the grandeur of French court life. It suggests, as well, the rigid formality that suffused every activity within its walls. A convergence of sculptural ornament, rich color, and costly materials, its sheer splendor is unmatched by any other style, in any other period of history. Though smaller in scale and freer in form than those of the Italian Baroque, these French interiors are designed to impress—and still do.

The Baroque room is high-ceilinged, rectilinear, and grandly symmetrical. Walls of boiserie, heavily carved wood paneling, are painted in light colors but given added weight with massive moldings, cornices, and classical elements like pilasters, entablatures, and arches. Decorations are applied to almost every surface, usually in high-relief carving, with fluid sculptural forms that create a feeling of dynamic movement. The upper parts of the walls are adorned with painted murals or tapestries, and ceilings are also decorated, often with celestial scenes. Cherubs, floral ornaments, and acanthus leaf motifs are often combined with architectural ones. Doorways and window frames are treated as architectural elements, and the enfilade—the alignment of doorways from one room to the other—enhances the visual flow of space.

Floors are wood parquet or marble, sometimes laid with luxurious Savonnerie carpets in intricate, symmetrical patterns. The fireplace, with a heavily carved mantel, has become an important decorative element, as well as a functional one.

Textiles are major elements of the decorative scheme. Windows, extending from floor to ceiling, are hung with heavy draperies befitting the grandeur of the space. They are made of sumptuous silks, velvets, or damasks in large-scale, formal patterns or intricate florals, executed in strong contrasting colors, and fringed or embroidered with gold and silver threads. Tapestries on the walls are produced by the flourishing industries at Gobelins, Beauvais, and Aubusson.

The colors in a Baroque interior are as rich as the materials themselves, tending toward intense hues of gold, crimson or burgundy, and deep blue or green.

Monumental chandeliers of crystal, bronze, or gilded wood, and wall sconces or torchères provide illumination and ornamental accents, although most rooms of the period are relatively dark. Helping to brighten and expand the space are tall mirrors,

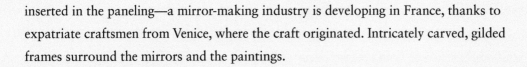

inserted in the paneling—a mirror-making industry is developing in France, thanks to expatriate craftsmen from Venice, where the craft originated. Intricately carved, gilded frames surround the mirrors and the paintings.

About the Furniture

Baroque furniture is grand in scale, to suit the proportions of the interiors. Too heavy to move, it is lined up against the walls of the room. Although essentially retaining rectilinear Renaissance forms, it has added extravagant decorations—carved cherubs and sea creatures, foliage, variations on columnar motifs, and sculptural mounts of hand-cast chased and gilt-bronze (ormolu)—so elaborate that it may obscure the outlines of the piece itself. Furniture is often made in matched suites.

Chairs are imposing, with throne-like high backs, ample seats, and ornate carved stretchers. Open arms and legs are also heavily carved. *Tabourets*, usually with X-base stretchers, are upholstered and fringe-trimmed. Elaborately decorated large storage pieces might be in the form of cabinets on ornate legs, or the marble-topped commode, which has replaced the Renaissance *cassone*. Tables are massive, generally marble-topped and trestle-based, and decorated with inlay or gilding. The console table is new in this period, as is the writing table or bureau. Four-poster beds, with testers, dominate the bedrooms. Furniture legs are generally square, evolving to cabriole shape in transitional years.

Major pieces of furniture are primarily made of oak or walnut, but other woods, including ebony for the most elegant objects, as well as chestnut, sycamore, and rare colored woods, are used for ornamental purposes. Most pieces are intricately decorated with marquetry, intarsia, *pietra dura*, lacquer, and gilding or parcel-gilding—every technique in the vast repertoire of guild-trained craftsmen has been employed to make each piece of furniture a virtual work of art.

French furniture is generally signed by the craftsman, and the names of the finest *menuisiers* (carpenters) and *ébénistes* (cabinetmakers) are often identified with particular styles or decorative techniques. In the Baroque period, the most significant of these is an intricate variation of marquetry in tortoise-shell and brass or occasionally pewter, combined with ebony and sometimes ivory. Perfected by André-Charles Boulle (1642–1732), the leading *ébéniste* of his time, it is so widely copied that the technique has become synonymous with his name.

PREVIOUS PAGE: In this depiction of the royal bedroom of Louis XIV at Versailles Palace, elaborately carved and gilded ornament exemplifies the extravagance of the French Baroque style.

BELOW: The fauteuil, an open-arm, wood-framed uphol-stered chair, was carved and usually gilded, as in these 17th-century examples.

LEFT: Typically ornate, this coffer on stand combines tortoise shell, tinted horn, brass, and pewter in marquetry on ebony, with ormolu (gilt-bronze) mounts. The c. 1710 piece is credited to André-Charles Boulle.

BELOW: Boulle-like marquetry was seen in work by several Baroque craftsmen; this bureau, with tinted horn, mother-of-pearl, brass, and tortoise shell, is attributed to Bernard Van Riesenburgh I, c. 1698. It has the characteristic ormolu mounts of the period.

RIGHT: Elaborately carved and painted, tabourets like this one would have been made in pairs. This design, parcel-gilt and white-painted, was made c. 1700.

BELOW: The console table, a form frequently seen in 18th-century France, was a wall-mounted piece often set between windows, usually beneath a tall, rectangular mirror. This one, carved and gilded, as was most Baroque furniture, is c. 1710.

One of the most celebrated forms devised in the workshop of André-Charles Boulle, whose skillful rendering of mixed-media marquetry gave his name to the process. This Mazarine commode is of ebony with tortoise shell and copper boulle-work, engraved ormolu mounts, and a marble top.

Style Markers

MOOD
opulent

SCALE
grand

COLORS
rich and saturated

ORNAMENT
profuse and elaborate

MOTIFS
columns, pilasters, pediments,
cherubs, masks

FURNITURE
massive, rectilinear, profusely
carved, often gilded

WOODS
ebony, walnut, oak

TEXTILES
rich damasks, tapestries or
velvets, large-scale patterns

LOOK FOR
gilding, Boulle marquetry,
large mirrors

Bragelonne, a densely patterned brocatelle fabric, reproduces a design dating to 1700, for an ideal complement to formal French Baroque interiors.

Damas lancé, delicately woven with gold threads, is reproduced from an archival document, dated 1700, in the design called *izarre*.

CHAPTER 2
English Baroque: William and Mary Style, c. 1688–1702

ABOUT THE PERIOD

With the return of the British monarchy after the puritanical Reformation, interiors in England began to shed the somber look of Renaissance and Jacobean décor in favor of lighter and more appealing styles. The Restoration (1660–1689) saw a revived interest in luxury and royal patronage, concepts adopted after Charles II's exile in France, and the Continental influence continued throughout the overlapping, and better-known, period that represents the Baroque in England.

William and Mary was an English translation of French Baroque, filtered through a Dutch sensibility. The reign of Dutch-born William of Orange and his wife Mary II, England's first constitutional monarchs (reigned 1689–1702), ended a long period of conflict between the crown and the nobility over religious issues by restoring Protestant rulers and bringing political stability, prosperity, and a burgeoning interest in design. The new rulers brought with them Daniel Marot (1661–1752), a French Huguenot, who became the period's most influential designer. Sir Christopher Wren (1632–1723), a follower of Palladian-inspired Inigo Jones (1573–1652), was its most celebrated architect, responsible for developing an English translation of the Baroque in buildings like St. Paul's Cathedral in London. This period of enthusiastic building included lavish town and country residences, extravagantly furnished in the height of the new fashion. In the years that followed, Britain's affluent aristocracy of landholding nobility and wealthy merchants would supplant the court as the country's arbiters of style and good taste.

Like other interpretations of Baroque, William and Mary design was characterized by grand scale and massive forms, but unlike the Italian and French versions of the style, it avoided extravagant ornament in favor of more conservative expressions. Fueled by the trade of the East India Companies, Asian influences began to appear in accessories and ornament.

As the period drew to a close, architecture retained its majestic Baroque proportions, but English interiors became less weighty and more relaxed, foretelling the advent of the understated Queen Anne style.

ABOUT THE STYLE

The English Baroque interior is an intriguing study in contrasts, reflecting both the sobriety of British tradition and the lightening-up influence of French style. Though somewhat somber and forbidding, with dark backgrounds and weighty furnishings, it is relieved by a palette of rich colors and luxurious materials, hallmarks of a style created for a privileged class.

Polished dark wood paneling, framed in heavy molding, defines the space and covers the walls, often extending to the ceiling. The monochromatic surround is relieved by rich tapestries, decorative painting, or, for the less affluent, new flocked wallpapers. In the most elegant rooms, walls and even ceilings are adorned by cascades of fruit and foliage carved by the Dutch-born master Grinling Gibbons (1648–1721).

The traditional truss-beamed ceiling associated with English Renaissance interiors has been supplanted by an elaborate plastered and painted one, with complex, curving forms that intermingle painting, sculpture, and architecture. The forms are less fluid than either Italian or French interpretations, giving a feeling of solidity rather than movement.

Floors are of dark oak, tile, or stone, with black-and-white marble squares in great halls and other important spaces. They might be accented with Oriental carpets, reflecting expanded trade with the Far East, which began after the establishment of the East India companies.

Windows are tall and narrow, often retaining the small, leaded-glass panes of earlier periods. They are hung with jewel-toned fabrics—damasks, tapestries, and velvets—over silk curtains that can be raised or lowered. In addition to their decorative function, heavy draperies help retain warmth in the chilly English climate. Printed chintzes are also used on window treatments and sometimes bed hangings.

Color schemes, although rich, are in relatively somber tones, perhaps deep blues, crimson, and green.

The fireplace remains a necessity in all European interiors throughout this century and is therefore treated as a major design element. In the William and Mary period, a heavy, carved, stone overmantel underscores its importance as a source of warmth and light.

A brass chandelier provides light and accent, and accessories of brass or silver are embossed with floral ornament. Displays of blue-and-white ceramics—real Chinese porcelain or Delft look-alikes—reflect the porcelain mania that began in this period and would obsess collectors until well into the 18th century, when Europeans at last discovered the formula for making the coveted material.

ABOUT THE FURNITURE

William and Mary furniture is straight-lined, massive, and sturdy looking. Oak has been supplanted by walnut as the primary wood, sometimes in patterned burl, and occasionally beech or boxwood are used, with lighter woods in marquetry ornament.

Chairs are narrow and high-backed, rounded at the top, and carved with floral or scroll motifs. Seats and backs of imported cane are gradually replaced by full upholstery. The draft-blocking wing chair, its side extensions serving also as headrests, has been carried over from Restoration designs. Settees, upholstered or with loose cushions, begin to appear in major rooms. Baluster, spiral, cup-turned, or trumpet-turned legs and serpentine-curved stretchers are alternatives to the elaborate carving seen in French and Italian styles, and gold accents are rare. Feet are most often finished in distinctive bun shapes or Spanish scrolls.

Case furniture remains relatively heavy, with rectilinear chests and cabinets set on sturdy ball or bun feet for a floor-hugging, substantial look. The weightiness is relieved by an extensive use of marquetry, rather than carving, as decorative ornament: delicate "seaweed" patterns and Dutch-influenced floral motifs are the most popular. Stronger and more densely grained than oak, walnut made it possible to create more refined pieces, as the cabinetmaker gradually replaced the less-skilled carpenter.

Brass hardware became decorative as well as functional. An important new furniture form has appeared: a chest of drawers has been mounted on a slightly wider and shorter chest, and raised on six legs—four in front, two in back—to create the tallboy. Also noteworthy are the elaborate carved and draped state beds, more lavish than the French objects that inspired them, seen in elite English residences.

The Asian influence has led to the invention of a technique called Japanning, in which shellac is applied over painted ornament to simulate the look of Japanese lacquer. Much furniture of this period, and even more during the Queen Anne to follow, was enhanced with this technique.

PREVIOUS PAGE: The interior of Baddesley Clinton, a manor house in Warwickshire, England, dates to the 15th century and combines elements of both Elizabethan and William and Mary styles.

ABOVE: High backs, carved ornament, and turned legs were characteristic of William and Mary chairs. The use of cane on seats and often backs reflected a burgeoning interest in materials imported from the Far East.

RIGHT: This chest on stand, c. 1700, would have been one of the most elaborate pieces in the home. The Japanned surface, simulating Asian lacquerwork, is decorated with *chinoiserie* figures, floral sprays, and birds, with gilt accents. It sits on six turned legs with bun feet, joined by stretchers.

LEFT: A William III parcel-gilt, scarlet-Japanned, brass-mounted cabinet on a stand, c. 1690.

BELOW: A chest of drawers with decorative veneered surface, in walnut and princeswood, c. 1690. In English Baroque furnishings, decorative veneering was preferred to carving, and applied ornament was generally avoided.

BELOW: A reading table, c. 1690, in walnut, which is replacing oak as the dominant wood for furniture. Turned legs and stretchers are typical of the period. The edge veneer is applied diagonally, in a technique called feather banding.

Style Markers

MOOD
grand but conservative

SCALE
monumental

COLORS
rich and somber

ORNAMENT
moderately heavy

MOTIFS
fruit, foliage, scrollwork

FURNITURE
rectilinear, massive, ball-turned legs

WOODS
primarily walnut, some burl

TEXTILES
heavy fabrics, tapestries, tassels and fringes on upholstery

LOOK FOR
wood-paneled walls, "seaweed" and floral marquetry

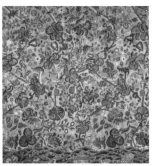

The fantastic landscape of this wool-on-linen crewel was influenced by imported Indian embroidery, reflecting the fashion for Eastern exotica.

Rich colors and fine hand embroidery suggest the type of textiles used to upholster furniture of this period.

CHAPTER 3
Early Colonial Style in America, c. 1620–1720

Early Colonial Style in America, c. 1620–1720

ABOUT THE PERIOD

The European settlers in the New World at the beginning of the 17th century (Jamestown, Virginia, in 1607 and Plymouth, Massachusetts, in 1620) were seeking both freedom from religious persecution and the promise of a prosperous life in a new land. Their first concern was with the bare necessities of food, shelter, and the simple amenities that would help them survive under harsh circumstances; their next objective was to create surroundings recalling those of the homes they had left behind.

The styles grouped under the general heading of Early Colonial include the period of the Pilgrims, incorporate variants of Jacobean design, and conclude with translations of William and Mary interiors and furnishings. Designs of furniture and objects were drawn almost entirely from English and also Dutch forms, but they were of a previous era reproduced from memory, rather than the most current fashion. These designs gradually evolved into styles that were distinctive to the new country.

The earliest Colonial homes were like peasant dwellings—single-story, boxlike structures that developed into wood-framed houses in English medieval style, covered with wood planks and clapboard siding, with brick chimneys. The classic Cape Cod cottage, a saltbox shape without a foundation, also evolved in this period.

The limitations of the new environment were considerable; with no established local trade, scarcely any skilled workers, and limited tools and materials—even nails—came over on boats with the settlers. The earliest furniture was almost medieval in its simplicity of form and almost primitive construction. But Colonial carpenters adapted quickly, devising their own substitutes for pieces they could not replicate and ornamentation beyond their skills, creating idiosyncratic pieces that were quaint, highly original, and often utterly charming in their individuality.

As the settlements grew, mercantile trade expanded and imports increased. By the turn of the 18th century, a growing market of potential customers encouraged European-trained craftsmen to establish businesses in the New World, and interiors and furnishings in the American colonies began to catch up with those they had left behind.

ABOUT THE STYLE

The early American Colonial interior seems almost primitive when compared to the European models on which it is based, and the sensation of cramped space and makeshift furnishings can make one overlook its considerable merits. In a single-story structure with only one or two rooms, a space must serve several functions, from kitchen and dining area, to guest parlor, to family room, to sleeping quarters. As the colonies develop, a second story and additional rooms will be added, but interiors for most of the 17th century remain simple, even spartan, with little planned or coordinated decoration. Utility is more important than appearance.

Despite its multiple functions, the main living space in the home is relatively small. Low ceilings with rough wood beams, walls of plain, whitewashed lath-and-plaster, and dirt or wide-plank wood floors create a bare-bones background for furnishings that are more assembled than designed. The miscellaneous mix of objects includes both items brought from home and those acquired or made locally.

Windows are small casement-style, the earliest having panes of oiled paper and later of leaded rectangular or diamond-shaped glass. They are fitted with plain wood shutters or simple sill-length curtains of cotton or linen. Homespun textiles—every Colonial housewife makes her own fabrics, for interiors as well as clothing—are supplemented by imported calico, India prints, and, only occasionally, English damask, brocade, and needlework. Floor coverings are simple handwoven or hooked rugs; imported carpets, too valuable to walk on, are used as table covers, if at all.

Like its counterparts in Renaissance Europe, the Colonial fireplace, here made of brick, is the most essential part of the main living space, providing the means for food preparation as well as heat and essential light. Flickering tallow candles are the only other source of illumination in interiors with such small window openings that, even on sunny days, admit little natural light.

Cheerful colors—bright reds, greens, and yellows—are the most appealing, and least costly, way to relieve the gloom.

Candlesticks, later supplemented by Dutch-style brass chandeliers, might be pewter (a tin-alloy substitute for silver), brass, or wrought iron. Pewter is also used for tableware and mugs. Pottery is made locally, but clocks and mirrors, available only as imports, are rare until after the end of the 17th century.

ABOUT THE FURNITURE

Furniture of the 17th century is basic and sturdy, requiring only rudimentary joinery skills, but its simplicity suits the Puritan ethic prevailing in the New England colonies. The few attempts at fashionable design reflect late Renaissance styles, with details and materials that vary according to the national origins of the makers—English, Dutch, and sometimes French in the New England area, Spanish in the Southwest. The earliest furniture consists of simple stools and benches, chests, and tables, of local woods like pine, maple, oak, elm, or cherry. The chest is the most important item of furniture; the blanket chest, made with basic frame-and-panel construction, is taller than European models, with a hinged top, and might be decorated with shallow chip-carving or brightly painted with stylized motifs like tulips and sunflowers. The Hadley or Connecticut chest, a more sophisticated variation, has a lidded top and two or three drawers, made with frame-and-panel construction. In addition to its other attractions, Colonial furniture is often painted to conceal the fact that it was assembled from bits and pieces of different woods.

Chairs are of two basic types, in the tradition of post-Renaissance oak furniture, and they are intended to denote status rather then seeking comfort: the turned chair, assembled from spindles, and requiring no special cabinetry skills, or the wainscot chair, with a paneled back and shallow-carved ornament. Loose seat cushions avoid having to accomplish the difficult task of upholstering. As Colonial woodworkers hone their skills, ladder-back and banister-back forms are added to the repertoire, and the age of the joiner progresses to the age of the cabinetmaker. Objects like the aforementioned Connecticut chest and the court or press cupboard, derived from a Dutch form as combination storage and display piece, are distinct Colonial inventions, as are combination table-chairs devised for their space-saving benefits.

William and Mary style appears at the beginning of the 18th century, in rooms that suggest the growing prosperity and sophistication of the colonials. As the settlements grow and prosper, life becomes more comfortable, living spaces become larger, and more attention is given to decorating them attractively. In more affluent homes, furniture is not necessarily more elaborate, but there is more of it.

Taller and more graceful than earlier Colonial furniture, American William and Mary pieces use more sophisticated joinery and have ball-turned or trumpet-turned legs with ball or Spanish foot and stretchers. Chairs may be upholstered or have seats and backs of imported cane, decorative Baroque carving—shallower than that in English pieces— and painted accents. The upholstered easy chair (adopted from the English wing chair) appears, as well as a daybed with a loose upholstered pad. Chests are likely to have brass mounts instead of wood knobs, and they may be decorated with a painted imitation of English Japanning to emulate Japanese lacquer. Gate-leg tables, developed earlier in England, are an indispensible space-saving solution in rooms that are still far smaller than their European counterparts. The tallboy chest, on six turned legs, has appeared on the scene, soon to become the classic American highboy.

PREVIOUS PAGE: Function rather than aesthetics dictated the interiors of early Colonial homes. This room from Plimoth Plantation, in Plymouth, Massachusetts, recreates the rough beams, whitewashed walls, and dirt floor of a Pilgrim interior.

RIGHT: Great chairs for the master of the house were turned of poplar or other local wood by Pilgrim cabinetmakers in Massachusetts. This Carver chair, c. 1685, has vertical spindles on the back; its counterpart, with spindles added to the sides, was the Brewster chair.

BELOW: Early case pieces in the Colonies reflected styles recalled from their European originals, as in this Jacobean-style chest, made in New England c. 1660.

LEFT: Generally intended to sit in a corner, the roundabout chair was adopted from English models. This piece, painted a dark reddish-brown, was made in New England, c. 1740. Much Colonial furniture was painted, adding color accents and covering pieces that might have combined several woods.

BELOW: The Hadley, or Connecticut, chest was named for the town credited with devising the form. It marries a lidded top section with a two- or three-drawer lower one. Made of oak, with shallow chip-carving or stylized naturalistic motifs, these pieces generally bore the initials of the recipient. This 45-inch-high example, unusually tall for the form, dates to 1700.

LEFT: The gate-leg table was practical for modest-sized, multifunction Colonial rooms. A rectangular form placed against the wall when not in use, it expanded via two hinged leaves that lift up and rest on pivoting supports to form a dining-sized oval.

ABOVE: Companion to the chest-on-tall-legged-chest called a tallboy, the lowboy generally had three drawers mounted on turned legs, with stretchers. This one, with trumpet-shape legs of the William and Mary era, was made in Boston, c. 1700.

RIGHT: Turned and carved, this banister-back chair is painted black, probably to conceal the fact that it was made of two different woods, maple and ash. Made in Salem, Massachusetts, c. 1720. Another popular form, the ladder-back chair, had horizontal slats rather than vertical supports.

Style Markers

MOOD
unassuming

SCALE
modest

COLORS
earth tones, bright accents

ORNAMENT
basic wood turning, split
spindles, chip-carving

KEY MOTIFS
sunflowers and tulips, hearts

FURNITURE
chests, benches, simple shapes

WOODS
local oak, pine, maple, cherry

TEXTILES
homespun wool,
handwoven cotton

LOOK FOR
spindles, chip-carving,
painted furniture

The bold floral
pattern of Istanbul
dates to c. 1640,
contemporaneous
with the period.

Charming wildflow-
ers embroidered
on a fine cotton
ground would
flatter a Colonial
interior.

Part II

18TH CENTURY:
From Rococo to Neoclassicism

CHAPTER 4
French Régence/ Rococo: Louis XV Style, c. 1710–1750

ABOUT THE PERIOD

As Baroque was the style of the court, so Rococo belonged to the nobility. Following the death of Louis XIV in 1715, his great-grandson, the heir apparent, was only five years old, and Philippe II, Duke of Orléans, served as regent until Louis XV was crowned in 1723. Philippe moved the court from Versailles back to Paris, where the nobles enjoyed a less restrictive lifestyle in the *hôtels particuliers*, the elegant townhouses that were the centers of life away from court. The pomp and formality of the Baroque gave way to the transitional Régence, evolving into the Rococo, a style of romantic imagery inspired by fantasy, fable, and the exotic Orient.

Rococo mirrored a new intimacy and informality, in fashions set by social leaders such as royal mistresses Mmes. de Pompadour and du Barry. The name Rococo, bestowed after the fact as a pejorative, combines the French words *rocaille* and *coquillage*, referring to the stones and shells that were among its most distinctive decorative motifs. Juste Aurèle Meissonnier (1695–1750) was the most prominent architect of the period, while Jean Berain I (1640–1711), his son Jean II (1678–1726), and Nicholas Pineau (1684–1754) were its most influential designers.

The Rococo style spread to other countries in Central Europe, most notably to Germany and Austria, where the Francophile princes, often employing French-trained designers, carried the style to its most enthusiastic expression. Italy remained mostly allied to classical forms, and Britain, save for the reserved interpretations of Queen Anne, rejected this charming, but undisciplined style.

The improvisatory freedom of the Rococo was ultimately its undoing, encouraging designers to frivolous expressions that were derided by critics as lacking in discipline and, more importantly, in taste. Rococo fell out of favor, to be supplanted by the more restrained neoclassical, whose popularity was also inspired by excavations at Pompeii and Herculaneum that awakened interest in the ancient world. Rococo, with its air of informality and nature-inspired ornament, is the most accessible of the French period styles; it would also prove to be the most influential, lending inspiration to styles that appeared centuries later. It is most frequently referred to as Louis XV style, after the king whose reign it dominated (1723–1774).

ABOUT THE STYLE

Smaller in scale than its pretentious Baroque predecessors, the Rococo interior is equally luxurious but far more inviting, beguiling the eye with graceful curvilinear forms and a variety of warm pastel colors. If linked to gender, Rococo is usually considered feminine, but its most uncontestable quality is that of charm.

The Rococo interior had more rooms than those in earlier periods, many designed for particular purposes, reflecting a new interest in defining separate public and private spaces. Opening off a central salon, the typical room is well-proportioned and might be in any of several interesting shapes, including ovals or octagons, depending on its intended function—as parlor, card room, or intimate boudoir. The ivory or pale-painted walls are of *boiserie*, without heavy architectural sculptured decoration; the tall rectangular panels are framed in low-relief, delicate foliate carving, touched with gilding. Later in the period, colorful wallpapers, in scenic patterns or *chinoiserie* motifs, might be set into the panels.

Over-door and overmantel panels have the same rounded corners, with inventive carved and gilded ornament; the Rococo uses more gilding than any other French period. Decorative motifs, drawn from nature, are distinctively asymmetrical—sweeping S- and C-curves expressed in forms like shells and rocks, stylized flowers and foliage, fish, wave-like scrolls, and trailing ribbons. Ceilings, joined by cove moldings rather than cornices, have arabesque patterns of plasterwork, often enhanced by painted motifs or occasionally the illusion of a cloud-dotted sky.

Floors are wood parquet or herringbone pattern, tile or terra cotta, most likely laid with elegant Savonnerie or Aubusson carpets in patterns designed with the characteristic floral and curvilinear motifs of the period.

At the full-height windows, cornice-topped draperies, generally in warm pastels, might be embroidered with patterns of flowers or foliage. Light is provided by airy crystal chandeliers, wall sconces, or *girandôles*. Baccarat, the first glass factory in France, was founded during Louis XV's reign, providing a local source for glass and mirrors, which were previously imported from Italy. The mantelpiece, still a focal point, underscores a tall, elegantly framed mirror, celebrating the French mastery in producing larger sheets of glass. Mirrors might also be installed between the windows, over a console table.

An important component of the Rococo interior is that colors are softer and more varied, in appealing combinations of ice-cream pastels, including warm blues, pale yellows, and lively seafoam.

Fanciful imagery also marks the decorative objects on tabletops and mantels, including gilded clocks, gilt-bronze (ormolu) candlesticks, Sèvres porcelain vases, and imported Chinese ceramics. Ornament is central to Rococo décor, often to the point of subsuming form.

ABOUT THE FURNITURE

Rococo furniture is far more sophisticated in construction than that of the Baroque. It is instantly identifiable by its graceful, rounded silhouettes and shapely cabriole legs, ending in small scroll feet. Invitingly curvy chairs and sofas, upholstered with loose seat cushions, are in a variety of forms, all bearing names such as *marquise, canapé a corbeille, veilleuse*, and *duchesse*. Elegant and light-scaled, with carved frames and shaped backs, they may be placed away from the walls of the room and moved around as needed. Stretchers have disappeared, and arms are set back from the front of the seat to accommodate the billowing skirts worn by ladies of the period. Rich upholstery, with overstuffed loose seat cushions that reveal a new concern for comfort as well as fashion, reflects the domesticity of this style.

In its fully developed form, the commode is also curvilinear, with splendidly bombé sides, undulating fronts, and short, curved legs. New forms have been invented: writing desks, card tables, music stands, dressing tables, and occasional tables, many with specialized functions in particular rooms. As with seating pieces, each has its own name: *chiffonier, bureau plat, bureau à cylindre*, and *sécretaire à abattant*. Although chairs are most often painted, case pieces employ a variety of decorative wood veneers, including mahogany, rosewood, cherry, pear, and ebony, and might be adorned with floral marquetry, inlaid porcelain plaques, paint, or Chinese lacquerwork. Musical instruments and pastoral images are also used, and many pieces are accented with the gilt or ormolu mounts that distinguish French period furniture. Leading craftsmen of this time included Charles Cressent (1685–1768), Martin Carlin (1730–1785), and Jean-Francois Oeben (1721–1763).

■ French Provincial

As the styles of the French court gained popularity, they were translated into simpler and often smaller-scaled adaptations for country homes and less ostentatious interiors. French Provincial, more informally known as French Country Style, mutes the exuberance of Louis XV design into a less showy, more serene, and considerably less labor-intensive rendering of Rococo.

The French Provincial interior strips off the elaborate Rococo framework of *boiserie* and ornament, replacing it with light wood or fabric-covered walls. The curvilinear silhouettes and asymmetry of the style adapt well to such understatement, which retains its outlines but avoids carving beyond simple panel shapes. In lighter and more accessible local woods, the furniture is better suited to the ambience of a country residence and more affordable as well. Finishes avoid the high-gloss, high-maintenance French polishes, gilding, and lacquers used in the more elaborate original style.

Window treatments are also simpler, often using the printed linen toiles in bucolic pastoral scenes that have become associated with French Provincial. It is an evolution of the country's most fashionable style, rendered with a lighter hand and a more casual air.

Warm fruitwood *boiserie* provides a backdrop for an informal arrangement of Provincial style furniture, with Louis XV forms, but minimal carving and no polish, paint, or gilding.

ABOVE: Graceful curvilinear form and naturalistic ornament distinguish the furniture of the Rococo era. This carved walnut *fauteuil* is a characteristic cabriole-leg form, with open upholstered arms, c. 1750.

PREVIOUS PAGE: The salon of the Chateau de Beaumesnil, a Baroque estate in Normandy, France, is furnished in Louis XV style, with light wood *boiserie* paneling and a pastel color scheme.

BELOW: This bombé-shaped commode, c. 1745, is decorated with black, gold, and colored lacquer panels, probably cut from a Chinese screen, set off by elaborate ormolu decoration of scrolling foliage and flowers; 53 inches long, with a serpentine marble top.

ABOVE: A variety of new furniture forms were introduced in this period, each with its own name. The wood frame of this *duchesse brisée*, c. 1760, is painted, as was most Rococo seating furniture.

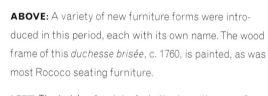

LEFT: The lady's *sécretaire à abattant*, another new form, presents an unbroken front, with a writing surface that drops down when needed. Made of tulipwood, fruitwood, and mixed-wood marquetry, with ormolu mounts, c. 1760.

ABOVE: The Louis XV commode is gently curved at the sides, with serpentine front and cabriole legs. The back is flat, because it stands against a wall. This one has cube marquetry of satinwood and tulipwood on the front, amaranth inlay on the sides, a marble top, and ormolu mounts, c. 1755.

ABOVE: A writing table in kingwood with parquetry surface, the veneers forming a geometric pattern, with ormolu mounts and gently curving cabriole legs, c. 1755.

ABOVE: Clocks were a prestigious accessory, fashionably encased as objects of furniture. The movement is a rope-winding system, with brass-weighted pendulum.

Style Markers

MOOD
relaxed elegance

SCALE
intimate

COLORS
warm pastels

ORNAMENT
copious and varied, asymmetrical,
veneers and lacquers

KEY MOTIFS
shells, florals, vines, naturalistic
forms

FURNITURE
curvilinear forms, veneered or
painted

WOODS
beech, walnut or cherry, gold leaf
and marquetry accents

TEXTILES
luxurious but light, tapestry,
brocades, silks, and damasks

LOOK FOR
cabriole legs, overstuffed
seating, gilding

This satin-background lampas latté is named *Les Chinois*, reflecting its Eastern inspiration.

The design of this satin-ground brocade dates to the time of Louis XV.

A floral toile with colorful wildflowers on an ivory linen ground.

CHAPTER 5
Rococo in England: Queen Anne Style, c. 1700–1720

ABOUT THE PERIOD

Under England's less autocratic monarchy, styles were not so determined by royal patronage as those in France, and were therefore less affected by transitions in the monarchy. English periods of the 18th century are not entirely contiguous with the reigns of their namesakes, and changes in design were more gradual, with considerable overlapping from one period to the next. During much of the 18th century, in fact, several styles were simultaneously at the height of fashion. Because the furniture often had similar design characteristics, it is sometimes difficult to place labels on pieces that may differ by date of fabrication rather than appearance.

As the century began, the Kingdom of England merged with Scotland in 1707 to become Great Britain. The Queen Anne style, named after the ruler who was the last of the Stuart dynasty (1665–1714), was the English version of Rococo (but the English did not use that term) and was the first style of that country to emphasize curving forms. Although the Queen Anne style was short-lived (as was Anne's reign, 1702–1714), its influence was considerable. When the overdecorated Baroque fell from favor, English designers sought a simpler, more refined style, one that reflected their aversion to the fancy French aesthetic. They accomplished this by translating French Rococo with characteristic British restraint, modifying the shapely silhouettes into more subdued curves and almost no decoration.

The simplicity of Queen Anne style was well suited to British taste. It was also lightweight, portable, and easy to produce; in the aftermath of the 1666 fire that had destroyed much of London, the need to rebuild and refurnish was critical. It was only a matter of time, however, before the fashion-forward aristocracy began to look for more elaborate expressions to furnish their imposing town and country residences. What ensued, at the beginning of the Georgian period, was the grafting of carved ornament and decoration onto basic Queen Anne silhouettes. The Queen Anne name also refers to a style of late-19th-century architecture, designated a revival style that bears little resemblance to that of the original Queen Anne period.

ABOUT THE STYLE

The Queen Anne interior suits its ladylike name: it is modest, understated, and evokes a sense of refinement. Lighter and more comfortable than William and Mary design, it reprises the curves of French Rococo but reduces them to their most pristine, free of the frilly asymmetrical decoration that marked the original. Rather than the frivolity of French Rococo, the English version projects a serious demeanor.

Queen Anne rooms moved away from the ornate plasterwork and pervasive ornament of English Baroque. Wood paneling, often cut down to dado height, gradually began to give way to painted surfaces and plaster decorations, bringing a lighter and more inviting aspect to the rooms. Ornament is restrained, but not entirely omitted.

Colors are softer and more inviting than the somber tones of the William and Mary period, with such shades as muted greens, ivories, and warmer reds.

Windows are larger, as are the glass panes within them, and drapery treatments have a lighter feeling, with fabrics in graceful floral or inventive patterns with exotic motifs from the Far East. In addition to China and Japan, India is a frequent source of inspiration, as crewels and chintzes begin their reign of popularity in English country houses.

Floors of polished wood parquet might be enhanced with Oriental carpets. Fireplaces, still important fixtures, follow the understated lines of the period, and lighting fixtures are predominantly brass, rather than the showier crystal favored by the French.

Accessories, too, are simple; silver, though shapely and sculptural, has relatively little adornment. The influx of decorative objects from the China trade has increased, with porcelain designed specifically for export in patterns and forms tailored to European taste. Most strikingly, the consumption of tea has transformed English daily life, requiring the creation of new objects linked to its use; these include not only tea services, strainers, and serving implements but also teapot stands and a variety of serving tables, particularly tilt-top versions that stand against the wall when not in use.

ABOUT THE FURNITURE

Queen Anne furniture reflects the increasing cabinetmaking skills of 18th-century crafts-men. It is characterized by restrained curvilinear shapes, where form is central, rather than ornament. The most frequent decorative motif is a simple version of the scallop shell. Symmetrical and flattened in its English translations, it is retained into the Geor-gian period despite its associations with the Rococo. Walnut remains the preferred wood, although after a blight on French walnut trees led to limited supplies, Parliament removed a tax on the import of mahogany, which would become the dominant wood in furniture by the mid- to late 18th century.

For chairs and tables in Queen Anne style, the defining feature is a bold C-curved cabriole leg, with a more pronounced out-curving knee, sometimes with shell carving, a narrower ankle than in the French form, and customarily a pad foot, though scroll, spade, or three-toed feet are also seen. Chairs have lower backs than in William and Mary designs, and they are curved to fit the body. Their distinctive silhouette features a double-curved hoop back, urn-shaped splat (derived from Chinese porcelain), and rounded front rail with drop-in horseshoe seat. Often, only the front legs are fully devel-oped and the rear ones left plain. Stretchers begin to disappear. The wing chair, with comfortably padded arms and back, will become a standard bearer of British style. Save for the feet, its design will remain virtually the same in the decades to follow. Sofas and settees reflect the interest in more comfortable furniture.

Queen Anne cabinet sides are straight, although the legs have adopted the new sil-houette, and the tops of tall pieces may have the double-hoop shape echoing that seen on chairs. New composite furniture forms have been introduced: the bureau-secretary, cabinet on chest, and bureau-bookcase, all crowned with double-domes, bonnet tops, or Rococo-curved, broken pediments. Consoles, wardrobes, bureaus, and occasional tables fill other furniture needs, as do card and gaming tables, new forms in this period. With almost no carving or intricate veneering, the wood—primarily walnut, but also elm and walnut burl—serves as its own ornament, although shapely brass escutcheon plates are added grace notes. The exceptions are the elaborately Japanned pieces, with *chinoiserie* decoration, which add dramatic statements to otherwise understated rooms.

PREVIOUS PAGE: The Blue Drawing Room at Melford Hall in Suffolk, England, has shapely Queen Anne furnishings and a Rococo-carved wood chimney-piece. The shapely silhouettes and cabriole legs seen in French Rococo style are more restrained in their English translation.

RIGHT: This bureau-bookcase, c. 1705, has a double-dome top that echoes the silhouette of the classic Queen Anne chair. The mirror-front doors conceal an elaborately fitted interior; the lower section has a slant-front secretarial drawer over short and long drawers; it sits on turned bun feet carried over from the William and Mary style. Made of walnut, burr walnut, and burr maple.

ABOVE: Grand proportions, finely turned stretchers, and vivid needlework distinguish this walnut settee, with the restrained design, newly introduced low back, and simple woodwork that mark designs of the later Queen Anne period.

RIGHT: The side table was customarily placed alongside a sofa. This one, made about 1710, is walnut, with a decorative frieze and shell-topped cabriole legs. The claw and ball feet began to appear as the Queen Anne style morphed into that of George I.

LEFT: The wing chair, also called the "easie chair," was designed for comfort rather than elegance. It varied little throughout the 18th century except for details such as the carving on the legs. This walnut one, c. 1710, has cabriole front legs, turned rear legs, and a turned stretcher.

BELOW: Queen Anne chairs were characterized by hoop-curved top rail and sides, urn-shape splat, cabriole legs, and pad foot, but within these parameters there was considerable variation. This compass-seat chair is a classic example of the form.

Some of the most elegant furniture of the period was Japanned—the English replication of Asian lacquerwork—reflecting the fascination with the exotic East, which reached its high point in this period. This striking brown and gold bureau-cabinet, with fine *chinoiserie* ornamentation, has an arched broken pediment and gilt finials. The interior is fitted with multiple small drawers and pigeonholes.

Style Markers

MOOD unpretentious	**SCALE** moderate
COLORS warm	**ORNAMENT** restrained
KEY MOTIF scallop shell	**FURNITURE** simple curving shapes, minimal carving
WOODS walnut, transitioning to mahogany	**TEXTILES** imports, Indian prints, and crewels

LOOK FOR
cabriole leg with pad foot,
tea furniture, Japanning

With multicolored motifs of Oriental imagery, Shanghai suits the period's fascination with the Far East.

This pattern of meandering lines and flower clusters is appropriately understated for Queen Anne decorative schemes.

CHAPTER 6
Early Georgian Style, c. 1720–1760

Early Georgian Style, c. 1720–1760

ABOUT THE PERIOD

The term Georgian in English style encompasses, if not three entirely different styles, the separate reigns of three rulers in the Hanoverian dynasty: George I (reign 1720–1737), George II (reign 1740–1760), and George III (reign 1760–1811). The Georgian era spanned most of the 18th century, a prosperous era of several coexisting styles and a society that intriguingly mixed elegance and dissolution. The reigns of George I and George II comprise what is designated as Early Georgian, the period when Rococo reigned supreme. The Late Georgian would see the revival of classicism.

Early Georgian interiors and furnishings, reflecting the influence of French styles, also reflected the growing sophistication of the English aristocracy, who were increasingly setting fashion standards. With London as its flourishing hub of creativity, England was for the first time in its history prepared to challenge French cultural dominance.

During these decades, the influence of a few prestigious architects and their affluent patrons initiated a Golden Age of English design, which saw the country's most exceptional design achievements. Architecture reigned foremost among the arts, and celebrated practitioners like William Kent (1685–1748) and James Gibbs (1682–1754) built showplace townhouses and the palatial country homes that epitomized the fashion of the day. An architect-designed and elaborately furnished residence was becoming a means of displaying the good taste and the social status of its owners.

Other factors contributed to the sophistication of Georgian styles. Advances in furniture workmanship enabled English craftsmen to produce objects of superb quality, and an integrated furniture trade had developed to market these objects to affluent clients. Perhaps even more significant in the long-range influence of English design was the development of widely distributed pattern books that made it possible for cabinetmakers in other parts of the country—and later, other parts of the world—to replicate the latest London styles.

After the middle of the 18th century, cultivated Englishmen, completing their education with a Grand Tour of the continent, would return with mementos of antiquity fueled by, and feeding, the new interest in classicism. Until then, however, the Rococo influence informed the design of English interiors and furnishings, as it did that of most of Europe.

ABOUT THE STYLE

The Early Georgian interior has moved away from the understatement of Queen Anne to assume the characteristics of a more assertive style. It distills the essence of Englishness, tempering aristocratic pomp with the restraint that distinguishes most British styles from those of their French neighbors. It is deservedly admired and consistently copied. While impressive and somewhat formal, it stops just short of stuffiness, walking a middle ground that mixes several elements of style. Richer decoration has been added to what is essentially the same type of well-proportioned space that began the 18th century. The application of ornament conveys greater formality, bespeaking affluence and status.

Walls of off-white or stone grey are finished with moldings and decorative cornices, all painted white. Dark wood paneling is giving way to lighter treatments, with carved swags or garlands on the dado, and perhaps faux-bois painting to suggest lighter woods. There might also be tapestries, and either hand-painted Chinese or flocked wallpapers.

Colors are deeper than in the Queen Anne period—blues, greens, reds, golds, muted or vibrant hues, as appropriate for each room: stronger in important public spaces, softer in private ones.

Floors are oak plank or parquet, and they might be stained or painted, though marble is preferred in the major rooms of grand houses. Oriental rugs are used in formal rooms, and perhaps canvas floorcloths in others.

Double-hung sash windows with rectangular panes or three-section Palladian windows with arched semicircular cornices are the latest style. They may be dressed in festoons of fabric ballooning underneath a carved and gilded cornice or draperies of heavy silk to match the upholstery fabrics, hanging to the floor. Toiles, chintzes, or printed Indian cottons are less formal alternatives to imported needlepoint or damask.

Fireplaces remain a focal point, with carved marble mantels and overmantels projecting into the room. Illumination is by means of candles or gaslights—tall candlestands in the corners, wall-mounted sconces, or massive chandeliers, perhaps of polished brass or French crystal. Elaborate framed mirrors might be carved with scallop or shell motifs, classical scrolls, or Rococo filigree.

Early Georgian Style, c. 1720–1760

ABOUT THE FURNITURE

The transition from Queen Anne to George I furniture, and in turn from George I to George II, are primarily transitions from simplicity to increasingly elaborate ornament. George I furniture looks much like that of the Queen Anne period, with carving and ornament grafted onto the same basic forms. Early Georgian chairs retain the Queen Anne silhouette but have become more elaborate. Their proportions are broader, with wider backs and wider, flatter seats, the fronts of which have lost their rounded shape. The cabriole leg remains, but the disappearance of stretchers requires the support of a broader knee, which is carved with graceful cabochons, volute ornament, and, in George II chairs, more prominent motifs that might include lion masks or foliage. A ball-and-claw foot, derived from an ancient Chinese image of a dragon holding a pearl, is a characteristic feature on early Georgian furniture, supplanting the simpler pad foot; a lion's paw is sometimes seen. Carved ornament appears on the splats and crest rail, and George II chairs have high-relief carving and decorated seat rails as well. Settees and sofas may have carved frames and aprons in addition to that on their short cabriole legs.

Tall cabinets have added finials to Queen Anne–style double-dome tops, or are crested with broken or swan-neck pediments for a more architectural look. The chest-on-chest, on a plinth base, replaces the tall chest on cabriole leg. In the Early Georgian period, a greater variety of furniture has come into use—tea tables are joined by several styles of drop-leaf and occasional pieces, and the card table accommodates the popular new pastime, with a folding frame that allows it to serve also as a side table. Console and side tables are often topped with marble. Beds are somewhat less elaborately draped than in Baroque times and have exposed, carved posts. In the George II era, bookcases and breakfronts often begin to reflect classical influences, with cornices and broken pediments.

A significant change in the appearance of George II furniture is the replacement of walnut with imported mahogany as the material of choice, walnut having become scarce after a blight that destroyed much of the European growth. But even more important, the strength of mahogany, a tropical hardwood, makes it stand up to intricate carving and piercing, encouraging the interest in more elaborate ornamentation. Its dark reddish tone and decorative grain are also ideal for the broad, carving-free veneered surfaces of tables and cabinet fronts. Japanning and *chinoiserie* ornament continue in popularity, appearing on many tall case pieces.

PREVIOUS PAGE: The dining room of Alnwick Castle, Northumberland, England, is a stately interior with the imposing character often seen in early Georgian interiors, combining classical architecture with Rococo silhouettes.

ABOVE: Rather than developing new forms, the early Georgian period drew on basic Queen Anne furniture silhouettes. Parlor chairs like this one, made of burr walnut, were embellished with shapelier sides and slate, carving on crest rail and knees, and ball-and-claw feet. C. 1725.

RIGHT: The Georgian periods saw the introduction of furniture combining two different forms in a single piece. The desk-and-bookcase was a frequent example; this George II piece, c. 1730, is made of burr and figured walnut, with gilded accents (gilding was seen in English furniture, though far less often and rarely as extensively as in French).

Upholstered armchairs were imposing and comfortable additions to the Georgian interior. This George II chair, c. 1755, has features associated with Thomas Chippendale designs: yoke-shaped crest rail, out-scrolling open arms with serpentine seat rails, and rich Rococo carving. Cabriole legs end in French-style scroll feet. The needlepoint upholstery is characteristic of the period.

LEFT: A pair of chairs meld into a double settee, of rich imported mahogany, in the Early Georgian period, c. 1740.

BELOW: The kneehole desk, so named because of the recessed central opening, was a frequent fixture in both English and later American interiors of the 18th century. This one is made of mahogany with gilded accents, c. 1750.

RIGHT: Mirrors became important accent pieces, as well as functional conveniences. Most were attractively framed, in carved and gilded wood, often with forms that echoed those of the furniture, like this swan-neck pedimented mirror with shell-carved apron, c. 1730.

BELOW: The pier table was generally placed between two windows, often with a tall mirror hung over it. This early 18th-century design is particularly elaborate for an English piece of the time, suggesting an interest in Italianate classical motifs. It is carved and gilded, with an alabaster top.

NEXT PAGE: Lord Burlington's Chiswick House, in London, is a superb example of Palladian-inspired design. The interiors, like the statue-filled Long Gallery here, are some of the finest extant by William Kent, the leading architect of the style. The apse was inspired by an ancient Roman temple.

■ Palladian, c. mid-1800s

ABOUT THE PERIOD

Concurrent with the relatively understated early Georgian style, the Palladian is an assertive and monumental style, clearly based on classical architecture. Palladian style had no relation to prevailing English fashion, but was created by architects and designers for wealthy clients who favored grandeur over understatement and could afford to commission whatever they chose.

The style was defined by the work of William Kent (1685–1748), who advised his patron Lord Burlington on the design of Chiswick House in London, and who executed commissions for dozens of churches and public buildings, as well as great country houses like Holkham Hall and Houghton Hall. Avoiding the sometimes ponderousness of the English Baroque, Palladian style drew instead on the more refined Italian classicism. Kent had studied the Renaissance architecture of Andrea Palladio and the 17th-century designs of Palladian-follower Inigo Jones, and he developed his own interpretations of the classical style. Though Kent's buildings were more elaborate than Palladio's country villas, the exteriors were still somewhat severe—and in striking contrast to the opulence contained within.

ABOUT THE STYLE

Palladian interiors are as grand in their way as almost anything in the French vocabulary of design. Their almost-monumental scale and symmetry reflect the English view of themselves, in the glorious days of the Empire, as inheritors of the Roman tradition. The typical Palladian room has an air of self-importance, intended to reflect the status of its owner.

In the high-ceilinged, symmetrical space, stucco walls have prominent baseboards and three sections: dado below, field above, and entablatures or massive cornices at ceiling level. The field might be painted or covered with patterned damask, tapestry, or occasionally wallpaper.

Ceilings, although not quite as elaborate as those in French interiors, are decorated with classical plasterwork that is often as three-dimensional as carving, and sometimes includes suggestions of Rococo. Doorways and windows have architectural detailing—chunky moldings, scrolled brackets, friezes, and reliefs. Most are painted white, with occasional gilded accents.

Grand overmantels have projecting cornices and imposing pediments that highlight the fireplace as the focal point of the room. Stairs and balustrades are given similar treatment.

Window treatments are complex, with multiple layers of ornate and costly draperies in rich, imported fabrics. Oriental rugs and magnificent accessory objects contribute to the sumptuous effect.

Colors, in a varied palette, are more assertive than those of the usual classical interior and reflect the preference of the individual client.

ABOUT THE FURNITURE

Kent was the first Englishman to design complete interiors, with furnishings and backgrounds that were carefully planned and coordinated. For these rooms, he and his followers designed furniture as imposing as sculpture or architecture. Chairs and sofas might be painted, or accented with gilding. Their forms are not new, but they are magnified, corniced, and pedimented, or enhanced with carved elements like volute supports, fish scales, shells, or lion masks. Case pieces and tables are grand in scale and clearly based on architectural forms. Kent designed distinctive consoles, which were heavily sculptured and often decorated with eagle motifs. Most of the furniture is mahogany, which takes well to the detailed carving.

Matthias Lock (c. 1710–1765), working in this period, produced distinctively weighty, ornately carved, column-legged console tables, typically with carved swags and classical faces, generally painted white and gilded. Unlike other Georgian furnishings adapted from pattern books, most Palladian pieces are individual and idiosyncratic works of art.

■Thomas Chippendale and "Chippendale Style," c. 1750s–1760s

Much English furniture of the mid-18th century is referred to as "Chippendale," but the designation properly belongs only to pieces made in the London workshops of Thomas Chippendale (1718–1779). Chippendale was the leading furniture maker of his time, but perhaps his greatest achievement was producing a series of books of designs, which were the first furniture catalogs. These books have made his name virtually synonymous with the period, and led to the first style named for a maker, rather than a ruler.

There is no single Chippendale style: *The Gentleman and Cabinet-Maker's Director*, published in 1754, 1755, and 1762, contained drawings for chairs, tables, commodes, and other objects of furniture in all the fashionable styles of the time, including many designs that were not Chippendale's own. They reflected several influences: French Rococo, Gothic, Chinese, and later neoclassical variants, all grafted onto what were essentially the same basic forms. Purely English pieces tended to be deeply carved; French-influenced ones were Rococo in form; Chinese-influenced styles used ornament from that country. *The Director* was distributed throughout England, as well as in other countries, most notably America, where it became the basis for meticulous copies, adaptations, and improvisations on the originals.

PREVIOUS PAGE: In the bedroom at Nostell Priory, *chinoiserie* wallpaper complements chairs whose openwork arms reflect the Chinese Chippendale style.

ABOVE: Illustration from *The Gentleman and Cabinet-Maker's Director* showing chair designs by Thomas Chippendale.

The variety of influences notwithstanding, Chippendale-style furniture, particularly the chairs, can usually be identified by several specific characteristics: the yoke-shape crest rail, pierced splat, straight sides, and (particularly if made at the Chippendale factory) skillfully carved ornament. Seat backs flare at the top and join directly to the seat stretcher. Upholstered seats are broad and flat. Below the seats, however, there is considerable variation. Early Chippendale designs have Rococo elements drawn from the French, like floriate carving and cabriole legs, but with ball-and-claw feet. Later ones are more rectilinear, with neoclassical motifs and square-section Marlborough legs with stretchers. Gothic-influenced chairs and tables are adorned with pointed arches, quatrefoil cutouts, and tracery-like carving. One altogether individual style that emerged from the *Drawing Books*, called Chinese Chippendale regardless of its maker, appears in furniture with fretwork or bamboo-like carving, and motifs like pagodas or Chinese figures.

Chippendale case pieces are less easily characterized. Commodes adopted the French curvilinear form, but are less elaborately Rococo, with carving usually the primary ornament in place of elaborate mounts. Bookcases and secretaries tend to be large architectural forms, with mullioned glass doors and cornices, and broken or scrolled pediments, often richly carved. Tables have carving on aprons as well as legs, and later designs may have classical pilasters. The primary wood seen in Chippendale furniture is mahogany.

Produced during both the George II and George III periods, Chippendale designs transition from Rococo to neoclassical, following the cycle of changing fashion from late-middle Georgian to late Georgian styles. In successive editions of *The Director*, Chippendale's designs become first more elaborate and then more refined as new styles take hold. After his death, Chippendale's son, also named Thomas, continued the business until 1796.

Style Markers

MOOD moderately formal	**SCALE** imposing
COLORS varied, muted, or bright	**ORNAMENT** relatively restrained, becoming more elaborate
KEY MOTIFS shells, ribbons, acanthus, lion's heads and paws	**FURNITURE** walnut, then mahogany ornamentation on Queen Anne forms
TEXTILES Indian prints, chintzes, imported silks and damasks	**LOOK FOR** ball-and-claw feet, heavy carving, Rococo elements

A tree-of-life pattern, like this one called Pondi, was often seen in the period.

Undulating lines, birds, and foliage printed in tones of lacquer red on a linen ground.

CHAPTER 7

Late Colonial Styles in America: Queen Anne, c. 1720–1780, Chippendale, c. 1750–1790

ABOUT THE PERIOD

Having survived the rigors of settling a new nation, Americans were steadily gaining ground, both in the amenities of day-to-day living and in the stylishness and sophistication of their homes. With the emergence of a prosperous class of merchants and ship-builders, and the arrival in the colonies of European-trained craftsmen, more people were able to afford fine furnishings, and more specialists were available to make them. Now the colonists could not only import fine things from abroad, but they were also increasingly able to copy, adapt, or commission entirely new objects. However, the combined inconveniences of British taxes and restrictions, the great distances involved in trade, and the uncertainties of ocean transportation led to delays in communication. Until late in the 18th century, styles in America lagged a decade or more behind those in England.

It is easy to describe American Colonial designs as scaled-down and simplified versions of European (mostly English) prototypes, but they are more interesting and more difficult to classify than mere attempts at reproduction. There are distinct differences between interiors and furniture in the two countries, reflecting both the changing taste, and the growing independence, of the young nation.

The Late Colonial period includes two styles: Queen Anne, beginning after that monarch had died and after the style had peaked in England, and Chippendale. In America, the two styles overlapped and intermingled, often with elements of both combining in the same interiors and objects. During this period, too, emerged the phenomenon of regional variations; although the designs were the same, they might be interpreted or ornamented differently in different furniture centers, depending on the skills of the local makers or the taste of their clients.

Furniture making tended to concentrate in the port cities. Boston was the original center, but Philadelphia caught up toward the latter part of the 18th century, when emigrant French craftsmen joined local makers and sparked a wave of creativity. By the end of the Late Colonial era, New York had become the largest port and also housed the country's leading furniture makers. Other centers developed in Newport, Rhode Island; Baltimore, Maryland; and Charleston, South Carolina. Although American furniture is generally unsigned, the names of exceptional craftsmen like Thomas Affleck (1740–1795),

Benjamin Randolph (1721–1791), and William Savery (1721–1787) of Philadelphia, and John Goddard (1724–1785) and John Townsend (1733–1809) of Boston, have become recognized.

Residential architecture also made great progress in the Late Colonial period, due in large part to the availability of the first pattern books for buildings. Brick or wood houses, styled after those in England, now had larger windows, symmetrical plans, and classical detailing. These developments were reflected in American interiors, as architectural details were added to the rooms, and the furniture that filled them.

In 1776, the American colonies declared their independence from England, leading to even more radical changes that would affect design, as it affected every other aspect of the colonists' lives.

ABOUT THE STYLE

As a general rule, the American interior is less elaborately decorated than its English Georgian counterpart. It is also less constrained by rules of fashion, and therefore somewhat lighter in mood. It has less architectural detailing but uses similar elements, and while the furniture appears to be much the same, the idiosyncratic variations of American furnishings lend diversity and individuality to the rooms they occupy.

As life in the colonies has become more stable and prosperous, the decoration of interiors has followed suit. Though ceilings remain low, spaces are more expansive, with paneled walls and floors of polished wood planks. Around midcentury, interiors take on classical detailing, such as moldings, pilasters, and paneled doors, but they are simplified to suit Colonial taste and craftsmen's skills.

Wallpapers—first, imported handpainted designs and later, locally produced ones—have become very popular, as they had in Europe. The Chinese motifs seen in England have been imported to America as well, particularly with Chippendale-style furnishings.

Windows are double-hung, with larger panes and accordingly more elaborate window treatments; floor-length draperies of imported textiles are used in more formal rooms, and chintz (an Indian influence), calico, or ruffled curtains are seen in more casual settings. Textiles are important and the costliest item of furnishings; although sturdy wools and horsehairs are being made in the colonies, the demand for richer fabrics has made these the single largest category of imports. Later in the period, Venetian blinds make their appearance, offering a more efficient means of light control.

Locally made floor coverings, once limited mostly to handwoven or hooked rugs, are now more varied and include floorcloths with floral and geometric patterns. Imported carpets, primarily Oriental, are used only in the best rooms.

Implements for serving and drinking tea are important symbols of a cultivated home, as Americans adopted the customs of the upper-class British—at least, until the Revolution.

Colors have become brighter and more varied—medium blue or shades of green, accents of white, and bright red are popular interior hues.

The fireplace stays a focal point, although its treatment is relatively simple, with a carved mantel often bordered in Delft tiles. Later in the 18th century, heavier moldings and architectural detailing become the norm.

Brass chandeliers and sconces are popular, being more decorative than wrought iron and less showy than crystal, reflecting the inclination of American taste toward a simpler aesthetic.

Oriental or other fine imported porcelains are displayed in glass-front cabinets or on mantels, along with decorative objects of brass or the new Sheffield plate that offers a middle-class alternative to silver. Clocks, imported or from local sources, are becoming popular—tall case clocks as well as wall-hung or mantel-sitting models—and gilt-framed mirrors may hang on the walls.

American furniture is now comparable to English in skillfulness of cabinetry and finishing, more closely resembling the designs that inspired it, though still lagging behind in style. But the resemblances are sometimes superficial. As American craftsmen have come into their own, form has become more important than ornament; the furniture is generally lighter in scale, slimmer, and more vertical than English pieces, which are horizontally oriented, weightier, and more deeply carved. These differences reflect not only the American dislike of pretension but also the inappropriateness of heavy-looking furniture to modest-sized rooms.

Beyond these general variations are more specific ones: the craftsmen in each furniture-producing community have developed particularities of form and decoration, from the silhouettes of Queen Anne chairs to the carving of shells or ball-and-claw feet to the placement of escutcheons on highboys. Differences in these and other details make it possible to identify the part of the country in which they were made, and often even the maker. Such highly individualistic departures from pattern-book models also make American furniture an intriguing study.

QUEEN ANNE FURNITURE

The silhouettes of American Queen Anne furniture are based on the S-curved forms of English designs, but they differ in several important areas: case pieces are slimmer, and the cabriole legs are curvier, with a pronounced knee, tapering ankle, and club or trifid foot. The archetypical Queen Anne chair is made in Philadelphia, a fluidly sculptural design with an elegant, shapely splat, balloon seat, and shell carving on knee and crest rail. The upholstered easy chair, with either scroll (from Philadelphia) or pillar arm (from the Boston area), is another adopted English form.

A particular invention of American furniture is the highboy, a chest-on-chest raised up on legs—for convenience and a graceful, taller silhouette—with a companion piece called a lowboy. The form continued until after the Revolution and became the most important item of furniture in most Colonial homes. The classic Queen Anne highboy is a bonnet-top form made in Boston, on four legs, without stretchers, and with vestigial pendants suspended from the apron. The highboy top may be flat, a less expensive option, or one for lower-ceilinged rooms. Brasses and handles are simple, shapely, and mostly imported.

Other furnishings are both more sophisticated and more varied. Tilt-top, tea, and card tables, drop-lid and slant-top desks (as literacy is more widespread), and chests of drawers are among the items of furniture produced in this style. Because the style began later in America, when walnut was less fashionable, much Queen Anne furniture is made of mahogany, although many American makers continued to use local woods like maple, pine, and cherry, especially outside of the major port cities.

Queen Anne furniture remained the most enduringly popular style in the colonies until after the Revolution, long after it had become outdated in England. Beyond the appeal of its grace and simplicity, there is perhaps another reason: their simple lines and less carving made Queen Anne pieces less costly than Chippendale ones, a fact that would appeal to conservative colonists. Americans, at that time, were more penny-wise than fashion-forward.

CHIPPENDALE FURNITURE

As styles moved from an American interpretation of English Queen Anne to variations on early Georgian, they also incorporated Rococo elements from France and the Far East. With the 1754 publication of Chippendale's *Director*, which was widely circulated in America, skilled craftsmen in the colonies could replicate the latest London fashions, although they often followed their own preferences and those of their clients. Most American Chippendale furniture is a free interpretation of Chippendale's originals.

The transition from Queen Anne to Chippendale design is seen in the replacement of curves with more linear forms, the addition of ball-and-claw feet, and a greater taste for ornament and carving. The new silhouettes, however, retain elements of the old. Chairs might marry Queen Anne–style cabriole legs with a Chippendale body—yoke-shape crest rail, straight sides, and an intricately pierced and carved splat. Carving is less three-dimensional than that on English chairs, seats are rectilinear rather than rounded, and generally not so broad and flat. In upholstered furniture, sofas are a larger, more comfortable, alternative to settees, while the easy chair remains, with squat cabriole legs, ball-and-claw feet, and no stretchers.

A new fashion appears: block-front furniture, in which desk, chest, or cabinet fronts are formed in three alternating concave and convex panels, each panel topped with a stylized carved shell. Although not an American invention, the form has become associated with Newport, Rhode Island, particularly in the workshops of the Goddard and Townsend families.

Chippendale highboys and lowboys show some of the most original stylistic touches of any American pieces. The tops have broken, curving, scrolled pediments, flanked with finials and centered with highly original variations of sculpture and ornament. Fanciful and finely executed carving, usually combining shells with intricate Rococo foliage, turns apron and tympanum into virtuoso works of art. Highly figured, imported crotch mahogany veneers make the smooth surfaces as decorative as the carved ones. Brasses, too, are more decorative, reflecting the Rococo influence, although Americans, like the English, limit their embrace of French frivolity.

Other furniture of the time includes tea tables with piecrust top and tripod column base with ball-and-claw foot, game tables, drop-front and slant-top desks, bookcases, and secretaries. Toward the end of the period, acanthus carving, fretwork, fluted columns, and gadroon borders reflect the growing taste for neoclassical forms.

ABOVE: The parlor of Hunter House, in Newport, Rhode Island, is furnished with mahogany pieces that reflect the warm appeal of Late Colonial furniture. Between the windows is a fine example of block-front furniture, the best of which was made in Newport.

BELOW: The Chinese Parlor at Winterthur, in Wilmington, Delaware, is furnished as an example of high style in the late Colonial period, with fine Chippendale furniture and walls covered in imported Chinese wallpaper.

The highboy was probably the most important piece of 18th-century American furniture. The wood and detailing varied with the region and the maker. This 88-inch-tall mahogany example has a bonnet top and spiral finials, with fanlike shell carving. It was made in Charlestown, Massachusetts, c. 1745.

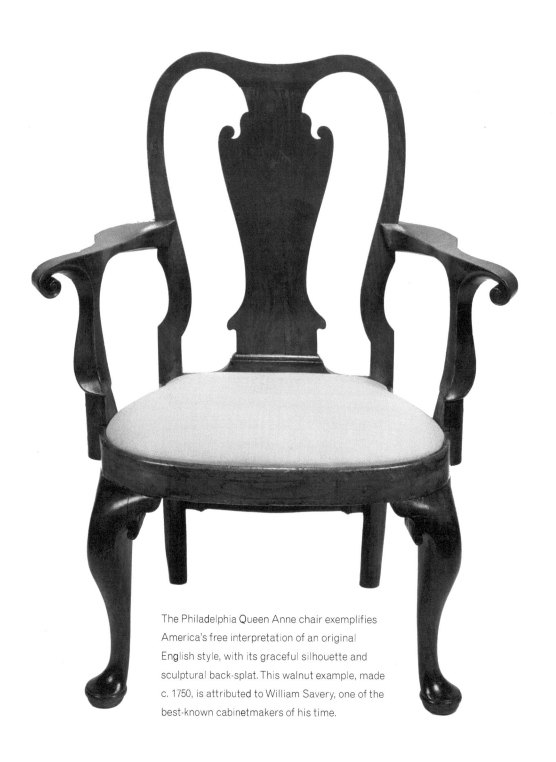

The Philadelphia Queen Anne chair exemplifies
America's free interpretation of an original
English style, with its graceful silhouette and
sculptural back-splat. This walnut example, made
c. 1750, is attributed to William Savery, one of the
best-known cabinetmakers of his time.

RIGHT: Another Queen Anne armchair, probably made in New England, is a more restrained variation of the style, with compass seat, straight front rail, and flat stretchers.

BELOW: The lowboy was a companion piece to the highboy, generally made with a complementary design on the apron and carved ornament, often a shell motif. This one, of walnut, was made in Massachusetts around the middle of the 18th century.

LEFT: The piecrust tea table, named for its decorative scalloped edge, was functional as well as decorative, the top tilting vertically when it was not in use. This mahogany one has a carved, fluted-column shaft and tripod base, with ball-and-claw feet. Made in Virginia, c. 1765.

RIGHT: The wing chair, brought from England and called the easy chair in America, was a luxury that required costly imported upholstery. This American Chippendale example has deep foliate carving and ball-and-claw feet on cabriole legs. Made in Philadelphia, c. 1770.

Chippendale chairs were translated in America directly from the pages of *The Director*, but they were freely interpreted by individual craftsmen. These chairs, in carved mahogany, were made by William Wayne, in Philadelphia, c. 1770.

LEFT: In the last and most spectacular interpretation of the form that disappeared after the Revolutionary War, Chippendale highboys are marked by virtuoso Rococo-style carving and ornament. This one, 89 inches high, combines bold foliate and shell motifs with scrolled pediment, urn finials, and fluted columns that foretell the coming of neoclassicism. Made in Philadelphia, of mahogany, c. 1765.

BELOW: In classic Chippendale form, this sofa has a serpentine back, volute arms, and Marlborough legs. Made in Philadelphia, of mahogany, c. 1770.

LEFT: The tall case clock, also called the grandfather clock, was a prestigious and relatively costly accessory in the late Colonial home. This elegant example was made in Connecticut, with works by an American craftsman, Lewis Curtis, c. 1795.

BELOW: Card tables were generally made with fold-open or otherwise expandable tops, to be placed against a wall when not in use. This mahogany one, in Chippendale style, was made in New York, c. 1770.

Style Markers

MOOD
understated and comfortable

SCALE
well-proportioned

COLORS
warm and varied

ORNAMENT
conservative

KEY MOTIFS
scallop shell, ball-and-claw foot,
decorative finials

FURNITURE
mahogany, English forms but
lighter

TEXTILES
Indian crewels, chintzes,
imported silks and damasks

LOOK FOR
highboy and lowboy, regional
variations in style

This silver-ground velour, whose design dates to c. 1730, was reproduced for Copenhagen's Amalienborg Castle.

Formal enough for the finest country house, this design is called Lovebird.

CHAPTER 8

Early Neoclassicism in France: Louis XVI Style, c. 1750s, Dominant 1774–1792

ABOUT THE PERIOD

As its name suggests, Neoclassicism marked a return to the traditions of the ancient world and the search for a more refined and enduring style than the undisciplined and frivolous Rococo. In its rationality, it was influenced by the intellects of the Enlightenment, but its more immediate impetus was the excavation of ancient ruins at Pompeii and Herculaneum in Italy. Beginning in the mid-18th century, these widely published archaeological findings became a rich source of inspiration for architects and designers, motivating a dramatic turnaround of style in France and a simultaneous one in England.

Coming into its own after some years of transition, when the Rococo mingled with the incoming style, the early phase of French Neoclassicism combined the best features of Baroque and Rococo, balancing the richness and symmetry of the former with the grace and delicacy of the latter. Considering its merits, it deserved to remain fashionable for many decades.

To its misfortune, Neoclassicism coincided with the reign of Louis XVI (1754–1793, reigned 1774–1789), grandson of Louis XV, by whose name it is also known. As politics intruded on fashion, the association of design and patronage with the monarchy ensured its downfall. When the French Revolution of 1789 dethroned Louis and his much-maligned queen, Marie Antoinette, the style that marked the era was discarded with the royals and their court. Their palaces and mansions were sacked or destroyed, and the trappings of wealth were disdained as inappropriate for the new proletariat. French design, however, would reassert itself under the rule of Napoleon.

Having avoided the excesses of its predecessor, the Neoclassicism of the mid-18th century influenced styles in many other countries, becoming the first of many revivals tracing its roots back to ancient Greece and Rome.

ABOUT THE STYLE

The Neoclassical interior is gracious and elegant, projecting an air of serenity that is achieved in large part from its emphasis on symmetry and order. It strikes a happy medium of mood: slightly more formal than the Rococo room but avoiding the pomposity of a Baroque one. It revives familiar classical ornaments but executes them with restraint and daintiness.

The space is generous but comfortably scaled, and it may take any of several shapes, although all of them are carefully balanced, projecting an air of calm sophistication. *Boiserie* on walls is framed in slim, classical borders that divide it into linear sections carved with classical motifs like acanthus scrolls, rosettes, swags, or Greek fretwork. The prevailing geometric forms of *Le Goût Grec*, the early stage of the style, progresses to more decorative Etruscan and rich floral ornament. Wallpaper might be a fashionable addition; papers replicating the look of handpainted silk are preferable to heavy tapestries, and scenic panels, newly introduced by Jean-Baptiste Reveillon, are attractive alternatives to frescoes or painted murals. Cherubs, nymphs, and figures inspired by classical legend are frequent subjects. High ceilings are less elaborately decorated than in previous periods. They are centered with plaster medallions, and they meet the walls with precise, geometric cornices rather than cove moldings.

To create the requisite symmetry, hidden doors or false openings might be created opposite real ones, and treated identically. Both doors and windows are framed in classical orders and topped with cornices, pediments, or decorative panels. The chimneypiece, which is less intrusive and more gracefully proportioned than those of earlier periods, is given similar treatment. Casement windows, to dado or floor, have arched or rectangular headings, and shutters to match the wall paneling. The glass panes are now larger, admitting more light to the interior. Drapery and *portières* are coordinated with the rich upholstery fabrics, for a unified look.

Floors, of parquet that may combine different woods, may also be *faïence*, marble, or terra cotta, and carpets are either imported Oriental designs or French-made Savonnerie or Aubussons, often with geometric patterns.

The soft colorations of Rococo are retained, with white or pastel walls, but a palette of livelier colors in fabrics adds sparkle to the scheme.

Still a focal point, the Neoclassical chandelier has a refined silhouette, more vertical than that of the Rococo, with strands of crystals clustered around the central post creating a waterfall effect.

Mirrors are still important accessories, framed in the paneling and contributing to the balanced proportions of the space. Other accessories, as might be expected, reflect the same type of classical ornament as the interior surround—porcelain shaped like Grecian urns, gilded clocks with columns and pediments, and candleholders with caryatids.

ABOUT THE FURNITURE

Having discarded the unrestrained forms of Rococo, Neoclassical furniture is slim and linear, with straight legs, gracefully fluted, reeded, or turned spirals, all tapering to neat *sabot* feet. In chairs and sofas, curves are controlled rather than voluptuous, with oval, medallion, rectangular, or square backs, wide seats, and legs jointed neatly to chair frames with rosette-carved corner blocks. The variety of forms introduced in the Rococo period continues, with silhouettes modified to suit the more restrained style. Exposed wood frames of beech are almost invariably painted, in part because the woods are not exceptionally decorative, and they may be gilded as well. On case pieces as well as chairs, more painted furniture is seen in this style than in any other in France.

Although it is light enough to be movable, furniture is set in precise alignment with the walls of the room, creating an effect that is in pronounced contrast to the informality of the Rococo period. Other than chair backs, the only curves are simple geometric ones, shaping corners or rounding fronts of cabinets and tables.

Cabinetry continues to be attractively varied—the *bureau à cylindre*, the *bonheur de jour*, and specialized pieces for a variety of serving needs. Larger commodes or tables are topped with marble in white or pastel tones. Small tables are in square, oval, or demilune shape, often drawn from ancient classical forms.

Mahogany (*acajou*) is the wood of choice, along with satinwood, ebony, tulipwood, and others with more varied and decorative grains. Linear cube marquetry, or more refined frieze veneer, are alternatives to floral marquetry to decorate commodes and cabinets, with graceful ormolu or gilt-bronze mounts shaped in swags or classical figures. Porcelain plaques, Japanese lacquer panels, and *pietra dura* are also used to decorate furniture. Wrought iron, inspired by Pompeii finds, is used for table legs, as are steel and brass trim.

Several celebrated craftsmen worked during this period, but Jean-Henri Riesener (1734–1806), *ébéniste* to the king, is considered the most exceptional. Others include Adam Weisweiler (1744–1820) and the *menuisier* Georges Jacob (1739–1814), who founded the workshop that defined fine French chairmaking for several decades.

PREVIOUS PAGE: The Grand Salon from the Hotel de Tessé, by Nicholas Huyot, c. 1700, in The Metropolitan Museum of Art, illustrates the elegant formality of Louis XVI style, with its rectilinear *boiserie* paneling to the tapering columnar legs of the furniture.

RIGHT: The *sécretaire à abattant* was an important and functional new furniture form; this example by Saunier, c. 1785, is of mahogany with marquetry ornament and gilt-bronze (ormolu) mounts.

BELOW: Reflecting the *Goût Grec* style introduced in France in the mid-18th century, this *bureau plat* has stylized classical-motif mounts.

RIGHT: From a suite of Louis XVI seating furniture by Henri Jacob, of the renowned makers of fine seating furniture over four generations. The *fauteuil*, dating to c. 1780, is covered in Aubusson tapestry depicting La Fontaine fables and pastoral scenes.

BELOW: A Louis XVI demi-lune commode *a l'Anglais* attributed to F. Schey, c. 1780, with marble top above a central frieze drawer inlaid with arches, above two trellis-veneered drawers. The curved mirrored-back sides have three shelves, each surmounted by a pierced gallery.

Sycamore, amaranth, tulipwood, and marquetry make this *sécretaire à abattant* a noteworthy example of the craftsmanship of French cabinetmakers who catered to royalty and nobility in the Louis XVI era, c. 1775.

Another of the specialized seating pieces given a particular name, the *canapé* was a small sofa. This one, carved and gilded, is a typical example of the form, c. 1775.

The console table continued to be a presence in French interiors during this period; this one, carved and gilded, dates to c. 1775.

A Louis XVI mantel clock in ormolu and biscuit porcelain, c. 1795. On either side, Sèvres figures depict the goddess Venus instructing Cupid in lessons of love.

Style Markers

MOOD
moderately formal

SCALE
generous

COLORS
lively and varied

ORNAMENT
restrained and linear

KEY MOTIFS
classical pilasters, swags,
rosettes, urns

FURNITURE
straight-lined, slim, and
symmetrical

WOODS
mahogany, exotic woods for
marquetry

TEXTILES
silks, damasks, velvets

LOOK FOR
fluted or reeded legs, motifs
from antiquity, cube marquetry

The rich damask fabric is Beaumarchais, a pattern in neoclassical Louis XVI style.

Dating to 1784, this fabric was made for Marie Antoinette's quarters at Rambouillet Castle.

CHAPTER 9
Late Georgian: The Style of George III, c. 1760–1810

ABOUT THE PERIOD

During the reign of George III (1738–1820, reigned from 1760), grandson of George II, English style entered a period of committed neoclassicism, which first overlapped and then supplanted the Rococo. Fueled by excavations at Pompeii and Herculaneum that made possible the accurate study of antiquity, it signaled growing interest in the ancient world and was contemporaneous with similar changes in French style. During these years, an increasingly sophisticated furniture trade produced some of the finest English designs ever made, by names like Adam, Chippendale, Hepplewhite, and Sheraton.

The first Hanoverian ruler actually born in England, George III was the longest-ruling monarch before Queen Victoria. He presided over a period when, despite losing the American colonies, England became a leading European power. Reaping the rewards of affluence, education, and travel, the English aristocracy became committed collectors, amassing artworks as souvenirs of their Continental tours. They acquired etchings by Giovanni Battista Piranesi (1720–1778), or paintings by artists such as Giovanni Antonio Canal or "Canaletto" (1697–1768) and Giovanni Paolo Panini (1691–1765), depicting the beauties of classical architecture, and they commissioned architects and designers to translate the timeless aesthetic in building, remodeling, and decorating their homes.

The most famous of these, Robert Adam (1728–1792), developed a design vocabulary that would dominate the Late Georgian period and is often called Adam Style. Adam brought a sophisticated sensibility to creating what he called "integrated interiors," in which every element was planned as part of a coordinated whole. Though William Kent had done this to some extent, Adam elevated the design of an interior into a fine art. Designing or specifying all of the furnishings in the room, he created a pervasive and enduring style that represents the English interior at its most fully developed. In furniture, early neoclassicism was linked to late Chippendale styles, and to furniture by George Hepplewhite and Thomas Sheraton, whose designs, particularly those of Sheraton, were adopted in American Federal interiors.

■ Robert Adam and Adam Style, c. 1760–1780

Robert Adam (1728–1792) was a Scottish-born architect and designer whose beautifully conceived "integrated interiors," designed during the Late Georgian period, represent the paradigm of early neoclassical design in England. The son of a celebrated architect, whose three brothers were also architects, Adam traveled to Italy to study classical buildings and the work of Palladio, whose designs he concluded were too weighty. He sought, in his words, to bring "novelty and variety" to the spirit of antiquity, and his interiors combine the lightness and charm of Rococo with the precision and symmetry of neoclassicism.

Most of Adam's architectural commissions were renovations rather than original construction, but his interiors were entirely his own, and they can be recognized by his meticulous attention to balancing all of the elements in a room and his finely executed vocabulary of ornament based on classical motifs.

An Adam interior feels spacious and airy, even when modest in size—the result of his delicate touch and superb sense of proportion. Walls, typically painted in white or warm pastels, are trimmed with white moldings and delicate low-relief plasterwork. The ceiling is an all-white composition of absolute symmetry, with plaster ornamentation that has its counterpart in the pattern on the floor. A hexagonal ceiling design, for example, is reflected in the hexagonal border of the Adam-designed carpet, probably produced in England's own Axminster factory, or in a similarly shaped motif inlaid into a marble floor.

Doorways and windows are balanced as well, each opening having its precise counterpart on the opposite side of the room. Where a door or window is not called for, a mirror of the same shape might substitute, or a tall recess for sculpture.

The mantel is an important element in the Adam interior; refined in scale and generally painted white, it is flanked by classical columns and decorated with ornament in *scagliola* that simulates marble or is patterned like *pietra dura* in familiar motifs like urns, rosettes, swags, ribbons, ram's heads, guilloches, and Greek keys. Though they are altogether distinctive and generally less rigidly formal, Adam interiors are related in their classical inspiration to those of French Louis XVI style. His selection of fabrics, though perhaps less elaborate, is equally elegant and refined.

Adam's color schemes favor warm-toned pastels, though he occasionally varies these with more saturated hues.

Elegant crystal chandeliers and graceful wall sconces provide the primary illumination in these interiors. Accessories include fine paintings and portraits, plaster casts of classical sculpture, and elegant silver objects by English or French craftsmen. Oval mirrors or girandoles, in delicate gilded frames topped with classical urns and swags, are another distinctive Adam touch. Wedgwood urns, bowls, and decorative plaques, inspired by or literally adapting objects from antiquity, are particularly appropriate complements.

Adam oversaw every element of each project, making drawings for painted ceilings, designing carpet to be woven to his specifications, specifying or selecting furnishings by the most skilled makers, or designing the furniture himself. His furniture is rectilinear in form, with straight, tapering legs. Commodes and consoles are typically oval-fronted, either veneered in rare woods like satinwood or tulipwood or painted in ivory or pastel shades.

Fully thought out and meticulously executed, Robert Adam interiors remain among the finest examples of coordinated design, establishing the foundation for the practice of interior design that would emerge as a serious profession, apart from architecture, more than a century later in America.

OPPOSITE: The Great Hall of Syon House is unmistakably Robert Adam, with the pristine symmetry of its classical surround, and the mirror-image floor and ceiling treatments.

PAGE 102: Adam's interiors for Saltram House in Devon, England, are some of his finest, and the dining room shows his skillful treatment of ceiling and floor covering as complementary designs. The classical fireplace and architectural recesses are also characteristic of Adam interiors.

The fates conspired to bestow England with new resources for luxury products—Axminster (founded 1755) for fine carpets, Royal Worcester (established 1751) for England's first porcelain, Waterford (established 1783) for cut glass to rival French crystal, Matthew Boulton's factory for Sheffield silverplate (established 1762), and Josiah Wedgwood's pottery (established 1759), developing basalt and jasperware, matte-finish stoneware in designs that channeled the look of Roman cameo glass. Georgian England also produced the painters Joshua Reynolds (1723–1792) and Thomas Gainsborough (1727–1788).

As the century drew to a close, neoclassicism continued to dominate English design, becoming even more explicit and sometimes exaggerated in the style that would be named Regency.

ABOUT THE STYLE

The finest Late Georgian interior can hold its own with the best of French style; in its most formal incarnations, it shares many characteristics with a contemporary French neoclassical room. There are, however, notable differences: although the same classical ornament is seen in both, the execution and the furniture details are very different. The Late Georgian room is elegant in its symmetry and refinement, balancing characteristic English restraint against the desire for ornamentation. In its sophistication planning, superbly crafted furnishings, and a worldly mélange of accessories, it represents the high point of English design.

The interior is grand, without assuming extravagant proportions. It is most often rectangular, though occasionally round. Avoiding heavy paneling, cornices, or tapestry, the walls are painted in pleasant colors, with a dado of plaster rather than wood. Above it might be an expanse of scenic wallpaper or patterned fabric. Moldings and plasterwork are white and relatively understated, and ceilings are treated in similar fashion. Doors are paneled or curved to conform to the shapes of circular rooms.

Tall windows with large rectangular panes are dressed in heavy drapery over sheer curtains and topped with a cornice or lambrequin, or they might have newly fashionable roller blinds. Bay windows have also come into fashion during this period.

Textiles are increasingly varied and less weighty, since England has begun producing fine woodblock or copperplate printed fabrics, as well as its distinctive printed chintzes.

By the final decades of the 18th century, all of the textiles and upholstery in the room are coordinated, giving the interior a more unified appearance. Colors are vibrant, with lively pastels lending warmth and variety to the scheme.

Floors of polished oak—stone or marble are more likely in halls or foyers—are covered with Axminster carpets, which are now as desirable as imported ones.

Chandeliers and candelabra in crystal, brass, or bronze provide light as well as decorative interest. And greater attention is given to fine decorative accessories: mirrors, most often gilded and often with *chinoiserie* motifs, clocks, busts of marble or bronze, *torchères*, and candelabra, along with souvenirs of foreign travel. Wedgwood objects may be joined by Sèvres porcelain vases or Meissen figurines.

ABOUT THE FURNITURE

Early Chippendale designs carry the Rococo influence into Late Georgian furniture, with finely executed carving that reflects the various influences seen in his drawing books. As the period progresses, however, neoclassical style takes hold, and furniture abandons asymmetrical ornament and foliate carving, returning to the symmetry and linearity of classical forms.

In the final decade of the century, Hepplewhite and Sheraton styles exemplify the full flowering of neoclassicism in Late Georgian furniture. Chairs are strikingly slimmer than those of the Early Georgian period. The cabriole leg and ball-and-claw foot have disappeared, to be replaced by slender, tapered legs, and slim vertical members. Some chairs recall French forms, though they are not always painted, and all have an air of delicacy.

In case furniture, heavy cornices and pediments are replaced by refined molding, and though cabinets are occasionally carved, the ornament is understated and generally is limited to panels or framing. Glass-doored cabinets are defined in shaped wood mullions, and even the largest pieces have a more refined, lighter look than in the Early Georgian period.

Though mahogany is still widely used, lighter-toned satinwood and fruitwoods are increasingly popular, often decorated with delicate inlays or contrasting banding. Characteristically, English designers continue to use wood as the major ornament, adding marquetry to introduce pattern and avoiding the gilt mounts that are a prominent feature of French period furniture.

PREVIOUS PAGE: Berrington Hall, a neo-classical country house in Herefordshire, England, was designed by Henry Holland, c. 1778. The library has fine plasterwork moldings and ceiling ornament, with furniture in Chippendale and Hepplewhite styles.

ABOVE: Late Georgian armchair with serpentine top rails, straight sides, and carved detail on the arms and legs; made of mahogany, c. 1765.

LEFT: Directly influenced by the "French-style" chairs of Thomas Chippendale, this extravagantly carved giltwood armchair, c. 1775, has a high arched crest and rounded, tapered legs with stiff leaf decoration.

This design combines a chest-of-drawers, bookshelves, and a drop-lid desk in one piece of furniture. Mirrored doors and the decorative finial are Rococo touches often seen in this period.

In the style of Thomas Chippendale, the top of this mahogany breakfront bookcase, c. 1760, has four etched-glass doors enclosing bookshelves, over a lower section with a secretary drawer containing small drawers and pigeonholes. The recess below is flanked by cupboards with drawers and folio storage. The plinth base becomes customary in this period.

ABOVE: This lyre-back chair, c. 1770, has all the hallmarks of Chippendale seating: straight sides, yoke-shaped crest rail, and pierced center splat.

RIGHT: A Hepplewhite-style armchair of carved mahogany, with a shield back on turned tapering legs headed by inlaid blocks that terminate in toupee feet at the front and splay feet on the reverse side, c. 1790.

ABOVE: The sideboard, a new form credited to George Hepplewhite, melded a center table with side pedestals to create a practical item of dining room furniture. This George III mahogany piece, 70 inches long, has a serpentine front and skirt.

BELOW: The demilune commode, a French form, was adopted in England with painted or inlaid decoration in place of applied ornament. This one attributed to prestigious London cabinetmakers Mayhew and Ince, c. 1815, has marquetry of satinwood, tulipwood, and rosewood.

A slim-line George III mahogany bowfront serving
table, c. 1780, with brass gallery on its cross-banded
and ebony strung top, and frieze bordered in satinwood. The use of lighter woods in delicate patterning
was associated with Sheraton style.

Interiors in the style of Robert Adam included neoclassical pieces like this graceful serpentine console table, c. 1740, in rosewood, satinwood, hardwood, and mahogany, its banded top decorated with marquetry and penwork depicting military and musical trophy motifs.

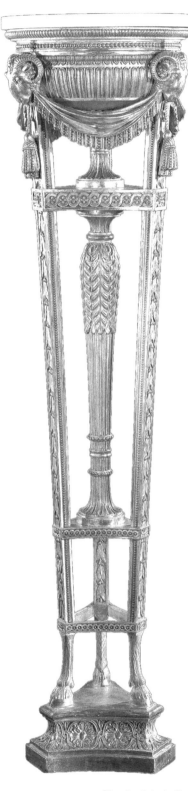

This carved torchère has a Carrara marble top and tripod base on a triangular plinth. The fluted border, ram's heads, and hoof feet reflect the neoclassical ornament favored in the Late Georgian period, particularly in interiors by Robert Adam.

■ Hepplewhite and Sheraton Styles, c. 1790–1810

George Hepplewhite (1721–1786) and Thomas Sheraton (1751–1806) were furniture makers in London during the time of George III, but their names are known primarily because of the pattern books they published, which together form an encyclopedic vocabulary of English neoclassical furniture. Like Thomas Chippendale, each of them illustrated a range of designs, but because the prevailing style was dominated by a single aesthetic, their furniture has many similarities. Both Hepplewhite and Sheraton pieces are light-scaled, slim, and graceful, though Sheraton's are generally more delicate, have more surface detail, and reflect a stronger influence from French styles.

George Hepplewhite died before the publication of *The Cabinetmaker and Upholsterer's Guide* in 1788, which was overseen by his wife, Alice. He is credited for the development of the sideboard, a new form of furniture that combined a cabinet and two flanking pedestals to form a single serving piece for the dining room, which had become established as a permanent single-purpose space. Hepplewhite style is associated with several specific shapes of chair backs—shield, oval, heart, wheel, and camelback—and the use of the Prince of Wales feather motif. Hepplewhite furniture may be mahogany or satinwood, with legs that are slim, most often square, and fluted or reeded, with spade feet. Veneering rather than carving provides ornamentation; classical figures or marquetry in contrasting light woods the most frequent means of ornamentation. Hepplewhite designs appear in many interiors by Robert Adam.

Thomas Sheraton published his *Cabinet-Maker and Upholsterer's Drawing Book* in installments between 1791 and 1794. Sheraton's well-proportioned designs tend to be more rectilinear and slimmer in silhouette than Hepplewhite's. His name is also linked to specific chair forms: light-scaled and rectangular, with delicately carved splats that may be decorated with urns, swags, lyres, or other classical motifs. Cabinetry is varied and graceful, with smooth expanses of fine-grained veneers, generally in lighter woods like satinwood or tulipwood. Ornamentation is delicate, often inspired by that on Louis XVI furniture, and includes marquetry in oval or lozenge shapes, string banding, or festoons. Sheraton case pieces may also have painted accents or graceful brass gallery trim and inlaid banding. His pattern books illustrate specialized accessory pieces such as tambour desks, folding tables, or tables with vanishing drawers, showing a fondness for multipurpose designs and mechanical elements. The legs of Sheraton furniture, like those of Hepplewhite, are slender, tapering, and finished in spade feet or sabots.

When furniture cannot be directly attributed to either of these cabinetmakers, pieces are designated as Hepplewhite or Sheraton on the basis of the book from which the designs were drawn, rather than the shop in which they were made.

Both Hepplewhite and Sheraton styles traveled to America, and their influence, particularly that of the latter, can be seen in American Federal style.

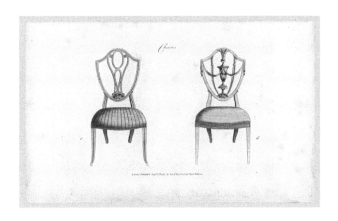

Illustration showing shieldback chair variations from George Hepplewhite's *The Cabinet-Maker and Upholsterer's Guide*.

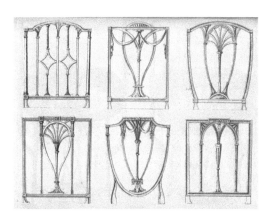

Illustration from *The Cabinet-Maker and Upholsterer's Drawing Book* showing the distinctive rectangular forms associated with Thomas Sheraton's chair designs.

Style Markers

MOOD moderately formal	**SCALE** generous
COLORS vivid and varied	**ORNAMENT** Chinese, Gothic, then classical
KEY MOTIFS pagodas and parasols, then urns, rosettes, festoons	**FURNITURE** light-scaled, drawing-book forms
WOODS most mahogany, lighter woods later	**TEXTILES** silks and damasks, English chintzes

LOOK FOR
Chippendale, Hepplewhite,
Sheraton furniture, Adam style

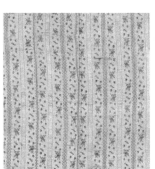

Pastel colors and a stripe-and-floral pattern would be appropriate for an interior in the George III period.

For a bolder statement, a neat pattern of foliage on a muted neutral-tone silk ground.

CHAPTER 10

Late Neoclassicism in France: Directoire/ Empire Style, c. 1790–1814

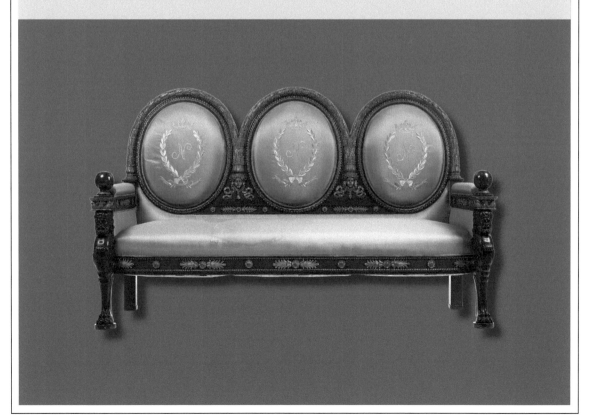

Late Neoclassicism | Directoire/Empire Style, c. 1790–1814

ABOUT THE PERIOD

The impact of the French Revolution of 1789 resonated through every aspect of life, in all sectors of society. The demise or departure of the monarchy and the nobles left designers and craftsmen without patrons for their luxury wares. In the search for new patronage, their designs became a reflection of the social climate, and the transitional Directoire style was named for the Directorate, the newly established legislature. Though retaining the aesthetic of neoclassicism, it distanced French styles from any association with the monarchy by adhering more closely to the forms and ornament of the ancient world.

The Directoire evolved into the majestic and overtly political Empire style, named for the reign of Napoleon Bonaparte (1769–1821), the general who declared himself Emperor in 1804, ruling France and casting his shadow over a good part of Europe until 1814. Napoleon sought to glorify his country, and more importantly himself, in the tradition of ancient Rome. Design became the visual expression of his political aims. His ideal classical world was celebrated in the politically inspired paintings of Jacques David (1748–1825).

Napoleon was the last French ruler to pursue the monarchy's tradition of patronage. He commissioned furnishings for the palaces he had occupied, mandating a style that mixed his personal motifs with those from classical Greek and Roman sources. After traveling with Napoleon's campaign in Egypt, his architects, Charles Percier (1764–1838) and Pierre Fontaine (1762–1853), published *Recueil de décorations intérieures* (*Collection of Interior Decoration*, 1801 and 1812), which included designs inspired by the exotic country and the Emperor's military achievements. They redecorated interiors in the Louvre and Tuileries Palaces and the Château de Fontainebleau for the Emperor and Empress, and in Josephine's Château de Malmaison.

Napoleon's followers in France, and in other countries under his influence, adopted the Empire style—possibly motivated as much by the desire to curry favor with its powerful progenitor as admiration of his taste. The exaggerated classicism of Empire spread across much of Europe and became fashionable in such widely separated countries as Italy, Austria, and Russia, each creating its own distinctive variations of the style. It also became a primary inspiration for Biedermeier style in Germany, which evolved after the

Empire had passed. Parallels to the Empire style included the Regency in England and the American Empire, an extension of the Federal period. With Napoleon's defeat, the Empire fell out of fashion, though an interest in neoclassicism continued to inform styles in France.

ABOUT THE STYLE

The Empire interior is a testament to imperial pomp and power, taking the basic elements of neoclassicism and magnifying their scale and ornament. Although amply furnished, these interiors are in many ways less elaborate than those of the Louis XVI period, but their imposing furnishings and richer colorations are more dramatic, and the result is an assertive, masculine air. A mélange of luxurious fabrics and dark, highly polished surfaces, Empire style projects palatial grandeur to rival that of the Baroque.

It is a grand space with strict geometric proportions, its linearity emphasized by prominent architectural details in place of the *boiserie* of 18th-century interiors. Walls are divided into sections by columns and pilasters, usually on ornamental bases and often topped with gilt capitals, flanked by large paintings or mirrors that create striking backdrops for the furnishings. The ceiling is flat or concave, sometimes suggesting barrel vaulting, and is decorated with classical moldings or other motifs drawn directly from those in Pompeii and adapted as precisely as possible. A circular room, or even a square one, may be enveloped in stripes, either with draped fabric or boldly patterned wallpaper, emulating the tents used in Napoleon's Egyptian campaign.

Doors and windows in the Empire interior are not overly elaborate, with restrained moldings and over-door panels. Windows have large panes of glass and are crowned with ornately sculptured valances and swagged over-draperies, pulled back to show secondary layers in contrasting color and fabric; each layer is weighted with tassels and trim. The invention of the jacquard loom has made the weaving of multicolored textiles easier and less costly, and such elaborate window treatments, as well as upholstery and wall hangings, are the result. Scenic wallpapers were another option.

The brilliant colors of Empire style are a striking departure from the softer tones of the preceding French periods. The patriotic Directoire tricolor palette of red, white, and blue has been supplemented with saturated shades like deep blue and green, golden yellow, rich red, and violet.

Floors of marble or wood parquet are polished and left bare, or covered with a carpet patterned in precise, geometric motifs of the ancient world, or symbols associated with Napoleon, such as the bee, the wreath with initial N, or Empress Josephine's swan.

The chimneypiece is classical in form, with a marble mantel flanked by prominent columns or caryatids. Mirrors are large and defined by similar motifs.

Most of the ornament is drawn directly from ancient wall paintings or Greek vases, although elements of Egyptian design often supplement the familiar vocabulary. Accessories in these rooms, from bronze chandeliers and sconces to classical statuary to Napoleonic plaques, reprise the same or similar motifs.

About the Furniture

There are actually fewer individual items of furniture in the Empire interior, but these are grander, even massive in scale—marble-topped rectangular armoires, pedestal-based tables, monumental sleigh beds, and the classic *Récamier* chaise, a new form named for a Parisian socialite pictured in a famous Jacques David portrait. Chairs have retained the shapes of the earlier neoclassical style, but they have broader proportions and heavier frames. Legs are columnar or adapting classical forms like curule, and armrests or arm supports may take the form of animal heads or mythical figures. In more explicit translations from the antique, objects like the *klismos* chair, the Egyptian X-base folding stool, and the tripod table underscore the classical theme.

On the cabinetry, highly polished expanses of richly figured veneers have replaced decorative marquetry: the emphasis on unadorned wood, begun in the austerity of the Directoire, is retained in the extravagant Empire. Woods, imported from the French colonies, include highly figured mahogany, with ebony as well as elm, beech, ash, and other less exotic accents, often ebonized or gilded. Underscoring many of the case pieces, plinth bases emphasize the rectangular forms, though sometimes exaggerating their severity.

Gilt-bronze (ormolu) ornament is applied in the shape of columns, swans, eagles, caryatids, and classical swags, as well as Egyptian, military, or Napoleonic motifs.

PREVIOUS PAGE: The library of Emperor Napoleon I, in the Chateau de Malmaison, France, creates a majestic effect with a domed ceiling painted with classical motifs. Built-in bookcases are of polished mahogany, and the furniture is fitted with ormolu mounts.

RIGHT: Napoleon I was associated with furniture reflecting the Emperor's power and his ambitions of conquest, as in this parcel-gilt fauteuil, c. 1810, with sphinx-shaped arms, scroll backs in the form of entwined serpents, and hoof-footed saber legs.

BELOW: This canapé in parcel-gilt mahogany was made from a design by Napoleon's architects, Percier and Fontaine. The center of the back is carved with a laurel wreath surrounding the letter N, and the apron has a figure of Hercules. Upholstered in blue-and-gold silk, a color scheme favored by the Emperor.

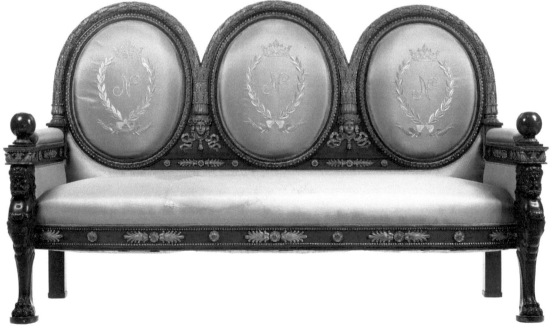

ABOVE LEFT: The curule form, dating to the time of the Roman empire, shapes a carved mahogany stool attributed to Georges Jacob, c. 1795, after a design by Percier and Fontaine.

ABOVE RIGHT: The primary wood in most furniture of this period was mahogany, with fine veneer and classical details. This ormolu-mounted demilune commode dates to c. 1805.

BELOW: This mahogany *lit en bateau*, with gilt-bronze mounts, is attributed to Jacob Frères and P. P. Thomire, c. 1800.

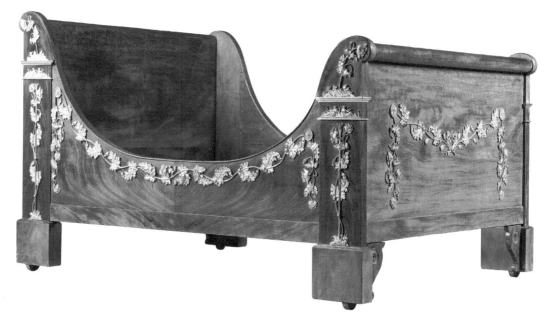

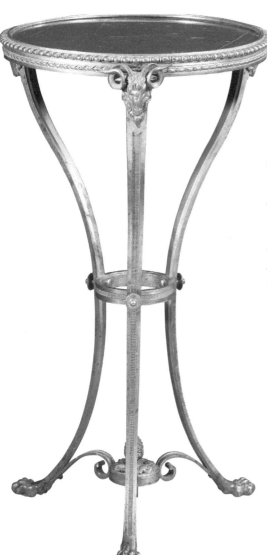

LEFT: The marble-topped *guéridon* table dates to the early 19th century. Its silhouette is closely related to pieces in the ancient world.

BELOW: Empire case pieces were imposing forms with large expanses of fine-grained wood and bold ornament, like this *sécretaire à abattant*, by Jacob-Desmalter, c. 1812, of Indian burl wood with gilded and patinated bronze mounts and ebonized columns, sitting on a broad plinth base.

The *surtout de table*, an elaborate centerpiece that
might be made of porcelain, silver, or gold, was likely
to be seen on formal dining tables in 18th-century France.
This ormolu piece, c. 1815, has been mounted to make a decorative low table.

Style Markers

MOOD pretentious	**SCALE** grand
COLORS rich and saturated	**ORNAMENT** selective, but imposing
KEY MOTIFS mythical figures and animals, military and Napoleonic symbols	**FURNITURE** massive, architectural, polished veneers
WOODS mahogany, ebony	**TEXTILES** sumptuous

LOOK FOR
tented rooms, Egyptian accents

On a fine satin ground, symmetrical motifs with a classical feeling to suit Empire style.

The bee motif, adopted by Napoleon as a symbol of the empire, was often seen on fabrics of the time.

CHAPTER 11
Early Neoclassicism in America: Federal Style, c. 1785–1820

ABOUT THE PERIOD

The American Revolution of 1776 created a new nation, but its effect on design was not immediate, though it would be considerable. When a new style emerged a decade or so later, its movement toward refinement and elegance reflected several aspects of the young republic: the search for a strong national identity, the presence of a consumer elite, and empathy with the French, the Revolutionary allies who had staged their own rebellion in 1789. The style was called Federal, after the name of George Washington's political party, and it represented the early phase of neoclassicism in America.

In the closing years of the 18th century, the classical aesthetic of Robert Adam became the height of fashion for the new and mostly native-born aristocracy of American merchants and ship owners who filled their homes with Hepplewhite and Sheraton furniture. Rejecting the heavy ornamentation and Rococo forms of Chippendale design, Federal style focused, like its European counterparts, on classical forms inspired initially by excavations at Pompeii and Herculaneum. As the style developed into what is designated American Empire, it drew more heavily on French designs like those of Percier and Fontaine.

New York was the center of trade and industry, and Federal furniture highlighted the skills of American craftsmen like Duncan Phyfe (1770–1854), Samuel McIntire (1757–1811) in Salem, and John Seymour (1738–1818) and Thomas Seymour (1771–1848) in Boston, though Phyfe became more closely associated with the Empire style that followed. Perhaps the most celebrated proponent of neoclassical style, particularly in its French-influenced interpretations, was Thomas Jefferson (1743–1826). His gentleman-architect designs included the campus of The University of Virginia and, more famously, his own home at Monticello, a translation that owed much to Palladian architecture. Jeffersonian buildings have smooth façades and gracefully detailed columns and portico at the entrance, precursors of the more exaggerated neoclassicism that would later captivate American architects.

Along with Queen Anne, Federal has been the most enduring, and most influential, of all 18th-century American styles.

ABOUT THE STYLE

More gracious and cosmopolitan than any previous American interiors, Federal rooms exude the confidence that came with independence and a sense of national pride. They are more sophisticated, though also somewhat more formal, than Colonial interiors, with symmetrical plans and straight-lined furniture completely erasing any remnants of Rococo.

The Federal interior is geometrically shaped and relatively spacious. Smooth plastered walls are painted white or warm tones of blue, green, or mustard—subdued in public rooms, much brighter in private ones. Moldings are white, classically detailed, and may have plaster ornament like swags, garlands, and rosettes. The dining room or parlor in this period will often have wallpaper with patriotic motifs or elegant handpainted scenics imported from France.

Tall windows, often Palladian style, will have fairly elaborate window treatments, perhaps with draped pelmets, swags, or tasseled pullback draperies over simple muslin or cotton curtains.

Floors are polished wood, graced with carpets. In wealthy homes, carpeting in geometric patterns might be laid in strips to cover the entire floor and finished with a decorative border.

Fabrics, many of them fine French imports, are richer than any used previously in America, in solid hues or patterned with appropriate classical motifs.

The classical revival has spurred the use of more varied colors, muted pastels most often combining with white—straw-yellow, oyster, dove grey, green, and fawn—blends with the lightness of Adam style.

Lighting has become more sophisticated, and formal chandeliers provide the requisite finishing touch in major rooms, either brass with crystal drops or cut-glass shades. Chandeliers and sconces still depend on candles, though the first oil lamp, the saucer-type "Betty," is introduced in 1790.

Decorations are more varied than in prior periods and more distinctly American. The eagle, the national symbol that was adopted after independence was declared, is the most frequently used ornament on mirrors and other accessories, and a circle of stars, representing the thirteen colonies, is also popular. The "Constitution mirror" is a popular style, a wood-framed mirror with a raised molding and pediment, often with an eagle finial. Clocks are now widely made in America, and tall case clocks—later called grandfather clocks—as well as the banjo form, have become symbols of status and national pride. Additional ornaments are silver by the smith and patriot Paul Revere (1735–1818) and portraits on the walls, suggesting the stability of family and home, by American painters like Gilbert Stuart (1755–1828) or Rembrandt Peale (1778–1860).

No longer multipurpose, the Federal interior reflects developments in room types and configurations. The parlor has emerged as the most important space, with its own type of furnishings, and the dining room is a newly designated space that also requires specific furniture and fittings.

About the Furniture

Federal furniture is distinguished by its geometric forms, slim lines, and smooth expenses of mahogany or lighter-tone woods, often accented with contrasting banding and inlays. The "skin" of veneer has replaced carved decoration. The new range of objects for specific rooms includes sideboards and large tables for the dining room, long sofas and matching chairs for the parlor, decorative tester beds, and a variety of occasional pieces like sewing or card tables, sofa tables, side tables, the desk-bookcase (used as a china cabinet), and ladies' dressing tables.

The American highboy has been supplanted by the chest-on-chest and various storage pieces on platforms or bracket feet. Brought over from England, the ubiquitous and inexpensive Windsor chair has become the most popular and varied all-purpose piece in America. Though introduced earlier, it is most closely associated with the Federal period—in fan, comb, loop-back, and other variations.

Despite the individuality of many objects, Federal furniture conforms more closely to pattern-book models than any previous American styles. With access to the finest imported veneers and skilled, often European-trained, craftsmen to execute the designs, American Hepplewhite and Sheraton furniture rivals the finest English pieces.

PREVIOUS PAGE: Homewood House, in Baltimore, Maryland, is a fine example of an elegant interior of the period, with Sheraton and other late-18th-century furniture, as well as collections of silver and ceramics.

BELOW: Translating an English form into American vernacular, this Federal secretary-bookcase from Massachusetts is made of figured mahogany with understated inlay, c. 1800.

LEFT: In a form derived from Sheraton drawings, this mahogany side chair from New York has a rectilinear back with swag and feather carving, c. 1800.

BELOW: A Federal-style, eagle-topped *girandole* mirror, of carved and gilded pine, c. 1815. The eagle was adopted as a symbol of the new government, appearing frequently as ornament.

RIGHT: The Windsor chair, and its many variations, was an inexpensive and versatile seating piece, made of any available wood and used in almost any room. This continuous-arm form is perhaps the most familiar of the genre.

BELOW: Of all the late-18th-century English styles, Sheraton was the most influential in America. This cabriole mahogany sofa, made in Massachusetts, c. 1790, reflects the slim lines and restrained ornament that characterized the style.

LEFT: This drop-leaf Pembroke table, a form originating in England, has cluster-column base and paw feet. Made in New York, c. 1810, it reflects the interest in ornament drawn from classical antiquity.

BELOW: The sideboard was extremely popular in Federal dining rooms. This straight-front, bellflower-inlaid piece in Hepplewhite style is attributed to William Whitehead of New York City, c. 1790.

Style Markers

MOOD formal, with Adam influence	**SCALE** relatively grand for America
COLORS varied and bright	**ORNAMENT** classical
KEY MOTIFS eagle, satinwood banding, and oval inlays	**FURNITURE** slim and rectilinear, with polished veneers and little carving
TEXTILES Indian crewels, chintzes, imported silks and damasks	**LOOK FOR** Hepplewhite and Sheraton forms, Windsor chair

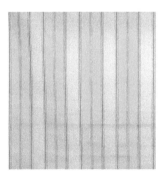

Striped patterns were a favored complement to neoclassical styles, such as this French *Matignon* taffeta rayé.

CHAPTER 12
Late Neoclassicism in England: Regency Style, c. 1811–1830

ABOUT THE PERIOD

The Regency denotes the late neoclassical period in England and was an evolution of the preceding style, rather than a break with it. Regency design incorporated the refinement of Late Georgian classicism with a growing emphasis on historical accuracy, based on the forms and details of Greco-Roman models. The result was a more explicit, and often more exaggerated, interpretation of classical style. The Regency has its counterpart in two other styles—the Empire in France and the similarly named style following the Federal period in America—and the three share many characteristics in interiors and furniture forms.

The style was named for the period (1811–1820) when George II was too ill to reign and his son served as Prince Regent, ending when the Prince ascended to the throne as George IV (1762–1830, reigned 1820–1830). Regency actually appeared several years earlier and continued after George II's death to overlap with the revival styles of the 19th century. During this period, Sir John Soane (1753–1837), long-time architect of the Bank of London, designed strictly classical buildings and interiors, like those of his own home, that moved away from the decorative neoclassicism of Robert Adam. Apart from the ancient world, much of the inspiration for Regency design came from the colonial holdings of England, France, and Belgium, which had spurred interest in design motifs from foreign lands. Regency style became a quixotic blend of familiar classical elements with fantastic ornament from such esoteric sources.

Thomas Hope (1769–1831), the name most closely linked to Regency furniture, was a wealthy dilettante and dealer who created an environment for his collections in his own home, Flaxman House. His 1897 publication, *Household Furniture and Decoration*, encouraged an interest in Greek and Egyptian styles, though most furniture of the period was less extreme than Hope's designs.

The most exotic incarnation of Regency style was the fanciful redesign of Brighton Pavilion, whose extraordinary combination of Moorish, Indian, and Chinese design was created, from 1815–1822, by John Nash (1752–1835), as a refuge for the Prince Regent from the formality of palace life in London. Its extravagantly overwrought interiors unleashed a passion for bamboo and reawakened an interest in exotica and all things

Chinese. Sadly, once becoming king, George rarely enjoyed his country retreat, which remains an exemplar of the Regency at its most whimsical and certainly most decorative.

ABOUT THE STYLE

A combination of refinement, classicism, and charm, the typical Regency interior is refreshingly bold for English style, with lively colors and more pronounced references to Greek and Egyptian sources than are seen in the Late Georgian period. It is more closely allied to Continental design than that of England, with lively color and refreshing touches of exotic ornament coexisting comfortably with classical motifs. A balanced and uncluttered arrangement of furniture and objects, it is more relaxed than its French Empire counterpart and less weighty than its American one.

The Regency room is a graceful, high-ceilinged space, punctuated with tall French doors and arched windows. The walls and ceiling, reflecting the classical aesthetic, might have white plaster rosettes, pilasters, and moldings, occasionally with subtle gilding. The walls are painted in more vivid tones than in previous periods—turquoise, salmon pink, emerald green, saffron, or cherry—often enhanced with decorative painting with *chinoiserie* or Pompeiian motifs. As an alternative, English or French wallpapers are patterned in stylized fruits, flowers, or classical stripes. Doorways and windows may have restrained classical trim.

Window treatments might be filmy curtains, hung on prominent brass rods and overlaid with deep swags of heavy silk in stripes or dark solids, generously trimmed with golden cord and heavy tassels. Fabrics are similar to those used in the Georgian era, although the designs, woven or printed, are more likely to be based on ancient motifs and classical architecture. Solids are seen more often than patterns, heightening the effect of simplicity and focusing attention on line rather than ornament.

Room-size, allover-patterned carpet is increasingly popular, or patterned oilcloth as a less costly alternative over parquet or black-and-white marble floors.

Color schemes are more vivid than the previous periods, and might include such tones as turquoise, salmon pink, emerald green, or saffron gold.

Lighting comes from chandeliers, similar to those used in French Empire rooms—perhaps of enameled metal rather than crystal, with brass accents in appropriate motifs from antiquity.

Classical urns and vases, in lively color, may be made of English bone china or ironstone. Plaster busts of famous Greeks and Romans and shapely framed mirrors are other popular accessories.

ABOUT THE FURNITURE

Regency furniture updates classical symmetry, combining straight lines with modulated curves. It draws on heavier Greek forms rather than slender Pompeiian ones, but modifies the larger scale with relatively simple decoration. Hope's pieces, notable exceptions to this rule, are unrestrained in their exotic detail: they are large-scaled, with animal heads and paws, columns and caryatids, or sphinx-like supports. Other Regency designs are considerably more understated, including extension dining tables with splay-legged tripod bases, round center tables on pedestal bases, or sideboards with brass galleries. Legs of tables and chairs often end in brass paw feet. Mahogany is still the primary wood, with rosewood or zebrawood veneers as accents.

Among the most typical Regency seating designs are bold Grecian-style sofas with scrolled head and footrest drawn from the French *chaise longue*. Highly decorative chairs appear in variants of the *klismos* form, some with arms or legs carved with classical figures like chimera or dolphins, and often gilded. Frames of highly polished mahogany or lighter rosewood and satinwood, are ornamented with brass inlay, trellised galleries, or star-shaped bolt heads and studs.

PREVIOUS PAGE: The upstairs drawing room of The Royal Pavilion, in Brighton, England, designed for the Prince Regent by John Nash. The interiors combine Regency furnishings and fantasy elements drawn from the Middle and Far East.

ABOVE: The *chaise longue*, perhaps the form most closely associated with early 19th-century styles in France as well as England, was designed for bedroom or boudoir reclining. This shapely piece is made of faux rosewood with brass inlays, c. 1810.

LEFT: Scrolled arms and sabre legs reflect the classical inspiration of this parcel-gilt *bergère*, c. 1810, its painted and gilt-accented wood frame giving it an imposing presence.

The sofa table was devised in the Regency period. Set along the back of a sofa, the table provided a place to place serving trays, hold a lamp, or stack books. This one, of calamander and ebony, dates to c.1820.

Pedestal-base drum tables, named for the shape of their center portions, were placed in the entry hall. In large estates with many tenants, they were ringed with drawers that housed tenant receipts. This rosewood piece, decorated with brass mounts, dates to c. 1815.

RIGHT: Objects like this convex mirror, c. 1815, were primarily decorative rather than functional accessories, hung over a side-board, mantel, or hall table.

BELOW: Sabre legs, first seen in the classical *klismos* chair, returned in Regency seating pieces, like this rosewood hall chair, c. 1810.

■ Biedermeier, c. 1820s–1850s

Described as both an adaptation of French Empire and a simplification of the English Regency, Biedermeier is a style of furniture that developed as those periods had passed their peaks. Not so much a specific aesthetic as a general approach to design, it was intended as a simplification of neoclassicism and a rejection of extravagant French style. Though generally less pretentious than those of the Empire style, Biedermeier pieces are often highly sophisticated.

Biedermeier is most easily recognized in case furniture with bold, geometric forms—fall-front desks with numerous compartments, armoires, display cabinets, and globe tables—framed by architectural elements like columns, pediments, cornices, and moldings that give the furniture a weighty, sometimes massive, look. In place of carving, highly polished, figured veneers are the primary ornament—rich mahogany, ash, native fruitwoods, and other lighter-tone woods—with veneers split to create bolder patterns. Ebonized columns are a frequent accent, as are applied gilt ornaments in the form of sphinxes, swans, and other stylized classical motifs.

Sidechairs in Biedermeier style are strikingly varied, in myriad and appealing designs with shapely, sculptural backs. Chaises, straight-back sofas, or settees have familiar classical silhouettes and polished wood frames.

The name Biedermeier, which like most style designations was bestowed after the fact, comes from a cartoon character satirizing the middle-class German *petit-bourgeois*, the presumed consumers of this type of furniture, who aspired to the trappings of the aristocracy. However, it is something of a misnomer, in that the furniture itself is finely crafted and generally costly to make. Though associated primarily with Germany, Biedermeier was popular in most of northern Europe, including Austria, Hungary, and the Scandinavian countries. It was produced until almost the middle of the 19th century and has been revived several times since.

NEXT PAGE: The bedroom of Queen Louise of Prussia, in Charlottenburg Palace, Berlin, has Biedermeier furnishings, clearly derived from French Empire style, against a backdrop of classical drapery.

Style Markers

MOOD	**SCALE**
relatively formal	restrained grandeur
COLORS	**ORNAMENT**
varied, saturated	overtly classical
KEY MOTIFS	**FURNITURE**
sphinx, caryatid, rosettes	graceful silhouettes, expanses of polished wood, some gilding
WOOD	**TEXTILES**
mahogany	luxurious

LOOK FOR
klismos, Grecian chaise,
exotic accents

This ribbed silk damask, called Fritillaire, was made in 1808 for Napoleon's bedroom in the *Palais des Tuileries*.

CHAPTER 13
Late Neoclassicism in America: American Empire Style, c. 1810–1830

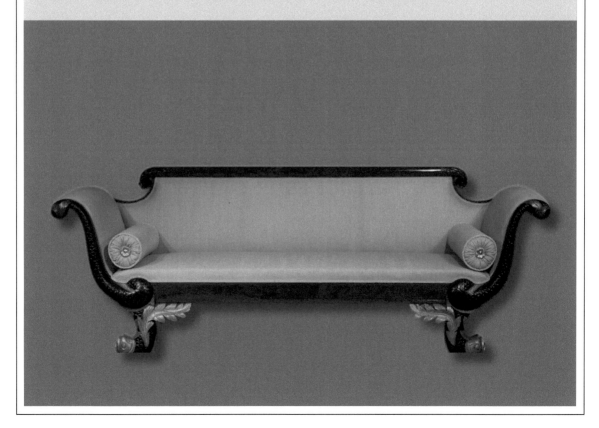

ABOUT THE PERIOD

America began to feel its strength as an independent nation, challenging the British again in the War of 1812, and starting its exploration of the uncharted Western territories. Empire seems an appropriate name for the style of this time. A counterpart to, and heavily drawing on, the Empire style in France, as well as the English Regency, American Empire overlaps the Federal style, of which it is often considered the latter part. More robust and overtly classical than its predecessor, American Empire was a once-removed continuation of the European romance with the ancient world. As always, however, American style began with inspiration from Europe and developed into a look that was uniquely its own. For the new republic, the neoclassical had implicit sociopolitical connotations, its symbolism suggesting a link to the democracy of ancient Greece.

Empire was also the first specifically French-influenced American style, the logical result of admiration for a country that had been an ally against England in the Revolutionary War. Many of the designs reflected the aesthetic of Percier and Fontaine's Napoleonic-era designs—most markedly the bold objects made by French emigrant Charles-Honoré Lannuier (1779–1819). Other important cabinetmakers in the major cities produced superb furniture in this period: the Seymours in Boston, Lannuier and Duncan Phyfe in New York, and brothers John and Hugh Finlay in Baltimore (working 1799–1833) were only a few of an increasing number in this now-established trade. Phyfe, who became established during the Federal period, was the largest and most prominent of these cabinetmakers, employing dozens of craftsmen, and his name is often used to designate much of the furniture of his era, as that of Chippendale was in mid-18th-century England.

Though classicism remained a constant in American architecture, interiors in the 19th century grew more diverse. American Empire evolved into a style with projecting pillars, exaggerated scrolls, and a sometimes-awkward weightiness. This Greek Revival style, by this time the paradigm of public architecture in America, was difficult to translate into interiors, which tended to repeat the same vocabulary of classical architectural details. It was, however, the first to be implemented in mass-produced furniture. Overlapping it, and more successfully translated into the interiors classified as Victorian, were several successive styles inspired by historic periods of the past.

About the Style

More striking than the Federal interior, though sometimes more pretentious as well, an American Empire room has strong overtones of French design but is less elaborate than its continental counterparts. It is more spacious, reflecting the affluence of an established society: its furniture and fittings are correspondingly larger in scale and enhanced with more elaborate ornament and a palette of deeper, contrasting hues.

Walls, with white baseboard, dado, and crown molding, might be painted a rich tone of mustard, blue, or brown, or will be covered in handpainted French scenic papers, with a motif that evokes classicism or patriotic events. Classical motifs might be added in friezes beneath the molding or above doors and windows.

Prosperity has made possible broader expanses of windows, with larger panes calling for assertive treatments. The drapery treatment is a simplified adaptation of French Empire designs, in rich fabrics like satin, damask, or velvet.

Colors, as noted, are richer and more intense than those of the Federal period—royal blue and gold, dark greens and crimson, or other warm and saturated tones.

Parquet or marble floors would be covered with imported rugs, or newly fashionable carpet—perhaps in a medallion pattern—laid from wall to wall.

About the Furniture

Furniture has grown larger in scale and more robust in appearance than earlier Federal designs, with strong geometric forms, darker woods, and broader expanses of polished veneer. Classical sideboards, chests, and wardrobes are low to the ground, sitting on broad paw feet or platform bases. Decorative carving is generally deemphasized in favor of a smooth surface in which the rich grain of fine veneers like mahogany, the material of choice, serves as primary ornament. The demand for more elaborate furniture has brought widespread use of brass inlays, ormolu and gilding, ebonized or faux-marble painted accents, and marble tops. Tables are important and varied: pedestal-base dining tables, sofa tables, pedestal-base center tables, pier tables, drop-leaf tables, or card tables all generally follow English forms but differ in their tendency to weightiness.

Decorative motifs are assertive and overtly classical: pillars or pilasters, lyre and acanthus motifs, sometimes lion masks. Nationalistic symbols like eagles, or classical ones like dolphins or mythological winged creatures and caryatids, are also used, as are massive animal paws or colonettes of carved leaves in place of feet.

Chairs, often suggesting the form of the X-base *curule* or saber-legged Greek *klismos*, might be upholstered or open-backed, the latter often with a lyre motif. Tightly upholstered, wood-framed sofas or chaises in curvy classical silhouettes are popular expressions of the American Empire style. Suites of furniture have been introduced, consisting of several pieces in matching design, particularly in parlor seating. The low-to-ground sleigh bed, with same-height head and footboard, is a variant of French models.

NEXT PAGE: Boscobel, an early 19th-century estate in Garrison, New York, is a fine example of Federal style architecture, but its interiors reflect the more elaborate décor of the early 19th-century American Empire style that succeeded it.

ABOVE: America adopted the Empire style from France, often improvising on the original with extravagant ornament like the dolphin legs on this curvaceous piece, in mahogany with cherry, maple, and white pine secondary woods. Painted *verde antique*, it is gilded and bronzed, with iron castors. Made in New York City, c. 1820.

BELOW: This card table, one of a pair, is typical of the striking furniture designs by French expatriate Charles-Honoré Lannuier, with its paw feet and bold classical ornament. Made of carved and parcel-gilt rosewood, in New York City, c. 1815. Many of Lannuier's pieces had winged classical figures.

RIGHT: Neoclassical card tables with eagle mounts, probably by Thomas Seymour, one of the leading cabinetmakers in Boston, c. 1815.

BELOW: The understated design of this 69 1/2-inch-high mahogany secretary is enhanced with mirrored doors, ormolu, and gilt-brass mounts. Attributed to Duncan Phyfe, New York City, c. 1815.

BELOW: Reflecting the taste for Sheraton-style details, this bowfront chest of drawers, possibly by Thomas Seymour, was made in Massachusetts, c. 1815, of cherry, mahogany, bird's eye maple, striped maple, and ebony, with pine as secondary wood (American furniture used available local woods, improvising individual variations on European models). Lion's-head pulls are gilt brass.

LEFT: A dressing table in the Sheraton style, made in the workshop of Duncan Phyfe, New York City, c. 1810, has the lyre ornaments often seen in Phyfe's furniture.

RIGHT: Reprising the ancient Greek *klismos* form, this shapely mahogany side chair has carved legs and paw feet. By the most celebrated designer of the era, Duncan Phyfe, New York City, c. 1815.

Style Markers

MOOD
formal, a bit pretentious

SCALE
grander than Federal

COLORS
rich, varied

ORNAMENT
overtly classical, often exaggerated

KEY MOTIFS
Greek and Egyptian figures

FURNITURE
weighty forms, expanses of wood, some carving and gilding

TEXTILES
French-type silks and damasks

LOOK FOR
furniture in suites, variants of Empire and English Regency

Gold medallion-like ornaments on red satin typify the kind of richly colored French textiles, often with classical motifs, that suited the style of the time.

Part III

19TH CENTURY:
Revival and Reform

CHAPTER 14
The Victorian Era: A Century of Revivals

The styles of the 19th century are often referred to collectively as Victorian, after the British monarch who reigned from 1837 to 1901, when that country led the Western world in industrial and social growth. But there is no single Victorian style; the period witnessed a battle between diverse and simultaneous styles, all reprising or reimagining designs from the past. Victorian eclecticism incorporated the Second Empire and the Restoration in France, and was seen in several European countries, but it is most closely associated with England and America. In America, especially, it saw the introduction of some half-dozen styles within one half-century, often in the same home, sometimes the same room, and occasionally the same piece of furniture.

The major cause of these profound changes was the Industrial Revolution, which began in the 18th century and affected every aspect of society in the next one. Industry had resulted in prosperity for merchants and factory owners, and poverty for underpaid and exploited workers. Nevertheless, more people had money to buy goods, and the expansion of production was inevitable. When objects could be made quickly and relatively inexpensively by machine, there was no reason to wait for handmade products, which were, in any case, far more costly. Moreover, consumers could choose from among many historic precedents rather than being restricted to a single aesthetic. The romantic return to the past offered an escape from the stresses of life in the newly urbanized industrial society. The result of these influences was a plethora of styles, each of which could be copied and amplified, with layers of ornament stamped out in metal, machine-carved, or stenciled. Some of it was charming; much of it was overdone.

The dominant influences were Greek, Gothic, Rococo, and Renaissance, each coalescing in a specific revival style, and all of them were popularized through widely published pattern books. The furniture forms remained essentially the same, varying only with the application of different ornament. In the search for novelty, a greater variety of woods were used in furniture, as well as alternative materials, including wrought iron (a new material), *papier mâché*, and wicker (made of rattan from China, or reed). New technology enabled greater seating comfort; the coiled spring for upholstery was invented in 1828, requiring deeper seats, which resulted in shorter chair legs. Other than that, little genuine innovation occurred until late in the century, with the introduction of inventive mechanical chairs and multifunction furniture.

In most revival-style interiors, particularly as the century progressed, surface decoration was the implement of design: furniture was almost overpowered by carving; upholstery was grandly overstuffed, tufted, and trimmed; draperies were layered, fringed, and tasseled. Carpets and textiles were made in a range of patterns to suit each revival style, and by mid-century, machine-printed wallpapers were ubiquitous, offering a new and relatively inexpensive way to envelop an interior with pattern, including coordinated panels and borders to suit any setting and style.

As industrial production increased, many accessory objects were available through mail-order catalogs, encouraging the impulse toward acquisitiveness and overdecoration. Mass-produced lithographs, using a process invented in late-18th-century Germany, made framed artwork available to a wide, if not always discriminating, audience.

As the decades passed, the lights of decorative oil or gas lamps faded in the enthusiasm for chandeliers, which waned in turn with the introduction of electric lighting in the 1880s. Colors shifted from soft to bright to dark, particularly in the final decade, when gloomy tones were considered the height of sophistication.

Several other influences were at work to bring even greater variety to furniture in the 19th century. The opening of Japan to the West by Commander Matthew Perry in 1854 stimulated interest in the exotic Far East, influencing England and to a lesser degree other European countries, and America as well. This led to a late-century vogue for decorating a particular room in one exotically foreign style. In the British colonies, traditional English styles were embellished with African and Asian motifs or Caribbean elements like pineapple carvings, while Indian colonial furniture used inlaid ivory and mirrors. In America, the Centennial Exposition in Philadelphia, in 1876, awakened a wave of nostalgia and an interest in America's heritage that brought a wave of Colonial Revival interiors. The same exhibition stimulated interest in objects from foreign lands. Expanded trade and travel generated a fad for such exotic conceits as Moorish smoking rooms or Arab halls. This wave of exotica did not itself constitute a style but was part of the mélange that made for a diverse and intriguing period in design.

The styles of the century conflated in America in what was called the Gilded Age, when the New York townhouses and Newport mansions of a new aristocracy evoked Beaux Arts and Baroque, exotica and eclecticism, in a fitting coda to the era that reprised the grandeur of centuries past.

Nineteenth-century interiors are often described in broad generalizations, most of them unflattering: a clutter of furniture and objects, a profusion of textiles, a plethora of pattern on every available surface—too much of not-good-enough things. But generalizations are misleading: albeit tending toward the overdone, these interiors are filled with life and personality. They are as creative in their way as any in history.

Queen Victoria's bedroom in Osborne House on the Isle of Wight, England. The private residence built for themselves by Prince Albert was furnished like any comfortable, upper-class residence.

■ Greek Revival, c. 1825–1855

ABOUT THE PERIOD

Primarily an architectural style, Greek Revival overlapped the American Empire, and its design aesthetic is similar, but with a shift in focus. The interest in neoclassicism that originated in mid-to-late-18th-century Europe changed as archaeologists and historians began to study actual sites and artifacts of ancient Greece, and it became obvious that the Roman architecture that had been copied since the Renaissance had actually been inspired by Greece. After Englishman James "Athenian" Stuart visited and wrote about it in the 18th century, Greece supplanted Rome as a source of inspiration, and the Elgin Marbles, showcased in the Grecian-style British Museum, reinforced awareness of the Parthenon's importance as an iconic historic structure.

There were other reasons for the growing interest in Greek design among Americans; the new country sympathized with the Greek war for independence (1821–1830), and the War of 1812 against England led to a rejection of the Robert Adam–inspired Federal style. But most important, Greece was associated with the idea of democracy and civic virtue—something of great significance to America. The new republic adopted the iconography of the ancient world to express the aspirations of a democratic, rational society and used this style for virtually every public structure, rather than styles associated with royalty or religion. Greek Revival became the patriotic expression of a new country, a national style of architecture popularized through architectural pattern books by Andrew Jackson Downing, Alexander Jackson Davis, and others. It spread throughout the Northeast, the mansions and plantations of the South, and even to the Midwest in all types of buildings, and it remained popular until the Civil War.

ABOUT THE STYLE

The typical Greek Revival house will have an entrance notable for its resemblance to a Greek temple—four, six, or eight columns in one of the Greek orders, topped with an entablature and a pediment. Failing that, it will at least have columns marking the entrance or lined up across the front of the building. Windows and doors are rectangular rather than arched, and if doors and window frames are ornamented, the motifs are drawn from a vocabulary that includes acanthus, anthemion, or patera, as well as Greek fretwork. The exterior is generally white; although Greek buildings and sculptures were actually painted, often in bright colors, the color had worn off by the time they were discovered by Westerners, so they are thought of as pristine white marble.

The interior of the Greek Revival home does not look specifically Grecian; the only Greek elements are ceiling medallions, mantels, occasional columns flanking doorways, and perhaps understated fluting or reeding on doors and window frames. Walls are white or near-white, floors are simple wood planks, and color is introduced with deep-toned upholstery and draperies. The interior, a symmetrical plan, generally has a central hall, twin parlors separated by pocket doors, and window shutters that fold back into the frame. The effect is stately and elegant, connoting good taste and dignity. Mantels, in every room, are usually marble, most often black or dark grey, with simple pilasters and no overmantel—a mirror or painting might hang above.

In general, interiors in the Greek Revival style tend to be more restrained and less object-filled than that of the later revival periods, which become increasingly exuberant, often to the point of excess.

Colors, as with all of the later classical revivals, are rich and intense, with understated patterns but elegant fabrics.

Furniture has strong silhouettes, generally of mahogany, with expanses of wood and little carving on forms that suggest classical models without specifically copying them, as had American Empire design. Pieces are somewhat more massive. The term "pillar and scroll" is often used to designate the most frequently seen motifs in this period.

PREVIOUS PAGE: The East Drawing Room in the Edmonston-Alston House in historic Charleston, South Carolina, uses Greek columns to delineate space.

BELOW: Attributed to Thomas Seymour of Boston, Massachusetts, c. 1815, this drop-leaf worktable with lyre base has the heavier lines and more explicit rendering of classical motifs that marked the Greek Revival. Made of mahogany, with gilt-brass drawer pulls, toe caps and castors, die-stamped rosettes, and fabric workbag.

ABOVE: This substantial mahogany-framed sofa, with gilt-brass castors and rich green velvet upholstery, was made by John and Joseph Meeks, c. 1836, and typifies the weighty look of Greek Revival, often called "pillar and scroll" style for its frequent use of those ornaments.

BELOW: Duncan Phyfe's workshop produced objects that transitioned from Federal style to Greek Revival, as indicated by this classically carved mahogany sideboard and cellarette, c. 1815, with antiqued gilded mounts.

■ Gothic Revival, c. 1830 and earlier, to 1870

About the Period

During the 18th century, a wave of architectural preservation in England stimulated interest in medieval architecture, leading to its revival as a style for the industrial age. Gothic Revival, or neo-Gothic, as it was called in England, was prefigured by Strawberry Hill (1758–1772), Horace Walpole's (1717–1797) fanciful reconstruction of his home in Twickenham, outside London. Its ultimate expression was Fonthill Abbey (1796), designed by James Wyatt (1746–1813) for the eccentric collector William Beckford.

For designers chafing under the strict symmetry of Greek Revival, the past of Arthurian legends, medieval poetry, and the novels of Sir Walter Scott seemed more picturesque and romantic. In addition to the aesthetic appeal of the style, there was the moral issue expressed by its most fervent proponent, Augustus W. N. Pugin (1812–1852), who saw the Gothic as a means of spiritual reform. The return to an ecclesiastical style could redeem industrialized society from degeneration. It was the godly alternative to the paganism of the ancient world from whom neoclassicism was derived. Pugin's heavily gilded interiors for the Houses of Parliament in London (1836–1868) and his exhibits in the Great Exhibition of 1851 are superb expressions of the Gothic Revival style.

The most striking and pervasive of the 19th-century architectural revivals, Gothic Revival was appropriated by the English as a national aesthetic, though the country had never altogether abandoned the Medieval style. It was translated for residential use in the villas and country cottages of Andrew Jackson Downing (1815–1852), and it appeared in France during the Second Empire of Louis Napoleon and Empress Eugénie, most notably in the architecture of Eugène Viollet-le-Duc (1814–1879). In America, it was interpreted in the gable-roofed, flat-cut, gingerbread-trimmed houses of Carpenter Gothic.

Later in the century, Modern Gothic followed the ideas of design reform as expressed by the Englishman Charles Locke Eastlake (1836–1906), whose *Hints on Household Taste* (published in 1868 in England and 1872 in America) was a response to Rococo excess, and helped middle-class consumers deal with the plethora of available styles by teaching them principles of good taste. The book supported simplicity of design and a craftsman-like look that spawned a popular range of machine-made, architecturally detailed furniture characterized by massive, rectilinear forms of solid wood, with medieval joinery and shallow-carved, flat decoration, that used his name but was rejected by Eastlake.

About the Style

The Gothic Revival interior has more personality than the sober Greek Revival with which it competed. It is less rigid and somewhat less formal, though considerably busier and characteristically cluttered, in the manner of the prototypical Victorian home. It is also costly to execute, requiring intricate detailing and considerable hand carving. At its best, it is winning; at its worst, weighty. It was most popular for decorating libraries and dining rooms.

Architects like Alexander Jackson Davis (1803–1892) switched from Greek Revival to interpretations of Gothic. Interiors are high-ceilinged, often ribbed, and walls are decorated with plasterwork tracery or dark wood paneling. Floors might be brick, tile, or marble in deep colors and geometric designs.

Windows and doorways are tall and slender, with pointed arches, sometimes with stained glass panels punctuating the mullioned panes. Curtain treatments are simple, perhaps of embroidered wool or velvet with horizontal cross-banding.

Stylized patterns on wallpaper or textiles might reproduce Gothic tracery or medieval panoramas, and carpets with medieval motifs are patterned in rich colors like crimsons and blues, or muddy tones of browns and olive, perhaps accented with gilding.

After the publication of books on color theory, it became the practice to select different palettes for particular rooms—darker for so-called masculine environments (e.g., the library), paler for feminine ones (e.g., the boudoir), muted for private settings and livelier for public spaces.

Elaborate mantels reprised the massive hearths of medieval halls. Flickering oil lamps cast a romantic glow that added to the romantic, if a bit somber, ambience. Accessories might include collections of armor, stag antlers, or accents of stained glass.

Gothic Revival furniture is massive, often made of oak, with similar detailing to that of the interior shell—tracery, rosettes, trefoils, and quatrefoils, even heraldic motifs. The reprise of medieval themes even includes some Elizabethan chairs, chests, and other cottage furniture, often with twist-turning on legs and chair backs.

PREVIOUS PAGE: The Grober Salon at Arbury Hall, in Warwickshire, England, is an enthusiastic rendering of Gothic Revival style. The intricate plasterwork ceiling, continuing down onto the walls, replicates those seen in early incarnations like Strawberry Hill.

RIGHT: A classic example of American Gothic Revival furniture, this hall chair has an unusually high back of cathedral tracery and distinctive carved front legs and supports. Of mahogany-finished oak, with hinged plank seat and glove box, it was made in New Orleans, Louisiana, c. 1850.

This marble-topped rosewood bedroom chest has Gothic arches on doors and apron, and an elaborately carved and pierced mirror frame. Made in New York by Charles A. Baudouine. c. 1845.

Objects like this would be the focal point of a 19th-century parlor. Made in England by Gillows of Lancaster, c. 1865, of mahogany, ebonized mahogany, purpleheart, burr oak, harewood, tulipwood, and boxwood; with cast brass grillwork and Carrara marble accents.

An understated hall chair, designed by Augustus W. N. Pugin, the British architect whose ideas shaped the Gothic Revival. Made of oak, with painted crest on the shield-like back, c. 1840.

■ Rococo Revival, c. 1840–1870

ABOUT THE PERIOD

Throwing off the moral component of Gothic Revival, this style reprised the voluptuous forms of its 17th-century antecedent. An exaggeration rather than a pure revival of Louis XV style, Rococo Revival drew on French pattern books and was fashionable in England and Second Empire France. It crossed the Atlantic into America, where it enjoyed a brief and flamboyant life, particularly in the South, where it was known as French Antique. Embracing florid scrollwork, marquetry, gilding, and fanciful ornament, it is undeniably appealing, despite the excesses committed in its name.

The Rococo Revival emerged when family life had become more informal, but strict conventions still ruled the manner of entertaining and receiving guests. Rooms were designed for specific purposes: the lady of the house received visitors in the parlor, the library was the husband's preserve, and the dining room denoted social and financial status in the luxury of a room used only at mealtimes. With many styles now available, there was no longer a reason to choose only one, and anarchy prevailed over fashion— interiors might vary from one room to the other, depending on the desired mood.

The Rococo Revival was too frivolous to enjoy a long life, and it began to undo itself with the kind of excesses that, a century prior, had led to the decline of its antecedent style and the return of Classicism.

ABOUT THE STYLE

The Rococo Revival interior is giddily charming and, despite its frills, very inviting. Recalling the grace of 18th-century French design, but considerably more quirky and unpredictable, it combines exaggerated curves and richly carved ornament, sometimes applying the gilding that characterized the earlier style. Seating pieces are extravagantly overstuffed and tufted and exceptionally comfortable. It was considered most appropriate for parlors and drawing rooms, as well as ladies' boudoirs.

Walls and ceilings are dressed in a muted version of Louis XV *boiserie* and plasterwork, framing machine-printed, flocked, or embossed wallpaper, usually with coordinated borders. The patterns are most likely colorful floral bouquets, swags, or ribbon-and-lace designs.

Windows have layered treatments; wood shutters beneath heavy woven or printed draperies, elaborately trimmed with fringe or tassels, and hung over lace curtains.

Portieres in similar fabrics are hung at doorways. Upholstery fabrics therefore include a range of vivid velvets and tapestries, in addition to popular horsehair and leather for seating pieces.

Floors are wood parquet or patterned and colored tile, with rugs in large-scale botanical motifs, machine-made carpet laid fashionably wall-to-wall, or linoleum (a new product) patterned to replicate carpet.

Bold, polychromatic color schemes predominate, made possible with aniline and synthesized dyestuffs that can replicate the hues of natural dyes or produce intense shades like mauve and magenta, increasing the available palette for interiors.

Mantels, which were still used for function as well as decoration, are usually marble, carved with Rococo ornament. Chandeliers and lamps, using kerosene, and by the 1860s gaslight, mix functional and fussy with painted-glass globes, brass trim, or crystal drops. Accessories include whimsical hat racks or whatnots with display shelves, arrangements of porcelain plates or figurines, specimens from nature, or framed prints.

Suites of furniture are the height of fashion; matching or coordinated case and seating pieces are designed for parlor, dining, and bedroom, each with complementary ornament and carving. Details translated from Rococo style include the cabriole leg, thicker than the original versions, and carved with shell and floral motifs. Coil-spring upholstery has brought new, comfortable seating forms such as the oversized tufted ottoman, the balloon-back chair, and the single-sided sofa. All draw on traditional Rococo silhouettes but are more exaggerated and often bulbous.

Woods are dark, rich, and highly polished, joined by other materials—iron and brass for ornate bed frames; real or faux bamboo and woven rattan for light-scaled seating and occasional pieces; and *papier mâché* for accent furnishings, glossy-painted and sometimes inlaid with mother of pearl.

The most inventive developments in furniture, however, have come from new manufacturing techniques: John Henry Belter (1804–1863) shapes furniture from layers of rosewood veneer, intricately carved in openwork floral patterns, and Michael Thonet (1796–1871) has patented a method for steam-curving beech into joint-free, curvilinear seating pieces. Belter's widely copied pieces are archetypes of the Rococo Revival, but Thonet's furniture prefigured *Wiener Werkstätte* modernist designs.

PREVIOUS PAGE: An archetype of the formal parlor in Rococo Revival style, this one at The Metropolitan Museum of Art, dating to 1852, is furnished with pieces by John Henry Belter, whose innovative techniques for making intricately carved, laminated rosewood furniture was widely copied by his competitors.

ABOVE: This parlor suite of seating furniture is made of rosewood with the floral carved ornament that marks furniture of this period, by Joseph Meeks, New York, c. 1850.

LEFT: The late-19th-century taste for the exotic in American interiors led to increasingly elaborate furniture, like this gilded *guéridon* table with gryphon motifs, made c. 1880.

RIGHT: Called a library chair, this velvet-upholstered piece, c. 1815, was designed for comfort as well as decorative appeal. Restrained carving on the mahogany frame draws the eye to the elaborate treatment on the crest rail.

BELOW: Cast iron, used extensively as a building material, found a new use in outdoor furniture, where it adapted well to Rococo ornament, as in this garden bench. Painted to prevent oxidation, cast iron could remain outdoors in all weather.

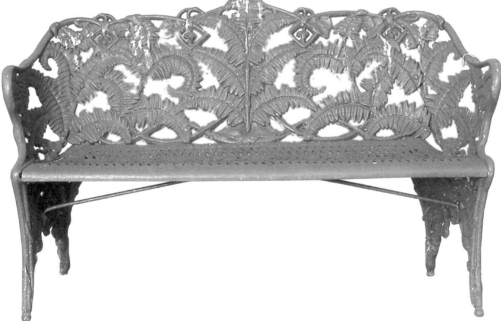

■ Renaissance Revival, c. 1860–1890

About the Period

Drowned in its own excesses, as had its original incarnation, the Rococo Revival was transmuted into an Italianate style known as Renaissance Revival. One of the cyclical reprises of classical ornament, this one made no attempt at authenticity, instead adopting elements of Renaissance architecture and French neoclassicism in mass-produced furnishings that might incorporate "*Neo-Grèc*" and Egyptian motifs with styles from other European sources. It was the most eclectic of all the revival styles. In Italy, Germany, and France, Renaissance Revival signaled a wistful nostalgia for regimes long past. In America, after the Civil War (1861–1865), it incorporated historic styles in a new show of diversity that gained strength after the Centennial Exhibition in Philadelphia in 1876, the event that also led to the Colonial Revival.

In architecture, a new style called Beaux Arts had emerged under the liberal French monarchy. Moving away from fixed classical forms, it fostered an aesthetic of classically influenced, but eclectically ornamented buildings of grand scale and great presence. Named for the *École des Beaux-Arts* in Paris, whose teachings it reflected, this expressive style spread to most of the Western world, lasting into the 20th century to compete with the first flowering of Modernism. Renaissance Revival interiors, encompassing a cornucopia of influences, were its perfect complement.

As the Renaissance Revival waned, the Edwardian era, named for English king Edward VII (reigned 1902–1919), brought the excesses of the Gilded Age, when opulence was valued over any particular style, and the townhouses and mansions of a new American aristocracy sought to recapture the glamour of European royalty. It was a fitting climax to a century saturated with extravagant design.

About the Style

The Renaissance Revival interior is distinctive for the imposing detail of its furniture, dominating the framework that surrounds it. Walls, ceilings, and floor treatments are similar to those of the Rococo Revival, though the decorative motifs are more classical than naturalistic. Moldings and pilasters, Pompeiian-style painted panels or wallpaper, porcelain plaques, and ormolu medallions evoke antiquity, adding pomp to accompany the clutter of furniture and objects.

Polished wood floors are covered with machine-made, patterned carpet or imported Oriental rugs, not necessarily having any relation to the style of the furniture.

At the tall windows, heavy tied-back curtains hang beneath elaborate lambrequins trimmed with loops, cords, or tassels. Textiles are more varied than in previous periods, thanks to new weaving machinery and roller-printing techniques, and the wallpaper might be hand-blocked French scenics, machine-made English patterns, or American interpretations of the most popular design motifs, including many inspired by Japanese design. Walls in three parts—dado, center panel, and frieze—if not papered or covered with fabric, are painted in deep, muted tones, as backgrounds for clusters of framed pictures or prints.

Toward the end of the 19th century, the invention of the electric light has revolutionized interiors and lighting fixtures, making chandeliers less popular and increasing the popularity of individual floor and table lamps.

The abundance of color and pattern reflects the riches of a thoroughly industrialized society, with schemes in rich, tertiary hues like olive, terracotta, and old gold.

Renaissance Revival furniture incorporates familiar forms in a variety of woods, and are often elaborately ornamented. The distinctive three-section parlor cabinet, on a platform base, is flanked with columns or caryatids and topped with pedestals for display. Sideboards, themselves imposing pieces, have upper sections with shelves to show off china or collectible objects. Many case pieces are accented with carved or incised decoration, ebonizing, gilding, or applied brass ornament, which can now be produced by machine—perhaps Egyptian or Greek motifs or cartouches with urns or classical profiles. The vogue for *japonisme* is reflected in ornamental details. Furniture is customarily purchased in suites: a set of sofa and chairs is crested with matched plaques and carving, and a mirror mounted to the bedroom dresser coordinates with the decoration on the bed. One factor in the design change was the difficulty of accommodating the curves of Rococo in machine production, which could, however, easily produce ornament and trim for the Renaissance Revival.

A range of ingenious designs in patent furniture has added to the vocabulary of furnishings available, even to homes of moderate means. By the 1870s in America, a thriving industry is developing in Grand Rapids, Michigan, to produce furniture for a broad consumer market that emulated the custom designs created for their affluent compatriots by firms like Herter Brothers.

PREVIOUS PAGE: Victoria Mansion, also known as the Morse-Libby House, is a National Historic Landmark in Portland, Maine, housing the most complete set of private interiors by Herter Brothers now extant. The downstairs parlor, shown here, is elegantly furnished in Renaissance Revival style.

The Wooten desk, a patented design, conceals multiple compartments and a hinged writing surface in its block-like form. The carved crest and applied ornaments adopt Renaissance forms. Made of walnut, in Indianapolis, Indiana, c. 1874.

This parlor cabinet is of rosewood with lighter wood inlays, handpainted decoration, gilding, and carving. The pedestal top is designed to hold sculpture or decorative objects; 70 inches wide and 51 inches high, it was made by Herter Brothers, c. 1870.

ABOVE: This side table is unusually elaborate, with intricately carved stretchers and decorative marquetry. It would probably have been placed alongside a seating piece, where much of the ornament would have been covered by a lamp.

LEFT: A large round table was often placed in the main stair hall, where it could hold a vase of flowers or a decorative bowl. This one is ebonized and gilded, made in New York, c. 1870s.

Style Markers

MOOD
extroverted, exhibitionistic

SCALE
grand as possible, even in
confined spaces

COLORS
increasingly varied, gradually
darkening

ORNAMENT
more than any other period

KEY MOTIFS
characteristic imagery
appropriate to the specific revival

FURNITURE
generally imposing, basic forms
with varying decoration

TEXTILES
myriad patterns, abundantly
varied

LOOK FOR
dark rooms, lots of furniture and
objects, lots of pattern

A lively floral-printed taffeta, *Guichard*, translates an 1853 design in the style of Napoleon III.

Aptly named Vivid Victorian, this wallpaper has the intense colors and floral patterns that were favored in 19th-century interiors.

■ Shaker, c. 1800–1860

In striking contrast to the other styles of the 19th century, a unique aesthetic developed in the modest communities of the Shakers, a strict religious sect that traces its origins to 18th-century English Quakers and early French Calvinists. Established in America about 1800, and almost extinct by the end of the Civil War, the Shakers followed a strict, simple, and celibate lifestyle, surviving on farming and the sales of products from their workshops.

The Shakers had no philosophy of design—for them, aesthetics were a frivolous consideration. A Shaker interior is severely plain, with white walls, board floors, and modest-size windows flanked by simple, painted shutters. The use of color is restrained, combining white backgrounds with calming earth tones, accented by occasional black-and-white, or muted primaries of red, blue, or yellow. The almost-spartan furnishings are made entirely by hand, usually of plain maple, cherry, or birch and woven straw. Shaker furniture, in natural wood or flat painted finishes, follows in the footsteps of early Colonial design: ladder-back chairs, benches, and plain square or rectangular tables. Storage is in plain chests with simple knob pulls, or oval boxes shaped of plywood. Every object is designed only for its function and is free of unnecessary adornment, although the uncluttered forms are themselves appealing to the eye. Flat-weave rugs and textiles are loomed from natural fibers, in simple geometric patterns.

Entirely without intention, these pristine objects are compatible with the Modernist aesthetic, and they are often cited as influences on contemporary design.

An interior in Shaker Village, Hancock, Massachusetts, is furnished in the spare style of the Shaker communities, with straight-lined, minimalist furniture of pine or maple that is often viewed as a precursor of functionalist modern design.

CHAPTER 15
Aesthetic Movement, c. 1870s–1880s

Aesthetic Movement, c. 1870s–1880s

About the Period

The Aesthetic Movement evolved during the period of design reform that followed the Industrial Revolution. Seeking to recapture qualities lost in the shift from handmade to machine-made goods, it was parallel and linked to Arts and Crafts, and like it, denoted an approach to style rather than any specific design vocabulary. It differed from Arts and Crafts, however, in rejecting moral values as a relevant issue in art or design: beauty was the sole consideration. The term "aesthetic," derived from the Greek word for perfection, referred to the appreciation of beauty in art, and "art for art's sake" was the movement's mantra. By appreciating beauty, one could transcend considerations of style.

Expressed in intricately patterned, meticulously detailed interiors and a lavish use of gold, tile, and intricate pattern, Aesthetic style exemplified the romantic excesses of the late Victorian era. Originating in England, it was inspired in part by medieval art, but also drew on exotic Japanese, Ottoman, and Moorish influences—particularly that of Japan, which had recently reopened its ports to Western trade, and whose design was perceived as exquisitely refined and respectful of artisanry. The most vocal spokesman for Aestheticism was the author and playwright Oscar Wilde (1854–1900), and its most celebrated practitioners were the painter James A. M. Whistler (1834–1903) and the designers E. W. Godwin (1833–1886) and Christopher Dresser (1834–1904), who drew heavily on Japanese presentations seen at international exhibitions in London (1862) and Paris (1867). *The House Beautiful*, published by Clarence Cook in 1887, defined the principles of the movement.

In America, fueled by Wilde's acclaimed 1882 national lecture tour, Aestheticism contributed to extravagant interiors in the city mansions and country estates of Gilded Age industrialists, designed by decorating firms like Associated Artists (Louis Comfort Tiffany's original company) and Herter Brothers. Unlike Arts and Crafts interiors, these eschewed claims of moral virtue and abandoned restraint, wrapping grand spaces in rich materials, intricately detailed furniture, and Eastern-influenced ornament. The Aesthetic Movement was too extreme to be long-lived, but its influence was considerable, and many of its elements were absorbed into early Art Nouveau.

ABOUT THE STYLE

The Aesthetic interior is beguiling in its exoticism and almost dizzying in its mix of color, pattern, and decoration. It mixes elements from diverse sources in idiosyncratic renderings that follow the designer's whim or the client's preference, resisting classification, but invariably providing an excess of visual stimulation. It can evoke instant enthusiasm or immediate disdain.

There are no specifics of shape or dimension particular to the Aesthetic interior. Rejecting the massive elements of the 19th-century revival styles, it avoids Baroque carved and gilded frames, ornate mantels, or heavy draperies over doors. Instead, pattern is the primary means of organizing and decorating the space. In many cases, the abundance of detail can make a large room appear deceptively small.

Wallpaper is the height of fashion for Aesthetic interiors, in coordinated patterns that designers use to create intriguing decorative effects. On walls divided into three sections— dado below, field or filling above, and frieze just below the ceiling—a different pattern and variation of color is applied to each area; the dado design is the most intense, the frieze the most elaborate, and the field the most understated, in order to provide a better background for hanging paintings or prints. The frieze is often defined by a wood rail that also serves as a shelf for china display.

Colors in wall coverings, textiles, and carpets tend toward deep, subtle hues, like dull greens, browns, and blues, with citrine as a frequent accent. Often, there are shimmery touches as well.

Window treatments probably use patterned fabrics, often in motifs reflecting the Asian influence that is a common theme throughout this period.

In accessories, Japanese and other Eastern sources provide many of the forms as well as the decorative inspiration for ceramics and metalwork; the Aesthetic movement produced many objects of exceptional charm and originality. Chandeliers and lamps, too, are as important, or more important, for their decorative value as for their function in providing illumination.

Aesthetic Movement, c. 1870s–1880s

ABOUT THE FURNITURE

The concept of art furniture, rejecting the commercialism of most industrially made design, is an important contribution of the movement. Aesthetic furniture avoids the weightiness of most Victorian-era pieces, and its light-scaled forms reflect the influence of East Asian design. Chairs, settees, and sofas are not marked by new forms so much as new decoration. The silhouettes of chests, exemplified by William Godwin's designs, often suggest Japanese cabinetry. Other pieces might be painted or incised with images of stylized birds and foliage.

Many items of furniture are painted or lacquered black, or, later in the period, made of light-toned mahogany or satinwood. They are often carved with openwork motifs drawn from Asian objects. Notwithstanding the disdain of manufactured objects as Philistine, most Aesthetic-era furniture is actually production-made, as differentiated from those of the Arts and Crafts movement, whose designers were committed to objects made by hand.

NEXT PAGE: The Arab Hall at Leighton House, in Holland Park, London. Designed for the painter Frederic, Lord Leighton in 1877 by George Aitchison, it is a two-story showcase for Leighton's collection of Middle Eastern tile.

PREVIOUS PAGE: In America, the Aesthetic movement was somewhat more restrained than its English counterpart. The library of the Mark Twain House in Hartford, Connecticut, where author Samuel Clemens lived and worked from 1874 to 1891, is an informal clutter of comfortable furniture, mixed patterns, and exotic accents.

LEFT: Architect Edward William Godwin is perhaps best known for his furniture designs based on Japanese forms, like this black-lacquer sideboard with drop-leaf sides and brass hardware.

BELOW: This three-seat settee, by Godwin, c. 1875, has detailing on the openwork sides that reflect the Japanese influence in his Aesthetic-era designs. Made of stained oak, with brass accents.

Christopher Dresser was a prolific designer of furniture and a variety of decorative objects. He designed this display cabinet of ebonized wood with insets of copper and cloisonné enamel, c. 1880.

Typically using a combination of woods and decorative media, this Aesthetic Movement sideboard is of walnut, rosewood, ebony, and fruitwood with carving and brass marquetry, made in New York, c. 1880.

This handsome walnut bedstead, more than 78 inches tall, is exuberantly carved with medallions and a stylized panel of songbirds and foliage. Made by Philadelphia cabinetmaker Daniel Pabst, c. 1875.

Framing an embroidered Oriental silk panel, this delicate ebonized fire screen, c. 1880, has graceful carved detailing that complements its Aesthetic form.

Vanities were customary items of furniture in 19th-century bedrooms. This ebonized piece by Herter Brothers has a patterned frieze with gilt-and-incised decoration featuring Egyptian-inspired motifs.

■ Herter Brothers

In 1858, German immigrant Gustav Herter (1830–1898), who had worked for Louis Comfort Tiffany, opened a furniture and decorating business in New York that became Herter Brothers when his half-brother Christian (1839–1883) joined him in 1864. By the 1870s, the firm had become the most prestigious producer and purveyor of furnishings in America, catering to a Gilded Age clientele. Herter Brothers created complete and elaborate interiors, producing the furniture and upholstery in its own workshops, and also sold accessories, much of which was manufactured to its own designs. Employing several hundred craftsmen, the firm designed and executed wall paneling, plasterwork and ceiling decorations, as well as all interior furnishings.

Herter Brothers designed in the revival styles that were popular at the time, but generally sought more original expressions for their demanding and affluent customers. Although many of the firm's opulent interiors reflect the influence of the English Aesthetic movement, the unique interpretations in furniture were its own. Herter Brothers created variants of Renaissance Revival and other styles, but are most celebrated for their intricately detailed marquetry pieces, with neo-Japanese motifs executed in multitoned wood veneers. Ranging from small tables and cabinets to sideboards or massive mirrored cabinets, every object was unique, designed and made for a particular client and a specific interior. Even in its more conventional designs, Herter furniture distinguished itself from its competitors by its exceptional quality and workmanship; each piece was superbly constructed of the finest materials, with hand-finished details.

Interiors for clients like William Vanderbilt, J. Pierpont Morgan, and Jay Gould were impeccably coordinated—and rarely understated. Commissions executed by the firm included work for the White House. Christian retired in 1880, and Herter Brothers ceased operations in 1906, perhaps the last vestige of America's most extravagant era in design. Unfortunately, most Herter interiors were destroyed in the San Francisco earthquake of 1906. In addition to Victoria Mansion, the Park Avenue Armory in New York has some of the few remaining examples of the firm's work.

RIGHT: One of the iconic pieces designed for a celebrated client, this side chair, of gilded maple with mother-of-pearl insets, was made by Herter Brothers for the New York mansion of William H. Vanderbilt, c. 1881.

BELOW: A six-foot-high ebonized bedstead has an Egyptian-inspired frieze with gilt-and-incised decoration, suggesting the variety of exotic influences reflected in the Aesthetic style and the versatility of the Herter firm.

■ Styles of the Exotic East

The art and culture of the Far East is as old, or older, than that of the Western world. It flourished for many centuries before the Europeans became aware of exotic lands like China and Japan. When Marco Polo visited Cathay in the 13th century, he led the way for other travelers to explore and bring back treasures and legends from the lands at the other side of the earth. By the 16th and 17th centuries, the East India trading companies were carrying silks, porcelain, tea, and carpets as well as decorative objects over land and ocean to decorate Western homes and to influence design, particularly in the form of ornament drawn directly from, or inspired by, exotic Eastern motifs.

In the middle of the 19th century, Japan began opening its doors to the West, negotiating treaties with America in 1854 and England in 1858 after two centuries when its ports were closed to all but a few Chinese and Dutch traders. The subsequent exhibitions of Japanese goods at exhibitions in London in 1862 and Paris in 1867 unleashed a wave of enthusiasm for the purity and simplicity of that country's design, inspiring the Aesthetic movement and influencing the movement for design reform. The use of natural materials and textures, the minimalist furnishings, and the refined ornament are also cited as precursors of a modern aesthetic—both Le Corbusier and Walter Gropius visited Japan in the 1930s.

Interest in design from East Asia has focused on India as well. Although it is one of the world's oldest civilizations, India's influence on the West began when the British East India Company essentially controlled the subcontinent, importing first spices and then also textiles and calico. Paisley and crewel, exotic silks, woodcraft, and metalwork in the West have borrowed or adapted decorative motifs and ornament that draw on traditional Indian crafts.

Most Far Eastern furniture is specific to interiors in those countries and less suited to those in the Western world, but several design elements—like the ball-and-claw foot and urn-shape splat of Queen Anne chairs, the yoke-shaped back of Chippendale, many of the decorative motifs in French Rococo ornament, and the English technique of Japanning—are all drawn from East Asian design.

Islamic design is not drawn from a single country, but from many. The term encompasses styles that began as far back as the seventh century and incorporated elements of Roman and Byzantine design. Its influence on Western design has been considerable, most strikingly in the form of ornament: calligraphy, arabesque patterns, diaper motifs, and intricate geometric ornament in glass, ceramics, and textiles. Elements of Islamic style appeared in many countries during the 19th-century wave of exoticism in design.

FOLLOWING PAGE: The Wang Family Courtyard, an interior furnished in classic 17th-century Chinese style, near Pingyao in Shanxi province.

PREVIOUS PAGE: Tatami mats dictate the dimensions of the rooms in Katsura Rikyu Imperial Villa, in Kyoto, Japan, an archetype of traditional Japanese design that inspired many Western architects, as a precursor of a Modernist aesthetic.

ABOVE: This interior in Egypt, with low traditional seating, is framed in intricately patterned blue-and-white Islamic tile.

Aesthetic Movement, c. 1870s–1880s

Style Markers

MOOD
fantasy

SCALE
varying

COLORS
subdued, but richly varied

ORNAMENT
delicate

KEY MOTIFS
Japonisme

FURNITURE
light-scaled, graceful, highly decorative

TEXTILES
intricately patterned

LOOK FOR
lots of pattern, wallpapers, gilded accents

The pattern of this luxurious satin-background silk lampas is from an 1880 design.

A pattern of interlacing branches and stylized blooms in monochromatic tones.

CHAPTER 16
English Arts and Crafts, c. 1860–1890

English Arts and Crafts, c. 1860–1890

ABOUT THE PERIOD

In the 1860s, designer William Morris (1834–1896) became an enthusiastic convert to the reformist ideas of art critic John Ruskin (1819–1900), who decried the taste of the Victorian public and the banality of mass-produced design. Arts and Crafts, a movement rather than a specific style, was one of several that rebelled against the impersonalization of modern life. It sought to create interiors and furnishings that would recapture the charm and personality that had been lost to industrialization. Morris favored a return to medieval craftsmanship, with honest finishes, nature-inspired ornament, and workmanship that revealed the hand of the craftsman and his pleasure in his work.

The movement was named after the Arts and Crafts Exhibition Society, founded in 1888, but it dates back almost three decades to 1860 and the completion of Morris's residence, "Red House," designed by architect Philip Webb with interiors by Morris. Joined by Webb and other fellow Oxford graduates, the artists Edwin Burne-Jones (1833–1898) and Dante Gabriel Rossetti (1828–1882)—members of the self-titled Pre-Raphaelites—he formed Morris, Marshall, Faulkner & Company and later Morris & Company to produce well-designed goods for the general public. The group believed that art should be useful as well as beautiful, adding a moral element that was in pointed contrast to the ideas of the Aesthetic Movement that paralleled it, though many designers of the period worked in both camps. Morris's Kelmscott Press, established in 1890, promoted his ideals and the writings of others believing in them, in England and abroad. He was unrealistic in his total rejection of mechanical production, insisting that objects be made entirely by hand, which necessarily made them more costly. Most of the interiors and furnishings produced by the Morris workshops were affordable only by a limited, affluent clientele. Only wallpapers and fabrics, in stylized patterns that were simpler and livelier than the pretentious Victorian-era designs, used some roller-printing techniques.

Morris and his associates in the Arts and Crafts movement failed in the objective of providing good design for all, but they awakened a new interest in handcraft that had been lost for almost a century. His ideas led to the formation of a variety of guilds and workshops, some of which used machine production.

As with most other 19th-century movements, Arts and Crafts overlapped with others of the time and paralleled the Art Nouveau style. Some designs of Morris's compatriots like Walter Crane (1845–1915) and Charles Voysey (1857–1941) might easily be classified in either camp. In its movement toward simplicity and its efforts to cope with the challenges of industrialization, Arts and Crafts was an important step along the road to Modernism.

ABOUT THE STYLE

The Arts and Crafts interior is studiously unpretentious and carefully avoids the suggestion of being designed for aesthetics alone. Evoking a medieval manor or a country cottage, it is charming in its simplicity, though that simplicity is often deceptive. Considerable time, effort, and often expense have gone into creating a room that looks artlessly unplanned but strictly follows the tenets of the movement. As William Morris famously cautioned, "Have nothing in your house that you do not know to be useful or believe to be beautiful."

Often, the simple rectangular shell of the interior is given the conceit of ceiling beams or timbering to reprise the look of a medieval hall. Walls are usually partially wood-paneled; above that, they may be painted white or wallpapered with stylized florals or patterns in medieval themes.

Sash windows might be shuttered or given simple curtains, in lively prints that complement those on the walls. Cottons or linen fabrics are likelier choices than pretentious silks or heavy wools.

Floors are generally wood, over which are deep-toned, flat-woven carpets that anchor the furniture arrangement and ground the mix of patterns. The inglenook, a recess with cushioned benches framing a fireplace opening, is a popular architectural feature.

Most Arts and Crafts interiors include some element evoking Gothic style—a genre that has remained enduringly popular in England. Other ornament is drawn from nature, although the heart motif appears frequently, in textile patterns or as a cutout element on furniture.

English Arts and Crafts textiles are intricate and colorful, depicting highly stylized flowers or foliage, birds, and other motifs from nature, rendered on backgrounds of white or subtly muted earth tones. Wallpapers, perhaps the most successful of Morris's designs, are meticulously printed with copper plates in delicate tints, and they often provide the starting point for the coordinated scheme of the interior, whose objective is to create a total environment—either highly decorative or crisply simple.

Even the most ordinary objects are important in achieving the desired effect. Arts and Crafts accessories, in ceramics, metalwork of iron or brass, and embroideries, emphasize a handcrafted look. Painted tiles and mosaics may decorate the walls or frame the fireplace. Decorative stained glass, another idea inspired by medieval design and an important product of Morris's workshops, is extremely popular, appearing as small roundels or elaborate scenic panels.

ABOUT THE FURNITURE

In contrast to styles of the Victorian revival with which it overlaps, the arrangement of objects in the Arts and Crafts interior is spare and uncluttered. Furniture forms are simple rectilinear shapes, most typically in oak, though other woods, including mahogany, are used as well, with detailing that emphasizes the handmade qualities of the furniture. Wood joints are deliberately exposed, and finishes replicate the rough-textured, hand-hewn appearance of medieval furniture. Even commercially produced Arts and Crafts pieces, later in the period, try to suggest the handcrafted look. Carving is rare, though decorative cabinets and chests might be elaborately handpainted with medieval figures and allegorical scenes.

Seating, in the form of straight-back chairs and open-back benches, is usually cushioned rather than fully upholstered, with cutouts, turnings, or through-tenons the only ornament. The most familiar designs are a simple rush-seat chair and the adjustable-back armchair designed by Webb but named for Morris, which prefigured the modern recliner.

PREVIOUS PAGE: In Wightwick Manor, Wolverhampton, England, one of Morris and Company's most important commissions, 1887–1893. The spindle-backed Sussex chair and floral wallpaper were Morris designs.

ABOVE: Philip Webb designed this upholstered chair on casters for Morris and Company. Called the Morris chair, it has become an iconic example of English Arts and Crafts furniture and the ancestor of the modern recliner.

LEFT: This charming cabinet by Mackay Hugh Baillie Scott has inlaid detailing with bird motifs and irregular drawer pulls that point up the handcrafted appeal of Arts and Crafts objects.

LEFT: A rare sideboard of oak and brass by Phillip Webb, c. 1862, shows the influence of the Gothic Revival style on early Arts and Crafts furniture.

BELOW: This simple oak writing table, c. 1906, is by architect Charles F. A. Voysey, who is perhaps best known for his distinctive textile and wallpaper designs and his houses influenced by English vernacular styles.

■ Craft Guilds and Associations

Emulating the medieval guild system, many British organizations were formed in the wake of the design reform movement, to carry out its principles by encouraging the practice of all types of handcrafts. Their objective was to reawaken interest in the rural lifestyle and to elevate the status of crafts to that of the fine arts. The most important of these groups were the Century Guild (1883–1892), established by Arthur Mackmurdo and Herbert Horne, the Guild of Handicraft (1888–1907), established by C. R. Ashbee (1863–1942), and Kenton & Company (1890–1892), whose founders included William Lethaby and Ernest Gimson.

Though these groups met with limited financial success, their efforts led to changes in design education that would strengthen the ties between the fields of art and crafts, and bring greater recognition of the value of handcraft. In America, Associated Artists (1879–1883), founded by Louis Comfort Tiffany, Candace Wheeler, and Lockwood de Forest, was the American counterpart of William Morris's firm, designing entire interiors as well as individual products. Later groups that followed a more rural Arts and Crafts model included the Roycroft Workshops (1895–1915 and later) and the Byrdcliffe Colony (1902–1915), and a number of smaller local associations made pottery, metalwork, and jewelry.

ABOVE: Charles Robert Ashbee established the Guild of Handcraft and produced furniture, textiles, and decorative objects inspired by the ideals of Morris and Ruskin. This simple but graceful wood cabinet is his design.

RIGHT: A landmark design, the Century Guild chair was designed by A. H. Mackmurdo, c. 1883. Made of Honduras mahogany with colored accents, with an undulating back whose openwork curves are considered to be the earliest precursor of Art Nouveau.

Style Markers

MOOD
unpretentious

SCALE
mostly modest

COLORS
muddy but rich

ORNAMENT
naturalistic

KEY MOTIFS
stylized foliage, birds, heart

FURNITURE
simple lines, rough finishes, hand detailing

TEXTILES
neat, stylized prints

LOOK FOR
medieval forms, handcrafted look

Strawberry Thief, one of William Morris's best-known designs for fabric and wallpaper. The muted coloration of his fabrics resulted from the use of vegetable dyes rather than artificial ones.

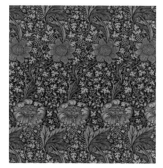

William Morris designed Kennet to be printed on cotton or silk fabric as well as wallpaper. Its undulating stalks can be viewed as anticipating the sinuous forms of Art Nouveau.

Charles F. A. Voysey's Donnemara wool carpet, distinctive for its stylized floral motifs.

CHAPTER 17
American Arts and Crafts, c. 1880–1915 and Later

American Arts and Crafts, c. 1880–1915 and Later

ABOUT THE PERIOD

Although inspired by its English namesake, the Arts and Crafts movement in America, also known as the Craftsman movement, began decades later. The styles are defined separately, but extensive intermingling and overlap occurred between them: the American practitioners shared the ideals of their English Arts and Crafts predecessors but differed in the execution of their designs. Focusing more closely on materials than on decoration, they were also far more practical than William Morris and his colleagues, utilizing the efficiency of industrial production to assemble furniture by machine and finish it by hand. This combination of operations made their designs more affordable, and therefore accessible to a wider market.

The most prominent figure in American Arts and Crafts was Gustav Stickley (1858–1942), one of four German immigrant brothers producing furniture in upstate New York. He opened his own firm in 1898, introducing his first collection of Craftsman furniture in 1900. Stickley also published designs for houses and interiors in his magazine, *The Craftsman*, and his catalogs included drawings that showed customers how to make the furniture themselves. Despite its initial success, Stickley's firm went bankrupt in 1916, but his influence was considerable in awakening an interest in Arts and Crafts ideals. Frank Lloyd Wright's early Prairie Style houses near Chicago, Illinois, reflected a similar aesthetic to that of the Arts and Crafts practitioners, but its translation into a more modern style was uniquely his own.

A subset of American Arts and Crafts, known as Mission Style, drew on the design of Spanish missions in Mexico and the American Southwest. In its willingness to move beyond the traditional forms of English style, it suggested America's growing confidence as an independent nation. The Arts and Crafts movement in America, like that in England, also spawned the creation of crafts communities, potteries, and other handicraft endeavors around the country.

Despite its large audience, Arts and Crafts in America did not survive the upheaval of World War I and the interest in modernism that arose after it ended. The style was rediscovered and enthusiastically revived in the 1970s, when the sturdy simplicity of its furniture, the charm of its ceramics and metalwork, and the worthiness of its ideals brought it back into favor.

ABOUT THE STYLE

The American Arts and Crafts interior is conscientiously rustic, simulating the rough-hewn surfaces of a preindustrial age, but making the most of its cost-cutting possibilities. It has overtones of Colonial style in its almost-strict simplicity and hints of English moderation in its lack of fussiness or frills. It combines the spare lines of almost-modern design with the warm appeal of handcraft.

White plaster walls and low ceilings are fitted with broad, exposed wood beams to create a cottage-like atmosphere. Modest-size square windows are cut simply into the walls without architectural ornament. They often have leaded-glass panes. Shutters or, more likely, simple woven or printed curtains are hung to sill height.

Ornament is relatively simple and applied by hand. Decorative stenciling is used as frieze-like trim on walls or to ornament otherwise unadorned furniture and curtains. Wright and the Greene brothers make sophisticated use of stained glass accents, evoking the Japanese sensibility that influenced both.

Plain wood floors, in planks rather than parquet, are fitted with hand-knotted Orientals or homemade rag rugs.

Color schemes replicate the soothing hues of the landscape: muted greens, browns, and deep golds. Plants are important, as another reminder of nature's bounty.

The Arts and Crafts interior, though relatively spare, is pleasantly accessorized. Lamps and fixtures in wrought iron, brass, or copper cast a warming glow, as do simple fireplaces, often faced with handmade tiles that may have been painted by the lady of the house.

Among the most successful products of the American Arts and Crafts movement are the ceramics produced by amateur and professional potteries, which sprang up in the wake of the new interest in handcraft. They offered an unusual, and previously unavailable, opportunity for women to earn money through their artistic endeavors. The best known of these are Rookwood Pottery Company of Cincinnati, Ohio (established 1880), Grueby Faience Company of Revere, Massachusetts (established 1894), and Newcomb Pottery of New Orleans, Louisiana (established 1895), but many others provided avocations for upper-class women and much-needed employment for others. Similar ventures produced decorative silver and metalwork in the Arts and Crafts style.

ABOUT THE FURNITURE

Furniture of the type produced by Stickley and others is relatively large-scaled and, despite its simplicity, can be imposing. Its sturdy, rectilinear lines are executed in rough-textured, quarter-sawn fumed oak, darkened by exposing the wood to fumes of ammonia, to simulate the natural weathering that comes from age and oxidation. The furniture is made with visible joints,and accented with metal hardware and occasional stenciled motifs. Despite looking handcrafted, it is made mostly by machine, then finished by hand.

Typical Stickley seating pieces include wide, low-seated chairs with broad slats, square legs, and loose-cushion upholstery, usually of dark leather. A few basic forms are repeated in variations of size and proportion, but always with the same silhouettes. Case pieces are similarly limited to craftsman-like, rectilinear forms, including square and rectangular tables with sturdy legs or trestle bases, chests, buffet servers, and bookcases with mullioned glass fronts. The few occasional pieces include desks, stools, and small tables. Hammered metal hardware and accents are in polished iron or patinated copper, sometimes suggesting medieval inspiration. Many of the most sophisticated designs are credited to architect and painter Harvey Ellis (1852–1904), whose furniture tended to be lighter in scale than most Stickley pieces and are often embellished with discreet decorative inlays.

Inspired by England's Arts and Crafts movement, several Utopian-like communities were established in America, among them the Roycrofters, founded by Elbert Hubbard in East Aurora, New York (established 1895), Byrdcliffe in Woodstock, New York (established 1903), and the Shop of the Crafters in Cincinnati, Ohio (established 1906). While pursuing a lifestyle that followed William Morris's ideals, they produced furniture as well as decorative objects in the Arts and Crafts style.

The homes designed in the first decade of the 20th century by the brothers Charles Sumner Greene (1868–1957) and Henry Mather Greene (1870–1954) in Pasadena, California, were a more refined American expression of Arts and Crafts style. Their interiors and furniture were distinguished by fine joinery, warm colors, softened rectilinearity, and lustrous finishes. Greene and Greene's interpretation of the Arts and Crafts aesthetic also shared the influence of Japanese culture seen in Frank Lloyd Wright's houses, and they also designed stained-glass windows and lighting fixtures.

PREVIOUS PAGE: The dining room of the Gamble House, in Pasadena, California, 1908, illustrates the refined interpretation of American Arts and Crafts style that marks the work of Greene and Greene. Warm mahogany, carved details, and distinctive Japanese-influenced stained glass are characteristic of the brothers' work.

This music cabinet with tapering form, of oak with pewter, copper, and inlays of dyed woods, was designed by Harvey Ellis for Gustav Stickley & Company, c. 1903.

LEFT: A drop-arm spindled Morris chair, a classic example of Stickley furniture, made by Gustav Stickley at his factory in Eastwood, New York, c. 1906.

BELOW: This lantern was designed by Greene and Greene for the Blacker House in Pasadena, California, c. 1907, in stained glass and mahogany.

The sturdy, unadorned furniture made by Gustav Stickley, like this bookcase of quarter-sawn oak, are the best-known expressions of American Arts and Crafts.

BELOW: Made of hammered copper with mica panels, the Warty table lamp is typical of designs by Dirk Van Erp, a Dutch expatriate who opened his San Francisco, California, workshop in 1910.

ABOVE: The Arts and Crafts movement in America produced distinctive ceramics as well as furniture. This stoneware vase, with trademark cucumber glaze, was made by Grueby Art Pottery, of Boston, Massachusetts, c. 1900.

■ Frank Lloyd Wright

Probably the most creative American architect of the 20th century, Frank Lloyd Wright (1867–1959) began his career in the last decade of the 19th century. His prolific and colorful career lasted almost seven decades and spanned several design aesthetics, from Arts and Crafts to International Style and biomorphic modernism. Although he designed more than 1,000 projects, at least half of them were never built. Those that were, however, have helped to shape the development of modern architecture and design.

At the beginning of his career, Wright designed a few houses in the then-fashionable Queen Anne style, but he quickly broke with the establishment, and most of his early work marked a radical departure from cluttered Victorian design. It was compatible with Arts and Crafts ideals but reflected his own distinctive aesthetic. The so-called Prairie Houses, in suburbs outside of Chicago, exemplified Wright's organic approach to architecture. He believed that a building should evolve naturally from its surroundings and the land on which it was built, and these houses did precisely that. Their rectilinear forms hugged the ground, emphasizing horizontals rather than verticals, with projecting rooflines and broad strips of windows that blurred the boundaries between interior and exterior space. In later designs, he carried his ideas even further, sometimes even reshaping the landscape in order to fit his objective of integrating site and structure. To Wright, a single-minded and autocratic man, the relationship between the elements of a design was more important than any specific form: every part must relate to the organic whole. He was adamant in controlling every element of a project including the smallest accessories and sometimes even the client's hostess gowns.

Most of the homes Frank Lloyd Wright designed share several characteristics. The typical Wright interior has a relatively low, beamed ceiling and rooms that flow seamlessly from one area to another. Stained glass inserts punctuate horizontal bands of windows that he called "light screens." They wrap around the house beneath an overhanging roof, in a configuration that both admits light and ensures privacy. A palette of understated colors, drawn from nature and the surrounding landscape, is varied with contrasts of tone and texture—unfinished wood grain, stone, rough plaster, and brick-work. The geometric-patterned stained glass in windows or lighting fixtures is usually the only strong color in the rooms.

Each piece of Wright's furniture is designed specifically for the interior in which it is placed; it is not necessarily graceful and is often not particularly comfortable. Objects are distinguished by sharply angular forms, often emphasizing horizontal lines, and some have cantilevered elements that echo the architecture. Highback chairs create a virtual enclosure when placed around a dining table, but their unforgiving lines make no accommodation for the body's contours. The furniture is made of stained or fumed oak, with surfaces that are matte-finished and minimally adorned. Intersecting horizontal and vertical planes, like those in his architecture, are largely free of ornament; the little ornament he added was either geometric or highly stylized.

In many Wright interiors, seating and storage are built-in, to provide the most efficient use of space and to ensure that clients would not rearrange his meticulously planned scheme. These serene and almost severe rooms reflect the influence on Wright of Oriental art, particularly the Japanese woodblock prints he collected. The Usonian houses of his later career translate his concepts into affordable, middle-class housing. Though he refused to acknowledge the influence of either history or other architects on his work, Wright's designs evolved throughout the course of his career. Many elements of his mature work, particularly the horizontal planes, the flowing spaces, and the continuity between interior and exterior, are compatible with the aesthetic of the International Style.

NEXT PAGE: In his Oak Park, Illinois, home and studio, Frank Lloyd Wright designed this Contemplation Chamber, with light pouring into the otherwise dark, wood-framed interior through a skylight.

The barrel-shaped armchair, its rounded shape and polished oak finish something of a departure for Frank Lloyd Wright, was designed in 1937 for the Johnson family residence.

Frank Lloyd Wright designed this desk chair for the Larkin Administration Building in Buffalo, New York, in 1904, of cast iron, bent steel, and leather.

One of the windows designed in 1903 for the J. J. Walser House, in Chicago, Illinois, by Frank Lloyd Wright, who conceived the idea of geometric-patterned light screens in his Prairie-style residences to admit daylight to the interiors without sacrificing privacy.

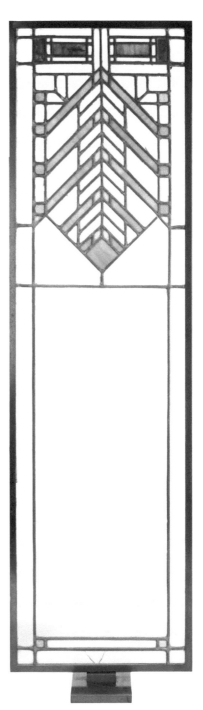

Style Markers

MOOD
refined simplicity

SCALE
modest

COLORS
limited palette, muted tones

ORNAMENT
restrained

KEY MOTIFS
nature, Japanese, some Gothic

FURNITURE
soft-edge forms of unfinished,
smooth oak

TEXTILES
handwoven-look

LOOK FOR
rough finish, brass fittings,
distinctive ceramics

Burnaby is a highly stylized abstract floral, complementary to an Arts and Crafts interior.

Clusters of birds in dense foliage, Savaric is in characteristic dulled green tone.

CHAPTER 18
Art Nouveau, c. 1890–1910

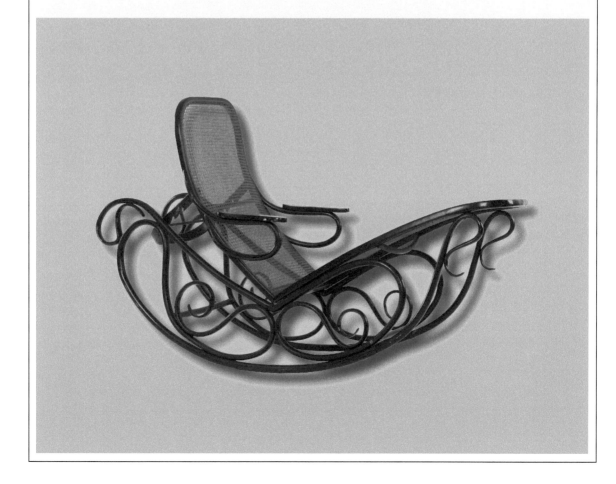

Art Nouveau, c. 1890–1910

ABOUT THE PERIOD

Art Nouveau is considered the first modern style. As its name suggests, it sought to throw off the restraints of tradition and historicism by inventing a design vocabulary for the industrial age. Born as the 19th century was ending, it flourished for a brief but glorious time in the early part of the 20th century.

Despite its rejection of historicism, Art Nouveau drew on such diverse sources as French Rococo, Gothic, the Far East, Symbolist art, and even Celtic manuscripts, making it more a blend of several related styles than a single one. Overlapping with Arts and Crafts, it took a different direction—instead of restrained evocations of nature, it used forms that vibrated with life; instead of rejecting modern materials and techniques, it embraced them. Its defining design motif was the undulating "whiplash" curve, designated by artist William Hogarth (1697–1764) as the "line of beauty."

Art Nouveau emerged in Belgium, in the architecture and interiors of Victor Horta (1861–1947) and Henri van de Velde (1863–1957), and in France, where its practitioners included designers Louis Majorelle (1859–1926), Émile Gallé (1846–1904), and Hector Guimard (1867–1942). It was named for the Paris gallery *L'Art Nouveau*, opened in 1895 by German-born art dealer Siegfried Bing, which became the major showcase for objects in the new style.

Embraced by a fashion-minded audience, *L'Art Nouveau* spread to many countries, assuming other names and national characteristics: it was *Jugendstil* in Germany, *Stile Liberty* or *Stile Floreale* in Italy, and Tiffany Style in America. It incorporated the eccentricities of Antoni Gaudí (1852–1926) in Barcelona, Spain, and Carlo Bugatti (1856–1940) in Milan, Italy. The primary example of Art Nouveau design in America was in the opalescent and favrile glass objects created by Louis Comfort Tiffany (1848–1933). At its apogee, the style was celebrated in the Paris *Exposition Universelle* of 1900.

Art Nouveau furniture began with established forms and sculpted them into variations expressing the organic, asymmetrical, and curvilinear characteristics that define the style. French-made pieces, in particular, combined masterful carving with elaborate marquetry; this work required a high level of craftsmanship and made most of the pieces too costly for any beyond the cosmopolitan coterie, who were, in any case, its greatest admirers. Furniture in other countries was generally less ornate, with a variety of interpretations that reflected a desire to develop individual national styles.

Art Nouveau architecture left a heritage of curvilinear façades in Brussels and Paris, as well as such diverse locations as Prague, Helsinki, Moscow, and Barcelona. It encompassed many other areas of the arts, particularly influencing jewelry and graphic design: illustrations by Alphonse Mucha (1860–1939) and Aubrey Beardsley (1872–1898) were among its most successful interpretations.

In their search for originality, Art Nouveau designers committed excesses of taste, and the style was as mocked for its frivolity as it was applauded for its flair. The outbreak of World War I dealt the final deathblow to the era.

ABOUT THE STYLE

Walking into an Art Nouveau interior is like entering a fantasy—it elicits a feeling of escape from reality, enticing the eye with exuberant celebrations of the whiplash curve.

The style is created by more than just furnishings; the entire room is designed as part of an ensemble that early German modernists called *gesamtkunstwerk*, a total work of art. The vertical and horizontal planes of walls and ceilings seem to dissolve into asymmetrical curves and undulating surfaces, transforming the shell of the room into a sculptural surround. Carved paneling might frame wallpapers patterned with stylized flowers, foliage, or Japanese motifs on pale grounds. Elaborate iron staircases resemble tendrils and vines, and the fireplace is framed in decorative tiles.

Window treatments are relatively uncomplicated, with shaped pelmets hung over draperies patterned with stylized floral motifs. Upholstery fabrics have the same stylized motifs, embroidered on linen, silk, or wool, and were often created by the same Art Nouveau designers.

Colors in the Art Nouveau interior seem luminescent; intense pastels like lilac, mauve, salmon, and indigo enhance the effect of a room enveloped in pattern. Notwithstanding their search for modernism, Art Nouveau designers shared the enthusiasm of the late-19th-century Victorians for elaborate decorative schemes.

Art Nouveau, c. 1890–1910

The ornament associated with Art Nouveau includes both nature-inspired and feminine motifs: nymphs with flowing hair, peacocks, dragonflies, irises and morning glories, waves, seaweed, and other botanical forms. These motifs are translated onto wallpapers, textiles, and woven rugs or carpets, laid over wood or tiled floors.

Lighting elements, using gas, kerosene, or now electricity, are organic brass forms or brilliant-colored Tiffany lamps and fixtures. On the walls are paintings, prints, perhaps Japanese woodblocks; on tabletops and mantels are many small objects of ceramic, silver, and pewter. Glass objects would include artware by the French firms Gallé or Daum.

ABOUT THE FURNITURE

Although its forms have clear references to 18th-century French styles, Art Nouveau furniture is another genre altogether. Unmistakable in its exaggerated curves and flowing ornament, it is as elaborately detailed, in its way, as its predecessors were. Yet the overall effect is one of lightness and delicacy, in part from the finely executed ornament, but also from the use of a variety of decoratively grained, light-toned woods. Virtually every object is designed as much for its visual appeal as for its function, with function sometimes secondary. Chairs and settees are strikingly varied, with sensual curves and carved wood frames that upstage even the most elegant upholstery.

Cabinets, in a variety of shapes and sizes, are sculpted with intriguing touches of asymmetry, so that their familiar forms seem entirely new. Some may have intricate marquetry ornament on door fronts; others have open glass shelves, sometimes unevenly arranged, for displaying the decorative ceramics and glass that are among Art Nouveau's finest expressions. Warm-toned, richly grained woods like mahogany, palisander, and exotics like amaranth are used. Gilt mounts are seen, as on traditional French furniture, though with naturalistic, asymmetrical motifs. Round or rounded-square occasional tables, nesting tray tables, and strikingly sinuous desks carry the distinctive lines and decorative detailing of the style. Notwithstanding the individuality of Art Nouveau design, many of the objects were not individually commissioned but were produced in multiples.

NEXT PAGE: The Salon of the Victor Horta home, now a museum in Brussels, Belgium, shows the sinuous lines of Art Nouveau design in the architectural surround as well as the furniture, exemplifying the *gesamtkunstwerk* (total work of art) sought by the designers.

Sweeping curves in a rocking chaise longue by *Gebruder Thonet*, Vienna, the firm that pioneered bentwood furniture. Made of solid beech and cane, c. 1880.

A French Art Nouveau mahogany and walnut buffet by Paul Bec, featuring two leaded glass doors depicting leaves and flowers, c. 1900.

■ Louis Comfort Tiffany

A multitalented artist, designer, and inventor, Louis Comfort Tiffany (1848–1933) was the only important American exponent of Art Nouveau style, and the first designer from America to become internationally celebrated. Trained as a painter, he spent most of his career working in glass, designing windows and then lamps, vases, and decorative objects using decorative processes of his own invention.

Of leaded glass with bronze bases, notable for their rich colorations and varied patterns, Tiffany lamps were among the most desirable accessories in early 20th-century interiors. Here, a tabletop Wisteria, c. 1900.

His work in designing interiors, however, spans the transition between the Aesthetic Movement and Art Nouveau style. In 1879, he formed the decorating firm of Louis Comfort Tiffany, Associated Artists in partnership with textile designer Candace Wheeler and then-furniture maker Lockwood de Forest. In its short existence, the partnership designed homes and interiors for Gilded Age clients in the Aesthetic style, although some of Tiffany's later work in stained glass leaned toward Modernism.

When Tiffany began, in 1883, to pursue his interest in glass, Wheeler took over the company, which closed in 1907. Tiffany continued to design interiors, but his most enduring contributions were in glass technology and in the objects he created in his preferred medium. In 1881, he patented a method for producing colored window glass that was opalescent rather than opaque, creating shimmering tonalities of color by combining several colors in making the glass rather than painting on it afterward. The process made possible remarkable contrasts of light and shadow in the leaded-glass windows he designed, although admirers of the monotone surfaces of traditional stained glass criticized it as too fanciful. Tiffany used the same material, assembling leftover glass fragments from his window commissions, into the leaded-glass lamps and lighting fixtures that his firm produced in great quantities until 1919. Customers had the option of pairing their choice of shade with any of several cast-bronze bases to customize what were essentially production goods. Other more elaborate designs were produced in limited numbers, made to order.

Tiffany's other major discovery, which he called *favrile*, was an iridescent glass whose luminous qualities gained immediate praise; it was used in brilliantly colored glass vases and other decorative objects. Tiffany exhibited his designs for windows and blown glass at international venues like the Paris gallery *L'Art Nouveau*, the 1900 *Exposition Universelle* in Paris, and the 1902 *Prima Esposizione d'Arte Decorativa Moderna* in Turin, Italy (where the Glasgow group and the Vienna Secessionists also showed). He also designed enamelwork and jewelry, and a variety of accessory items, but he is best remembered for his extraordinary work in glass.

Louis Comfort Tiffany's firm began by making stained-glass windows, like this strikingly colored three-panel example, in Magnolia pattern, c. 1910.

LEFT: Louis Majorelle, one of the French masters of Art Nouveau, designed this *bombe* vitrine, c. 1900.

BELOW: Both the form and the ornamental motifs of this étagère by Émile Gallé, made in France in 1900, are derived from plant forms. The inlay depicts a landscape of reeds and orchids while the legs and shelves suggest branches and pond lilies.

LEFT: This French Art Nouveau carved walnut and fruitwood marquetry Narcissus side table was made by Émile Gallé in 1900.

BELOW: Part of a suite that included two matching armchairs, this shapely carved mahogany settee, called *Ombellifères*, was designed by Louis Majorelle, c. 1900.

RIGHT: The *Bloemenwerf* chair, designed by Henri van de Velde, one of the most important Belgian Art Nouveau designers, was made for his own house, of elm, with leather seat and brass tacks. In 1905, Van de Velde established an Arts and Crafts school in Weimar, Germany, which later became the Bauhaus.

BELOW: Art Nouveau produced a few idiosyncratic designers like Carlo Bugatti, whose unique furniture showed Oriental and Moorish influence. This settee, like most of his designs, combines ebonized wood with parchment, mixed-metal inlays, and fringe; made c. 1900–1910.

Style Markers

MOOD
exuberant

SCALE
generous

COLORS
jewel tones

ORNAMENT
fine marquetry, asymmetrical

KEY MOTIFS
nymphs with flowing hair, vines
and foliage

FURNITURE
extravagantly curved, highly
decorative

WOODS
mahogany, palisander, amaranth

TEXTILES
rich and richly patterned

LOOK FOR
"whiplash" curves, Tiffany lamps

A silvery gray feather-motif wallpaper, Havana Platinum, could be a flattering accompaniment to Art Nouveau.

A sophisticated interpretation of a nature-inspired pattern, with calla lilies and undulating lines.

■ Glasgow Style, c. 1890–1910

ABOUT THE PERIOD

Named for the birthplace of Scottish designer Charles Rennie Mackintosh (1868–1928), with whose name it is most closely associated, this style is unique but extremely difficult to categorize. It straddles the fence between Arts and Crafts and Art Nouveau, but it is also linked to the modernists of the Vienna Secession. Mackintosh, his future wife Margaret MacDonald (1864–1933), her sister Frances MacDonald (1865–1902), and Frances's husband Herbert MacNair (1868–1955) were fellow art students who developed the elements of the Glasgow design aesthetic. "The Four," as they were called, worked together on several projects, but the partnership of Mackintosh and Margaret actually defined the style, with furniture forms and construction that recall Arts and Crafts objects, and curvilinear ornament that vividly prefigures Art Nouveau.

Despite its connections to both strains of design reform, however, Glasgow Style is also a precursor of Modernism. The celebrated "Rose Room," designed by the Mackintosh group in the 1902 *Prima Exposizione d'Arte Decorativa Moderna* in Turin, Italy, was enthusiastically received by the Vienna Secessionists, who saw in Mackintosh a kindred spirit rebelling against the design establishment. His use of linearity and intersecting planes, his progressive spatial planning, and his imaginative contrasts of solids and voids were clear explorations of an avant-garde aesthetic.

In his architectural commissions, Mackintosh drew on elements of Scottish vernacular design, combining them with more modern notes: asymmetry, cast-iron ornament, and plate-glass windows. Although critically acclaimed in Europe, his work drew little interest in England, and his architectural and interiors projects were limited to the Glasgow area. His most noted designs include the Glasgow School of Art (1897), Hill House (1902), and four tearooms for Miss Kate Cranston, the most admired of which was the Willow Tea Rooms (1904).

The combination of severe form and sensual decoration—the yin and yang of male and female elements seen in the collaboration of Margaret MacDonald and Charles Rennie Mackintosh—make the Glasgow Style a genre of design that, while drawing on influences of the past, translates into something unique. Despite a relatively brief and intermittently successful career, Mackintosh is an important early participant in the modern movement.

ABOUT THE STYLE

An interior in Glasgow Style is in a class by itself. Entirely original, it is identified by the strong geometry of its attenuated furniture forms and the bold contrasts of light and dark. The Mackintosh interior is striking for its minimalist simplicity in an era of clutter and pattern-filled rooms. Elegantly understated, it embellishes spare furnishings with sophisticated ornamental accents.

The room might be almost delicate in ambience, with all-white backgrounds and slim-lined white- or black-painted furniture. In a bedroom or parlor, white walls and carpeted floors form a backdrop for slender chairs and cabinets, arranged with spare precision in a linear composition, relieved by occasional accents of color. In other spaces, a more robust mood might be evoked by the use of dark woods, posts, and beams. Mackintosh's predilection for white interiors, however, especially in public places like the tearooms, were a refreshing and unexpected amenity in a smoke-filled industrial city.

Mackintosh rooms have no specific shape, but they are articulated around the furniture arrangement with built-in cabinetry, Arts and Crafts–style inglenooks, or small alcoves. These irregularities are reflected in the exterior of the building, which might be punctuated by randomly placed windows, curving bays, and turrets recalling Scottish Baronial architecture. Walls are most likely enhanced by gessoed or silvered panels painted by Margaret with romantic fantasy figures, sinuous floral forms, or motifs including a stylized rose.

Making skillful use of light and shadow, Glasgow Style interiors are deliberately simple, yet the spare elegance accounts for their appeal. Window treatments are light and airy, and apart from the contrast of furniture against background, there is relatively little additional decoration and minimal accessories. The characteristic color scheme of white with black is sparked with accents of lively pastels. Mackintosh designed fabrics as well as furniture, in precise and unpretentious patterns that complement the simplicity of his interiors.

ABOUT THE FURNITURE

Furniture by Mackintosh is more distinctive for its design than for its workmanship. The silhouettes are bold and the ornament highly refined, but most of the cabinetry is relatively unsophisticated and the construction undistinguished. It is consistently rectilinear, with visible joints, straight legs, and rough-textured finishes. The forms of storage pieces are not unusual, though the decoration is—geometric cutouts that contrast solids and voids; inlays of mother of pearl; doors with stained-glass inserts or painted motifs on exterior and interior faces, presenting different aspects when open or closed. The furniture is generally of simple oak, often painted white or black, ebonized, or sometimes silvered for decorative effect.

Mackintosh chairs are severely rectilinear, with ornament that includes hearts, crescents, or openwork grid pattern similar to the motif used frequently in *Weiner Werkstätte* silver. Several of the angular forms, with assertive high backs and distinctive openwork, have become iconic images of early Modernism.

NEXT PAGE: A section of the master bedroom in Hill House, Helensburgh, Scotland, designed in 1902–1904 for Walter Blackie. The white interiors, abstract-rose motifs on the closet doors, and tall black-painted ladderback chair are hallmarks of Mackintosh's style.

ABOVE: The chairs designed for a series of Glasgow tearooms are among Mackintosh's best-known designs: here, the barrel-shaped cashier's chair from the Willow Tea Rooms, 1904.

RIGHT: This chair was made for one of Mackintosh's first major commissions, the Argyle Street Tearooms in Glasgow. The unusual high back gave a feeling of privacy to diners. Made of oak and rush, c. 1897.

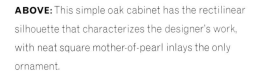

ABOVE: This simple oak cabinet has the rectilinear silhouette that characterizes the designer's work, with neat square mother-of-pearl inlays the only ornament.

RIGHT: The interiors of the Glasgow tearooms varied, and Mackintosh designed different furniture for each. Here, a highback chair from the White Dining Room of the Ingram Street Tea Rooms, c. 1900.

Style Markers

MOOD
serene

SCALE
modest

COLORS
white and black, jewel-pastel accents

ORNAMENT
recalls both Arts and Crafts and Art Nouveau

KEY MOTIFS
stylized rose, square cutouts on furniture

FURNITURE
angular rectilinear forms, distinctive silhouettes

TEXTILES
understated patterns and textures

LOOK FOR
white rooms with black or white furniture, flowing painted panels

Mackintosh's designs for textiles were brightly colored and often used floral motifs, like this pattern of stylized roses, which also appeared as ornament on his furniture and interiors.

Part IV

20TH CENTURY:
Modernism and After

CHAPTER 19
Early European Modernism: *Wiener Werkstätte* and Avant-Garde Style, c. 1900–1930

Early European Modernism, c. 1900–1930

ABOUT THE PERIOD

Although the reformers of the 19th century took the first steps away from tradition, their designs did not break entirely with the past. The early years of the new century, however, marked a time of genuine change. The secessionist movements of the early 20th century—the 1897-founded *Wiener Sezession* is the best known of these, but there were earlier similar groups in Berlin and Munich—sought to separate themselves from the art and design establishment, to seek a new modern aesthetic, to erase the distinction between the fine and applied arts, and to improve public taste. In these objectives, they had much in common with the English reform movement. In their designs, however, are visible the first clear iterations of Modernism.

The key concepts for these and other avant-garde designers were the understanding that industrialization had radically changed the process of design and the acceptance of the machine as a valid alternative to handcraft, though not necessarily a replacement for it. This view opened an ongoing conversation about how to reconcile the two, a challenge that would be faced by designers and theorists well into the 20th century.

One of the tenets of the new Modernist aesthetic was expressed in a widely published 1908 essay by architect and theorist Adolph Loos (1870–1933). Entitled "Ornament and Crime," it posited that ornament was not a natural product of modern society and was therefore no longer appropriate. The essay was used to justify the rejection of ornament by Modernists. "Form follows function" and "less is more" would become battle cries of the Modern movement—though it was neither formally organized, nor a single movement, but a series of independent and often loosely connected groups.

One of the most influential of these groups was the *Deutsche Werkbund*, founded in Germany in 1907, which brought together all those involved in design—artists and designers, artisans, and manufacturers—to collaborate in meeting the new design challenges brought about by industrialization. Some of the most innovative designs of the time were introduced at *Werkbund*-sponsored exhibitions in the period before the outbreak of World War I, after which Germany was ostracized by much of the Western world.

Influential early Modernist groups included *De Stijl*, in Holland, which decreed that design should be impersonal and abstract, as seen in the paintings of Piet Mondrian

(1872–1944) and the angular forms and primary colors of buildings and furniture by Gerrit Reitveld (1888–1964). Other early modern movements included Russian Constructivism, which translated the vocabulary of abstract art into graphic design, and Italian Futurism, which celebrated the aesthetic of the machine and speed, and produced Antonio Sant'Elia's (1888–1916) vision of the glass-towered modern city.

Only one of the early Modernist groups, the *Wiener Werkstätte* (Vienna Workshops), developed a fully realized style. Founded in Vienna, Austria, in 1903 by designers Josef Hoffmann (1870–1956), Kolomon Moser (1868–1918), and their patron Fritz Warndorfer, the *Werkstätte*, whose key members also belonged to the Vienna Secession, established a series of workshops for applied arts, modeled somewhat on C. R. Ashbee's Guild of Handcraft (1888–1907) of the Arts and Crafts era, and rejecting the excesses of Art Nouveau. The *Wiener Werkstätte* took a functional approach to design, employing linear forms and its own vocabulary of ornament, which was almost entirely geometric, although the designs later became more exuberant and decorative. The group sought to bring good design, meaning modern design, to all categories of objects, but like so many early attempts at design reform, their products were costly and therefore available to only a small market of affluent clients. The designs, however, represent an important step along the path to a modern aesthetic.

ABOUT THE STYLE

For the *Werkstätte* designers, all elements of a project are part of a coherent plan—the *gesamtkunstwerk*—and are designed to coalesce into an integrated whole. Although Secessionist design often includes elements of Art Nouveau, Hoffmann and his colleagues, with rare exceptions, rejected curvilinear forms. *Werkstätte* interiors are notable for their striking rectilinearity and their elegant simplicity.

The space itself is defined by the interplay of horizontal and verticals: white walls might be slashed with bold vertical lines that form an enclosure of slim rectangular panels, each accented with stylized floral or geometric motifs. A string-like design runs horizontally to visually connect the windows. Despite the severity of the individual elements, Hoffman's interiors for important clients are luxurious, enriched with rich materials like marble and rosewood, parquet flooring, mosaics, and suede or velvet upholstery.

The *Werkstätte* designers did not eschew pattern, but they stripped it down to the barest essentials: the pure geometry of checkerboards, squares, and sometimes circles. A favorite grid pattern is applied to floors, windows, and vivid textiles, appearing most intriguingly on pierced silver accessories. The most characteristic color scheme is primarily black-and-white, although an interior might include accents of red, brilliant yellow, deep blue, or other high-intensity hues.

Small-scale geometric motifs or dense clusters of stylized florals are arranged in symmetrical patterns on the fabrics and carpets designed by Hoffmann and Moser and produced by the workshops, in one of their more successful ventures. An interior might also use Hoffmann-designed geometric wallpaper.

Among the most recognizable designs produced by the *Wiener Werkstätte* are metalwork accessories: silver and silverplate are used for elegant lighting fixtures, clocks, bowls, boxes, and vases decorated with hammering or perforated grid patterns—a motif also used by Charles Rennie Mackintosh. The workshops also produced striking works of color-accented glass, as well as ceramics and jewelry.

ABOUT THE FURNITURE

Furniture by Hoffmann and his colleagues follows a similar reductivist aesthetic, with angular construction, sometimes decorated with inlays of contrasting materials. Moser, in particular, devised sophisticated effects with a minimalist vocabulary, using rare woods and sometimes mother-of-pearl or semiprecious stones. The most famous pieces of *Wiener Werkstätte* furniture, however, are the distinctive bentwood objects designed mostly for J. & J. Kohn, using the process developed by the German-born Michael Thonet (1796–1871) 50 years earlier. These factory-made chairs, settees, and tables, several of which have become iconic symbols of Modernism, are the only designs that achieved the objective of creating modern furniture that was accessible to a broad market.

PREVIOUS PAGE: The house where Josef Hoffman was born, in Brtnice, Czech Republic, is now a museum. Here, one of the interiors, showing some of his bent-wood chair designs.

RIGHT: This chair was designed for the first-floor dining room at the Purkersdorf Sanatorium in Austria, c. 1905. Like many other of Hoffmann's designs at this time, the decorative elements have a functional aspect. The punched and geometrically arranged decoration can be found on many other Hoffmann pieces.

BELOW: The *Sitzmachine*, by Josef Hoffmann, c. 1902, combining straight lines and bentwood curves, has an adjustable back. Made of stained beechwood with ply-wood seat and back.

This cabinet of lacquered beech, mirrored glass, and brass was designed by Josef Hoffmann, c. 1905, and made by the Austrian firm of Jacob & Josef Kohn, who were competitors of Thonet.

ABOVE: Shaped of bent beechwood, the frame of this settee has a circular motif, rather than the more familiar diamond shape. Designed by Josef Hoffmann for Thonet, c. 1908.

LEFT: This armchair was designed for the Director's Office of the Post Office Savings Bank in Vienna, Austria, by Otto Wagner in 1906. Wagner was one of the founders of the Vienna Secession, with Josef Olbrich, and *Werkstätte* members Hoffman, Moser, and Klimt.

LEFT: With the distinctive checkerboard motif often seen in *Wiener Werkstätte* design, this glitterwerk dessert basket of silver and lapis lazuli is by Koloman Moser, c. 1906.

BELOW: Josef Hoffman designed these barrel-shaped armchairs for the Fledermaus Cabaret, in Vienna, Austria, in 1905. Made of black-painted bent beechwood with brass accents.

Early European Modernism, c. 1900–1930

Style Markers

MOOD
severe

SCALE
varies

COLORS
bright, bold

ORNAMENT
minimal, stylized

KEY MOTIFS
grid pattern

FURNITURE
simple linear forms, dark wood,
no carving

TEXTILES
flat-weaves, bold symmetrical
patterns

LOOK FOR
bold black-and-white, gridwork,
bright accents

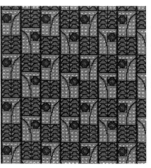

Paradis is one of the distinctive patterns, mostly small-scale geometrics, designed by Josef Hoffmann for the *Wiener Werkstätte*.

Kolomon Moser, a co-founder of the *Wiener Werkstätte*, designed *Orakelblume*.

CHAPTER 20
International Style, c. 1930–1970

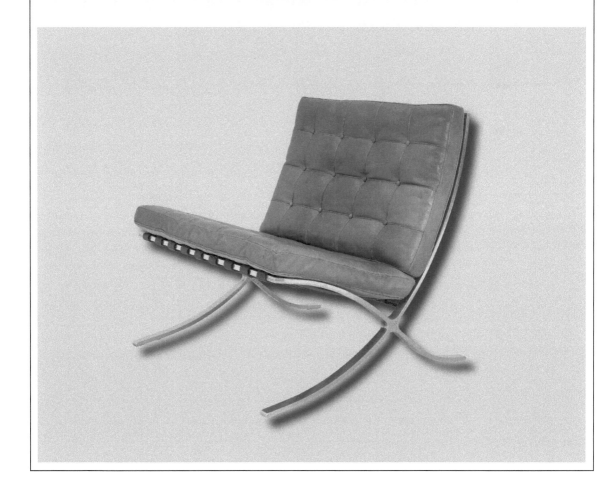

International Style, c. 1930–1970

ABOUT THE PERIOD

In 1932, Philip Johnson and Henry Russell Hitchcock curated *Architecture: An International Exhibition*, at The Museum of Modern Art in New York City. The style it documented, named after the accompanying book, is considered the purest expression of 20th-century Modernism. Functionalism was a dominant concern, and the book outlined three principles to be followed: (1) architecture as volume, rather than mass; (2) regularity of form; and (3) the avoidance of applied decoration. The International Style in architecture was not intended as a style but as a rejection of the idea of style, although it was ultimately applied as a formulaic approach to building that led to its decline in popularity and the rebellion of Postmodernism.

Among the names most associated with the International Style's principles of design were Bauhaus masters Walter Gropius (1883–1969), Ludwig Mies van der Rohe (1886–1969), and Marcel Breuer (1902–1981), and their contemporary Le Corbusier (Charles-Édouard Jeanneret-Gris, 1887–1965). International Style architecture celebrated geometric form and modern materials. Its buildings were glass curtain–walled skyscrapers or flat-roofed structures of steel and concrete with broad swaths of windows and entirely without ornament. The revolt against traditional architectural styles launched a new look in interiors that were open, light-filled, and furnished with objects that followed the tenets of functionalist design.

The International Style was embraced as a statement of modernity in the rectilinear, curtain–walled corporate headquarters that dotted the American landscape in the prosperous years after World War II. The form was ideally suited to the demands of postwar construction: both economical and efficient, it provided maximum floor space and facilitated the use of machine-made modular elements.

Emphasizing structure and functionality rather than warmth and creature comforts, International Style failed to gain the acceptance in residential design that it did for office structures, like Mies van der Rohe's celebrated Seagram Building (1958) in New York City, the paradigm of 20th-century corporate culture. It was more successfully applied to high-rise apartments than single-family residences, except perhaps for the innovative California homes designed by Rudolf Schindler (1887–1953) and Richard Neutra (1892–1970), both briefly associates of Le Corbusier.

■ Bauhaus, c. 1919–1933

Founded in 1919 in Weimar, Germany, under the direction of Walter Gropius, the Bauhaus was a school founded on the principle of the equality of all the arts: fine and applied arts were of equal merit and should be treated equally. The school's name means "a house for building," and its revolutionary approach was to combine the teaching of art with that of craft, beginning with a hands-on foundation course taken by all students and individual workshops for each discipline. Its faculty was drawn from the leading names in art and design—Mies van der Rohe, Wassily Kandinsky, Josef Albers, Paul Klee, and others—and its ambitious objective was to develop products for industrial production, representing the first of the Modernist groups to truly embrace industrialization. In the craft workshops, however, art was often favored over function, and few of the prototypes were actually produced. Despite failing to achieve its primary goal, the Bauhaus developed a new educational approach and formulated the fundamental design vocabulary of Modernism.

Faced by internal squabbles and political pressures, the Bauhaus moved first to Dessau and then Berlin, but its life was cut short by the rise of National Socialism. When the Nazis closed the school in 1933, its masters fled to other countries. Many found refuge, as did other forward-thinking designers, architects, and artists, in America. In teaching positions at leading architecture and design schools, Walter Gropius and Marcel Breuer at Harvard University, Mies van der Rohe at the Illinois Institute of Technology, and others passed on their Modernist principles to an entire generation of young designers.

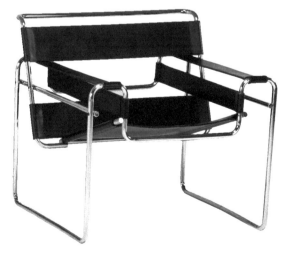

One of the best-known furniture designs emanating from the Bauhaus, Marcel Breuer's Wassily Club Chair, made of tubular chrome-plated steel and leather, was named for Wassily Kandinsky, one of the Bauhaus masters.

The Bauhaus design legacy is considerable, in furniture by Mies van der Rohe (1886–1969) and Marcel Breuer (1902–1981), textiles by Anni Albers (1899–1994) and Gunta Stolzl (1897–1983), and graphic design by Herbert Bayer (1900–1985) and Laszlo Moholy-Nagy (1895–1946). Equally important is its contribution to education. By the mid-20th century, the Bauhaus "foundation course" became the new prototype for design curricula and enhanced the prestige of the applied arts. Perhaps even more enduring is the association of Bauhaus with Modernism: although there was no specific Bauhaus style, the name has been adopted to refer to designs in the machine aesthetic and is linked to the architecture of the International Style.

Like the architecture that surrounded them, the design of International Style interiors was sometimes limited by the constraints of the Modernist vocabulary. Though the interiors were often surprisingly sumptuous, they were seen by many critics as severe and impersonal. Despite its high profile, the International Style was considered passé by the 1970s; its principles were too demanding to sustain in the pendulum swing of fashion.

ABOUT THE STYLE

The International Style interior is dramatic, expansive, and suffused with light. Walking into the space becomes not one but a series of experiences, with the conventional layout of separate rooms replaced by an open plan of interlocking volumes, articulated by screens or wall sections. Individual areas are defined by islands of furniture in precisely arranged compositions set away from the walls. Following Mies van der Rohe's often-quoted dictum "less is more," the room is furnished with a carefully edited selection of industrial-age accessories. One drawback of International Style interiors is the predictability of their furnishings, which are drawn from a limited store of acceptable designs.

Smooth white walls, stripped of moldings or other architectural detailing, enhance the seamless flow of unbroken space. Ceilings are flat and often not overly high, emphasizing horizontal rather than vertical space. Glass is an essential element in International Style architecture, and it dominates the interiors as well: the concept of exterior as extension of the interior is expressed in floor-to-ceiling walls of glass that erase any feeling of separation or enclosure, bringing the landscape indoors. Curtains, if any, are as unobtrusive as possible, or clean-lined blinds may provide an alternative covering for light control.

Colors are primarily neutrals such as grey, beige, or black, with careful and limited accents in clear, assertive hues. The textiles of choice are either tightly woven natural fibers or smooth leather in natural colors—primarily black or brown. Occasionally, a more luxurious fabric may be used for dramatic effect, but prints are studiously avoided. Pattern is more likely to appear on the walls or furniture, with materials like marble, rosewood, and ebony, while steel and chrome provide light-reflecting accents.

Lighting is for the most part concealed, to avoid interrupting the linearity of the space, although an occasional clean-lined lamp or fixture may be used. There are few judiciously placed accessories, and the walls provide an ideal background to set off large abstract paintings or modern sculpture.

ABOUT THE FURNITURE

The most prominent furniture in International Style interiors is likely to be designed by one of the celebrated Bauhaus masters—iconic pieces that follow the strict parameters of the Modernist aesthetic. Even the most costly of these, in sharp contrast to earlier styles, have been industrially produced. The most dramatic of these pieces are the chairs, benches, or chaises by Mies, Breuer, or Le Corbusier, with bold silhouettes of tubular or flat steel and upholstery in leather, cane, or wicker. Cabinets are low and rigidly linear, of polished rosewood or walnut with steel hardware and legs. Storage is often built-in, to minimize clutter. Tables are steel-based, topped with glass or perhaps marble. The pure International Style interior avoids combining its Modernist furnishings with those of other periods, though occasionally an antique piece might be inserted as a contrasting work of art.

Philip Johnson's Glass House, in New Canaan, Connecticut, built in 1949, is a celebrated example of International Style architecture, with its Mies-inspired open plan and Bauhaus furniture.

ABOVE: The cantilever chair replaced conventional legs with a framework of continuous tubular steel. The Cesca armchair, the most widely copied of the genre, was designed by Marcel Breuer for Thonet in 1928, with stained beechwood arms and a woven cane seat.

BELOW: Swiss architect Le Corbusier, born Charles-Édouard Jeanneret-Gris, shared the aesthetic sensibility of the Bauhaus designers. His lounge chair, 1928, frames thick leather cushions in slim, tubular chrome-plated steel.

LEFT: The Thonet firm, best known for bentwood furniture, also worked in other materials. This chair, a rare example by a less familiar designer, Walter Knoll, was made by Thonet in 1932.

BELOW: An International Style classic, this *chaise longue* was designed by Le Corbusier, Pierre Jeanneret, and Charlotte Perriand in 1928, of chrome-plated tubular steel, with natural hide on painted steel and rubber base. The body of the piece shifts on the base with the movement of its occupant.

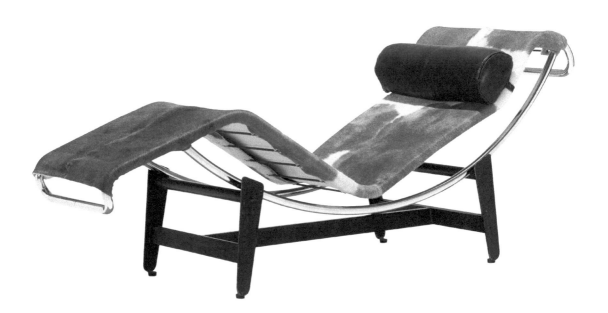

Companion to the X-base chair designed for the German Pavilion at the Barcelona World's Fair in 1929, Mies van der Rohe's Barcelona table is of polished steel and plate glass.

The iconic Barcelona chair, designed by Ludwig Mies van der Rohe, made of polished steel, leather, and horsehair.

Style Markers

MOOD
serious and intellectual

SCALE
varies

COLORS
black-and-white or neutrals

ORNAMENT
avoided

FURNITURE
sleek forms, industrial materials

TEXTILES
leather, flat-weave solids

LOOK FOR
open-plan interiors, expanses of
glass, iconic Bauhaus furniture

The Bauhaus workshop revolutionized textile design, introducing new approaches to woven fabrics by women such as Gunta Stölzl (1897–1983), one of whose patterns is shown here.

Bold and surprisingly floral, this design dates to the Bauhaus workshops.

CHAPTER 21
Modernism in the Workplace

Modernism in the Workplace

International Style buildings proliferated across America in the decades after World War II. Designed by architectural firms like Skidmore Owings & Merrill, they translated the Mies aesthetic into iterations to suit every city and any climate, creating not only new architectural archetypes but also a new type of interior. Conventional office furniture was too pedestrian for these sleek surroundings, and even fine traditional pieces would be out of place. Even in older buildings, more offices needed furniture and decoration, as postwar prosperity had generated new businesses offering goods and services to eager and affluent consumers.

The first to take advantage of the new market segment was Florence Knoll (1917–), who founded the Knoll Planning Unit in 1943 as the first of a new genre of design groups specializing in space planning and contract (as opposed to residential) design. Knoll, Herman Miller, and other furniture producers began to focus their attention on this specialized field, designing new types of furniture to accommodate the needs of employees, who needed to be productive as well as comfortable in their workday environments, and their bosses, who needed modern versions of executive office furniture.

In the early decades of the 20th century, engineer Frederick Taylor did extensive research on efficient operation of offices, which led to the practice of arranging workers in an open central space, surrounded by executives in private offices around the perimeter. This configuration changed with the more democratic office landscape, a concept introduced in Germany in the 1950s. It applied the open plan to workspaces, eliminating walls and doors in an egalitarian environment that has gone in and out of fashion in subsequent years.

In modern buildings, as air-conditioning and heating systems made natural light and ventilation less essential, and although glass walls admitted ample sunlight—sometimes even more than was comfortable—they also mandated different types of dividing walls. The office landscape might eliminate walls, but some divisions were required both for privacy and to enable employees to concentrate on their work.

Midcentury offices adopted a new type of furniture: the office system, with desks and storage units built into movable panels that also included wiring for telephones, lighting, and electronic equipment. These enabled designers to rearrange the interior into various configurations that could change according to the need of each occupant and each office environment. The first of these systems was the Action Office, designed by Robert Probst in 1964, and many others followed, from manufacturers such as Steelcase, Haworth, and others in America and abroad that catered to the increasingly profitable field; a home needed only one sofa and a limited number of chairs, but an office required dozens of each.

The science of ergonomics, which studies efficiency in the working environment, also examines the physiological effects of various postures and movements to provide standards for furniture that is easy to use, comfortable, and beneficial to workers' health. It began to influence office furniture design in the middle years of the 20th century. Industrial designer Henry Dreyfuss (1904–1972) published *The Measure of Man* in 1960, documenting the measurements of the average male and female to guide designers in planning the dimensions of seating pieces. Chairs that accommodated a variety of body types to offer good support throughout the workday became the focus of ergonomic research, the benefits of which were later applied to furnishings for homes as well as businesses.

The midcentury workplace leaned in one of two directions: either toward pristine Bauhaus furnishings and a black-white-neutral color scheme or versions of Midcentury Modern furniture and office systems with bright, saturated primaries against natural wood. The former was seen primarily in reception areas and lobbies; the latter in the more typical midcentury office space. Lighting was generally fluorescent and mostly concealed—dropped ceilings were popular—and floors were normally carpeted. Low-pile, durable carpets and sturdy flat-weave fabrics were developed and engineered for high-traffic, heavy-use areas.

The development of specialized products for commercial spaces, which eventually included hotels and restaurants as well as offices, led to a network of producers and products that ran parallel to those designed for residential use, though this would change toward the end of the century, when office design became less conventional, and the same furniture could cross over from home to office.

ABOVE: In the middle years of the 20th century, many interior designers began to turn their attention to the office, often devising open-plan arrangements like this one.

LEFT: The Knoll Planning Unit, headed by Florence Knoll, was one of the pioneering office design firms. This straight-lined sofa was designed for the Alcoa Building, in Pittsburgh, Pennsylvania.

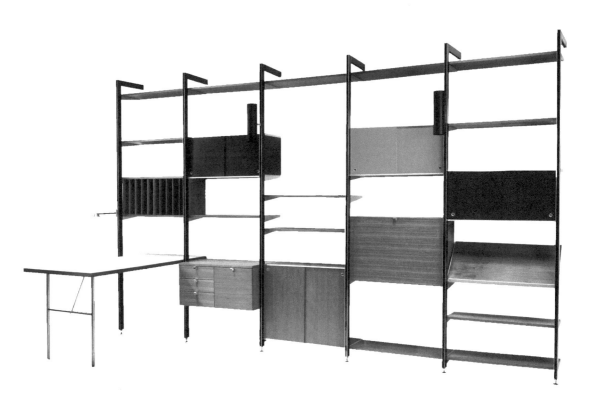

Flexible shelving systems provided efficient storage and display space in the modern office. Here, George Nelson's Five Bay Comprehensive Shelving System (CSS), for Herman Miller, incorporating desk and shelving space.

RIGHT: Danish designer Hans Wegner designed this swivel-base office chair, first made by Johannes Hansen, of teak, leather, chrome-plated steel, and bakelite, in 1955

BELOW: Robert Propst invented the Action Office for Herman Miller in 1968. It was the first open-plan system, with components that could be reconfigured according to individual requirements.

CHAPTER 22
French Art Deco Style, c. 1920–1940

French Art Deco Style, c. 1920–1940

ABOUT THE PERIOD

Often referred to as the last of the great period styles, Art Deco began to develop in Paris in the first decade of the 20th century, as a reaction to the excesses of Art Nouveau. With antecedents in Glasgow Style and the *Wiener Werkstätte, Le Style Moderne*, as it was originally called, found immediate inspiration in the avant-garde—cubist forms, Fauve colors, and the dazzling sets and costumes designed by Leon Bakst for the *Ballets Russes*—but it also drew from sources as diverse as ancient Egypt, Africa, and the Jazz Age.

The designation Art Deco was bestowed long after the fact, on the occasion of its revival in America in the late 1960s. It was named for the 1925 Paris exhibition that provided its most prominent showcase. *L'Exposition Internationale des Arts Décoratifs and Industriels Modernes* sought to reassert France's fashion leadership in the face of German innovations in modern design, but the exhibition actually celebrated a style that, in its embrace of luxury and rich materials, was already behind the times.

Despite its wish to express modernity, and its stated rejection of ornament, *Le Style Moderne* was closely linked to the guild-based tradition of 18th-century French design. Embraced by style-setting couturiers like Jacques Doucet, Pierre Poiret, and Jeanne Lanvin and interpreted by Paris *ensembliers* like Émile-Jacques Ruhlmann (1879–1933) and the design studios of the great department stores, French Art Deco design was impeccably executed, costly, and elitist. Its extravagant interiors and labor-intensive objects were the antithesis of democratic design for the industrial age. Some designers sought another direction. The *Union des Artistes Modernes* was formed in 1930, and avant-gardists like René Herbst (1891–1982), Irish-born Eileen Gray (1878–1976), and Robert Mallet-Stevens (1886–1945) would help to bring new vitality to French design in the years to follow.

Le Style Moderne was brought to an untimely end by the Wall Street crash of 1929, after which such extravagance was no longer either tasteful or affordable. Tied to a heritage of artisanry and requiring time-consuming handcraft techniques, it proved too costly to survive the Depression. It would be translated in other European adaptations, and altogether transformed in its equally striking, but more egalitarian American counterpart. Long after it had gone out of fashion, Art Deco would be preserved for future generations in the fantasy interiors of great ocean liners, grand public spaces, and glamorous Hollywood films.

About the Style

The French Art Deco interior is a study in soigné sophistication, possessed of generous proportions, and wrapped in rich and exotic materials. Even in period photographs and faded drawings, the splendor of these interiors is striking. They are discernably modern, but the most luxurious modernity imaginable, and they were clearly designed for only the most elegant, and affluent, occupants.

Grand geometric volumes of space are defined by stylized architectural elements, distilled from the classical vocabulary. Columns, moldings, recessed coves, and often, elaborately tiered ceilings create a dramatic background. Despite a professed avoidance of Art Nouveau excesses, almost every surface of the space is decorated, but in a manner so subtle that the overall effect, despite its richness, is rarely excessive.

The walls are most likely upholstered or covered with velvety, flocked wall coverings, and rich damask and velvets are used on furniture and window treatments. At the tall windows, draperies are either hung straight or in fluid pullbacks.

Floors of dark polished wood are covered with carpets in intense colors and large-scale, stylized patterns that enhance the sumptuousness of the surroundings. The patterns on textiles, walls, and floor coverings are stylized motifs from nature and classical sources, or sweeping curves that suggest abstract painting. The same stylization lends refinement to three-dimensional decorative effects such as reliefs, murals, and mosaics, which are often applied to walls.

Color schemes may be chosen for theatrical effect—with unexpected combinations of intense, almost-clashing hues—or use more conventional schemes keyed to deep tones like brown, purple, or black.

Focal-point lighting fixtures create their own drama, with cascading, multilevel crystal chandeliers, wall sconces, *torchères*, or table lamps, often of frosted or etched glass, as well as intricately worked metal. Metals like bronze and wrought iron, most notably in the work of Edgar Brandt (1880–1960) and Raymond Subes (1891–1970), are used for screens, fireplace ornament, and accent furniture. Finishing touches might include enamel-on-copper bowls or vases by Jean Dunand (1877–1942), bronze-and-ivory figurines by Dimitri Chiparus (1886–1947), silver by Jean Puiforcat (1897–1945), and frosted-glass objets by René Lalique (1860–1945).

ABOUT THE FURNITURE

Exquisitely crafted furniture by masters like Ruhlmann, Louis Sue (1875–1968), André Mare (1887–1932), André Groult (1884–1966), Pierre Chareau (1883–1950), and others have conservative silhouettes in the tradition of Louis XV, XVI, and Empire design. Chairs, chaises, and loveseats are either variations of Rococo and Neoclassical models, stripped of extraneous ornament, or angular geometric forms, framed in polished wood.

Case furniture, too, is rectilinear, with cabinets and armoires massed on platform bases, desks on shaped and saboted legs, and tables on pillars or trestle supports. Many of the pieces drew on classical models, and their linear symmetry is a conscious departure from the asymmetrical curves of Art Nouveau. The French designers considered straight-lined shapes more modern than curved ones, and they used extravagant finishes more often than applied ornament or marquetry for decoration. Cases might be sheathed in exotic woods like amboyna, macassar ebony, amaranth, and zebra, layers of mirror-finish lacquer, or exotics like shagreen (sharkskin or galuchat). Unable to resist the intricacy of detail that characterized traditional French design, they often added precise inlays of ivory or accents of gilt-bronze. Other surfaces may be covered in silver-leaf or parchment. Elegant detailing avoids a massive look, even on larger pieces. The Art Deco period also produced a variety of unusual desks and vanity tables, coffee tables, consoles, and occasional pieces inspired by African sculpture.

ABOVE: A shapely pair of armchairs, framed in mahogany, designed by André Groult, c. 1920, suggesting the enduring influence of French 18th-century style.

RIGHT: Another piece by Émile-Jacques Ruhlmann, this cabinet from 1920, made of amaranth, ivory, and ebony, has the distinctive ivory inlays around the top and down the tapering legs that mark many of this designer's pieces.

RIGHT: Jean Dunand was celebrated for his skillfully crafted accessories in lacquer, copper, and other metals, though he also designed furniture. This vase is made of patinated brass and silver gilt.

BELOW: The *Gondole* daybed, c. 1925, reprises a classic French form in a more modern vein. Of rosewood-veneered oak, by Émile-Jacques Ruhlmann.

Pierre Chareau, another important French
designer of the period, designed this cabinet
in walnut burr and patinated metal, c. 1928.

LEFT: Among the many unusual materials seen in *Style Moderne* furniture was parchment, which was treated as a patterned surfacing material. This cabinet is made of sycamore with parchment squares, c. 1930.

BELOW: This richly figured coffee table, by Maxime Old, is a later design in the tradition of French Art Deco style.

■The French Modernists

While established French designers continued to produce luxury goods for an exclusive clientele, the iconoclasts of the *Union des Artistes Modernes* (UAM; founded in 1930), and others who shared their commitment to a modern aesthetic, embraced technology and the use of new materials. They designed furnishings that accepted the realities of modern materials and production techniques, balancing traditional elegance with sleek functionalism, and often crossing over into avant-garde innovation.

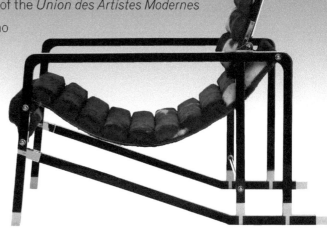

Eileen Gray, a Scotswoman who spent most of her career in France, designed the Transat Chair, 1927.

The furniture and interiors they designed stand with the best of early Modernism, and have drawn increased recognition during the past decade. The most familiar of the UAM designers are René Herbst (1891–1982), Jean-Michel Frank (1895–1941), who also worked in America, Charlotte Perriand (1903–1999), and Jean Prouvé (1901–1984). After the decline of Art Deco, they were major contributors to the revival of French design.

This E1027 telescoping side table designed in 1927 by Eileen Gray is one of the most copied designs in modern furniture, although only a very few of the original version were made, since she fabricated them herself.

LEFT: Side table from the Paris apartment of René Herbst, one of the leading French modernists, of nickel-plated tubular metal, ebonized wood, and glass, c. 1930.

BELOW: This bookcase was one of many similar pieces made of pine and painted aluminum in varying configurations for *Cité Universitaire*, Paris, in 1953. Designed by Charlotte Perriand and made by Les Ateliers Jean Prouvé.

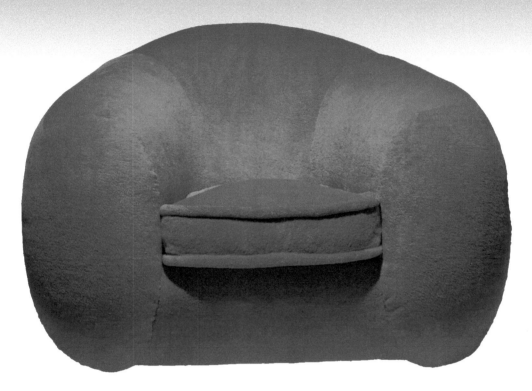

A modernist designer who favored organic forms, Jean Royère designed the velvet-covered *Ours Polaire* arm-chair, c. 1950.

Style Markers

MOOD
soigné sophistication

SCALE
grand

COLORS
deep, saturated

ORNAMENT
stylized, with classical overtones

KEY MOTIFS
waterfall, stylized flowers

FURNITURE
symmetrical linear forms

MATERIALS
exotic woods, parchment,
shagreen, lacquer

TEXTILES
as rich as possible

LOOK FOR
lacquer surfaces, exotic finishes

The pattern by Benedictus, from 1925, shows the waterfall motif often seen in French designs of the period, and later in America as well.

The French designer Louis Sue designed this damask, *la Vigne*, an abstraction of grapes and grape leaves, in 1913.

Designed by Henry Stephany for Émile-Jacques Ruhlmann's *Hôtel du Collectioneur* at the 1925 *Exposition des Arts Décoratifs et Industriels Modernes*, this rich design, Pigeons on Flower Basket, shows the most elegant aspects of the style.

CHAPTER 23
Modernistic and Streamline Style in America, c. 1930–1939

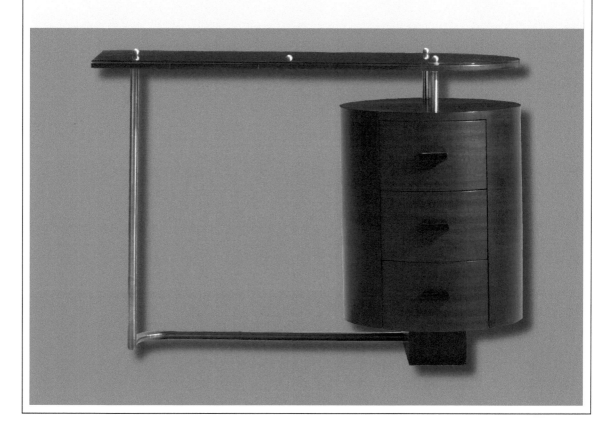

ABOUT THE PERIOD

America's enthusiastic expression of Art Deco absorbed the country's infatuation with speed, transportation, and the machine age into what was variously called Modernistic, Streamline, Jazz Age, and Skyscraper Style. It offered welcome relief from the gloom of the Depression, with positive imagery and an optimistic attitude. In objects whose come-hither packaging was calculated to stimulate consumer purchasing, the period also saw the birth of the new profession of industrial design.

The United States had been conspicuous at the 1925 Paris exhibition by its absence, declining to exhibit on the grounds of having insufficient good modern design. Secretary of Commerce Herbert Hoover's judgment was accurate, although the decision was a blow to national pride. The exhibition, and its glorification of *Le Style Moderne*, became a catalyst for change in America, awakening the incipient Modern movement and leading to exhibitions in museums and department stores to showcase the new style.

American translations of *Le Style Moderne* were less luxurious, more subdued, and more democratic than the original. Furniture was produced in pared-down, populist versions of the formal French designs. Most successfully, the new fashion stimulated an explosion of affordable, mass-produced objects like tableware, cocktail sets, small appliances, and decorative accessories that were at best witty reflections of popular culture and at worst disposable kitsch.

America's most ambitious, and most successful, innovations of this period were in architecture, where motifs from machinery, transportation, and Jazz Age geometry created a new design vocabulary—one that was then replicated in textiles, graphics, and decorative accessories. At its most fully realized, American Art Deco produced iconic structures like the Chrysler Building, the Empire State Building, Rockefeller Center, the colorful hotels of Miami's South Beach, and the elegant interiors of theaters, hotels, and train stations in many major cities.

At Cranbrook Academy in Bloomfield Hills, Michigan, Finnish-born Eliel Saarinen (1873–1950) brought his Scandinavian sensibility to the new style, teaching Modernist design principles to students like Charles and Ray Eames, Eero Saarinen, and Harry Bertoia, who would become the first generation of American-born designers. And, encouraged by manufacturers seeking to repackage their products with more consumer appeal, early industrial designers like Donald Deskey (1894–1989), Raymond Loewy (1893–1986), and Norman Bel Geddes (1893–1958) created designs in the modern vernacular that could be identified as uniquely American.

Their accomplishments were considerable in helping to stimulate sales of consumer products during the Depression years and, more importantly, in introducing new forms and new industrial materials like plastic laminate and tubular metal in mass-produced decorative objects and furniture. The New York World's Fair in 1939 was the last real showcase for Art Deco, as an excess of poorly conceived and tasteless objects brought it into decline. The same event, however, saw the first stirrings of a fresh new direction—one that would develop fully after the interruption of World War II.

ABOUT THE STYLE

The American Modernistic interior is essentially a pared-down version of its French antecedent, though with its own note of sleek sophistication. It is glamorous, but more lively, welcoming the Machine Age instead of rejecting it. Backgrounds are generally light: crisp white walls, with areas of glass block to create intriguing interplays of light and shadow. The archetype of the American interior in this period is the movie-set-like penthouse apartment with gleaming white tile floors or fluffy carpet, heavy silk draperies, and comfortable chairs and sofas.

Fixtures might be brass or crystal. Colors are lively, and pattern is overscaled and stylized, with many similarities to that seen in *Style Moderne* interiors.

Accessories in American Art Deco proliferated: clocks, mirrors, lamps, cocktail sets, and even kitchen appliances like toasters and irons carried the streamlined look to the point of excess.

ABOUT THE FURNITURE

Early modernists like Austrian émigré Paul Frankl (1886–1958) introduced a new look in furniture that rejected historicist influence and began to move in new directions, though designs by Frankl and Warren MacArthur (1885–1961), both European émigrés, did not have the elegance associated with French Art Deco style.

More in keeping with its Gallic predecessors is American furniture of polished dark wood with rounded corners and silhouettes inspired by the streamlined shapes of ocean liners or aircraft. By designers such as Gilbert Rohde (1894–1944) and Eugene Schoen (1880–1957), it simplifies the too-fancy French styles into machine-made symmetrical forms with very little ornament. Luxury woods are combined with new materials like Bakelite and brushed aluminum that proclaim modernity, as do accessory items that eschew any suggestion of historic style.

Industrial designers Deskey, Loewy, and Bel Geddes also designed furniture as well as accessories, translating the forms of Art Deco into a uniquely American and very sophisticated, though non-elitist, style. Adapted during the Depression years into chrome-tubing-framed chairs and painted-metal cabinets, American Art Deco provided the first modern furniture style that could be afforded by a wide consumer public.

PREVIOUS PAGE: The suite designed for impresario Roxy Rothafel in Radio City Music Hall, New York, is an archetype of America's translation of French Style Moderne in sleek lines and modern materials. Designed by Donald Deskey, 1930.

BELOW: Among the first American-made designs in a new modern style were a series of ziggurat-shaped desks and storage pieces by Austrian-born Paul Frankl, which he called Skyscraper furniture. This mahogany bookcase, 49 1/2 inches tall, is from 1928.

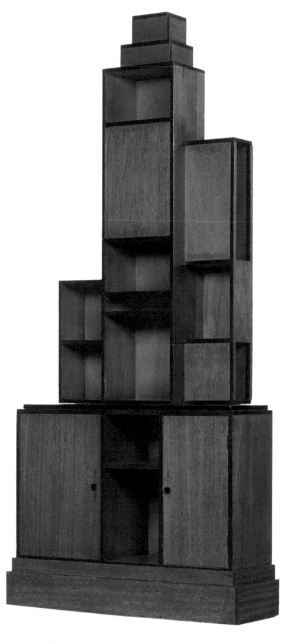

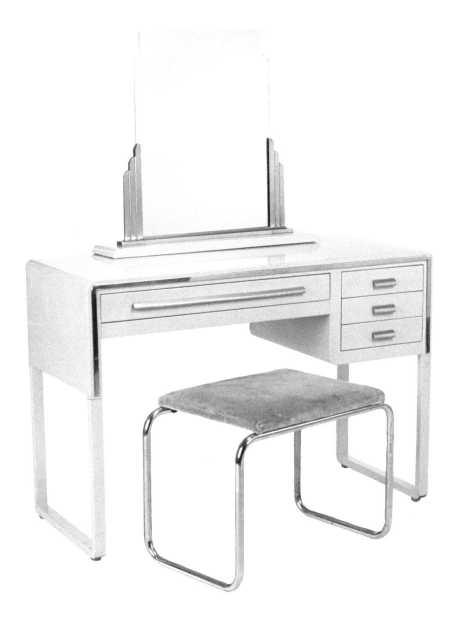

During recession years, manufacturers sought to upgrade mass-produced furniture with streamlined modern design. This vanity set made of aluminum and lacquered wood was designed by Norman Bel Geddes for Simmons in 1935.

ABOVE: The rounded form of this desk shows the influence of French Style Moderne. Made of macassar ebony, maple, chrome-steel, and glass, designed by Gilbert Rohde in 1934 for Herman Miller.

LEFT: Donald Deskey designed this occasional table of mahogany and lacquered wood for the Brown Palace Hotel in Denver, Colorado, in 1936.

ABOVE: Furniture was often named to suggest an association with aircraft and flight: Paul Frankl's Speed chair dates to 1934.

LEFT: Raymond Loewy, the most famous of the first generation of industrial designers, used streamlined form and bright color to add appeal to furniture made with inexpensive materials, as in this 1960 cabinet of plastic, laminate, and enameled aluminum.

Style Markers

MOOD
soigné sophistication

SCALE
moderate

COLORS
lively

ORNAMENT
minimal

KEY MOTIFS
sunburst, cogs and machine parts

FURNITURE
symmetrical linear forms

MATERIALS
dark woods, laminate, brushed aluminum

TEXTILES
solid flat weaves, velvet, stylized pattern

LOOK FOR
streamlined silhouettes, smooth finishes

This design suggests the ziggurat and Machine Age motifs seen in architecture of the period.

This pattern of palm trees and building images suggests Miami or Los Angeles, cities where Art Deco was popular.

CHAPTER 24
Midcentury Modern in America, c. 1945–1965

Midcentury Modern in America, c. 1945–1965

ABOUT THE PERIOD

America was the last of the major Western countries to embrace Modernism, although American designers had long been aware of the developments in Europe, largely through translations of German design publications. When it first emerged in the 1930s, Modernism in America was a battleground between opposing camps: on the one hand were the Bauhaus expatriates and those with architectural leanings who favored spare, functional design; on the other hand was a tradition-minded public and followers of the French approach, for whom aesthetics were the priority, and functionalist design seemed too austere and dehumanized. The conflict for dominance in the new market came to an abrupt conclusion with the outbreak of World War II.

As the war ended, a second wave of modern design swept across America. It drew on elements of its Bauhaus and Art Deco predecessors but developed its own aesthetic in a range of new materials. Now known as Midcentury Modern, it was a homegrown style made possible by new petroleum-based plastics, foam and fiberglass, and technologies developed for wartime. Spearheaded by the innovations of Charles Eames (1907–1978) and his wife Ray Eames (1912–1988), Eero Saarinen (1910–1961), and George Nelson (1908–1986), and supported by the Museum of Modern Art and the media, it was embraced by a victory-proud public that was open to new ideas. It offered the right products, at the right time, at the right price. It was also the first original American style.

The period of postwar prosperity ushered in a building boom and new kinds of living space: high-rise urban apartment buildings in the cities and ranch-house residences in the suburban developments that sprang up to fill the need for housing in an exploding postwar economy. Prefab construction was born in these years. In the new suburban homes, whether budget-priced or custom-built, a new generation of young families lived a casual lifestyle that precipitated changes in both the look and layout of interiors. As an alternative to the cookie-cutter tract house, the Case Study Houses, sponsored by *Arts & Architecture Magazine* beginning in 1945, commissioned a series of architect-designed model homes, most of which were built in Los Angeles, to show that good, modern housing could be had at affordable prices.

With the evolving design climate came a sharper definition between the roles of furniture and product designers and those who created interiors. Interior design was coming into its own, maturing from its origins with Elsie de Wolfe (1860–1950) at the turn of the 20th century into a serious and financially significant profession that mirrored the explosive growth of the American furniture industry.

Midcentury Modern coexisted with more historicist-based styles, and it overlaps the International Style in interiors. Despite its originality, it did not become dominant in America, although a half-century later, it has become old enough to enjoy a major revival in the early years of the 21st century.

About the Style

Midcentury Modern interiors are bright, inviting, and refreshingly unpretentious. Reflecting the happy optimism of the postwar era in America, they are casual, comfortable, and generally reflect the easy-to-live-with air that suits a space designed for family living and informal entertaining.

The flowing, open plan, first conceived by Frank Lloyd Wright and brought to its full flowering by Mies van der Rohe, is a hallmark of the Midcentury Modern interior, as it is in those of the International Style. The basic enclosure is a simple, rectilinear shell, easy to build and generally painted white, though often accented with warm-toned wood paneling. Decorative moldings have been eliminated as a relic of the premodern era. Wall screens or wall sections define living areas without entirely separating them, bringing continuity from one room to another and adding a feeling of spaciousness, even in homes of modest size. In these easy-living, casual interiors, privacy, except in bedrooms and bath, is not as critical as togetherness, and the boundaries between inside and out are erased by sliding-glass doors, floor-to-ceiling windows, and the use of natural colors and materials that link interior spaces with those beyond. (A similar type of indoor-outdoor residence had been pioneered by Schindler and Neutra in California two decades earlier.)

The kitchen, seen through a pass-through into the dining and living areas, is now the highly visible center of home life. It is outfitted with the newest labor-saving modern appliances, products of the postwar boom in consumer-product manufacturing, and a necessity for an era of servant-free homes.

Wall-to-wall carpeting is almost ubiquitous, although in warmer climates, natural wood, stone, or linoleum provide a similar feeling of continuity throughout the interiors. Furniture is often pulled away from the walls and set in free-floating, asymmetrical arrangements. It might also be grouped around colorful area rugs that offer an alternative to carpeting or are placed over it.

Window treatments follow the clean-lined look of the space, with straight hanging, floor-to-ceiling draperies pulled back to reveal simple sheer curtains or shades. Colors, apart from the predominating neutrals, are lively and clear, and patterns are relatively simple, with abstract geometrics or other stylized motifs rather than representational ones. Textured woven blinds, printed velvets and linens, and nubby natural-fiber upholstery add contrast to avoid the monotony of an overly simplified space.

Illumination is provided by concealed lighting or light-scaled fixtures that might include floor-to-ceiling pole lamps or textured ceramic ones. Decorative accents include colorful ceramics, wall hangings, or lively abstract paintings and prints.

ABOUT THE FURNITURE

The spare modern furniture in these interiors has abandoned any traces of traditionalism in favor of new forms and modern materials. "Good Design" is the mantra proposed by the Museum of Modern Art in a series of exhibitions from 1950 to 1955. Good design must utilize new materials and technology, serve a practical need, avoid unnecessary ornament, and be affordable to the average consumer. The scale of the furniture is relatively modest, in keeping with the size of the average contemporary room.

Armless sofas and sectional upholstered pieces are the popular centerpiece of the living-room furniture arrangement, offering many options for rearrangeable seating. Modularity is a new idea in case pieces as well, making it possible to create different configurations from a limited number of individual units. Cabinetry emphasizes function over decorative effect—silhouettes are linear, laminates fashionable, metal an acceptable alternative to wood, and carving or decorative hardware altogether avoided. Flexible built-ins, open shelving, and items that serve multiple functions, like folding or stacking tables and serving carts, are increasingly popular. During this period, a parallel strain of historicist design offers forms evoking traditional styles from designers who refused to altogether abandon the past.

Midcentury Modern chairs are refreshingly varied and designed in accordance with ergonomic research on the human proportions and comfort. Dozens of imaginative and now-iconic furniture designs have been conceived in this period by America's first generation of homegrown talent and produced by forward-thinking companies—most notably the venerable Herman Miller and the brand-new Knoll, both committed to producing furniture in the Modern style. Many of the new designs, like Eames's molded plywood chair and Eero Saarinen's Tulip chair, looked relatively simple, but in their use of new materials and technology were almost shockingly avant-garde.

PREVIOUS PAGE: In a Palm Springs, Florida home, the open kitchen-dining area, lively colors, and light-scale modern furniture set a Midcentury Modern mood.

LEFT: Of laminated plywood in varying thicknesses, this slim-legged design by Norman Cherner, made in 1958, reinterprets the earlier Pretzel chair by John Pile of the George Nelson office.

BELOW: At home in the Midcentury Modern living room or office, the Thin Edge cabinet is made of rosewood with metal legs by George Nelson for Herman Miller, 1955.

RIGHT: The ESU (Eames Storage Unit) offers many options for varying configurations and colors in flexible shelf-and-cabinet units, designed c. 1950 by Charles and Ray Eames, for Knoll. Made of laminated plywood or masonite, zinc, and aluminum.

BELOW: Molded fiberglass, a new material developed for aircraft in World War II, was adapted for seating pieces by Charles and Ray Eames, perhaps the best-known of the first generation of American-born modern designers. This 1948 design was available as armchair and sidechair as well as rocker.

BELOW: Molded rosewood forms the three-section shell of this lounge chair, with leather upholstery and brushed aluminum swivel base. Designed by Charles and Ray Eames, for Knoll in 1957.

RIGHT: Eero Saarinen, a Cranbrook Academy classmate and frequent collaborator of Charles Eames, designed the Womb chair in 1948, with upholstery stretched over a fiberglass shell, on an enameled steel frame and legs.

ABOVE: An iconic coffee table by a sculptor and designer who preferred organic to straight-line forms, Isamu Noguchi designed this wood-and-plate-glass piece in 1948.

BELOW: Using plastic-coated welded steel rods, sculptor Harry (Arieto) Bertoia designed a collection of furniture based on a wire grid. Here, the Bird chair, designed for Knoll in 1952.

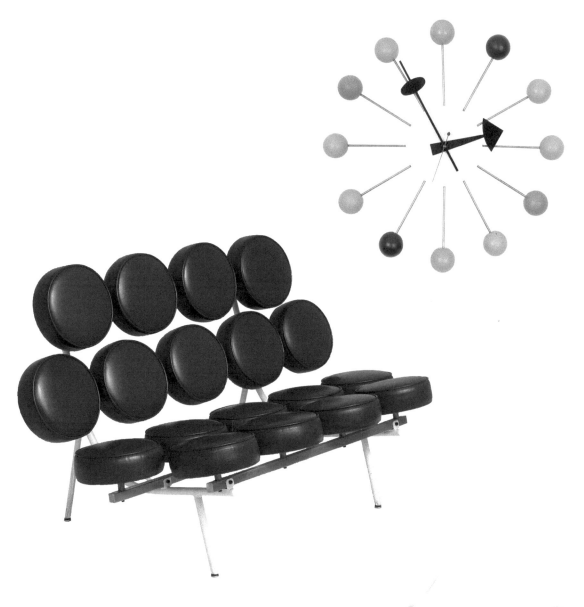

TOP: As America became intrigued by atomic energy, modern designers adopted the imagery into objects, like George Nelson's Ball Clock, designed in 1948.

MIDDLE: The Marshmallow sofa was actually assembled using elements being produced for barstools. Made of vinyl and painted metal, designed by George Nelson for Herman Miller in 1956.

BOTTOM: The pedestal-base chair followed the cantilever in providing an alternative to four-legged seating pieces. Eero Saarinen's Tulip, of molded plastic with cast aluminum, painted base, was designed for Knoll in 1957.

ABOVE: A curved pedestal of welded steel rods form the base of a dining table. Designed by Warren Platner 1966 for Knoll, this was part of a collection that included seating and occasional tables.

LEFT: The classic Eames Chair, from 1946, is made of laminated molded plywood and shaped to fit the body. The design developed from Charles and Ray Eames's experiments in bending veneers when they were designing splints for the U.S. Navy during World War II. Made ultimately by Herman Miller in dining and lounge chair versions, with metal rods or molded wood base and legs, this chair is still being produced.

■ Historicist Modern, c. 1950–1970, Ongoing

Notwithstanding the enthusiastic reception awarded Midcentury Modernism, a concurrent strain of design refused to abandon its traditional heritage. In the heyday of America's first modern design, historicists like Edward Wormley (1907–1995), T. H. Robsjohn-Gibbings (1905–1976), and Harvey Probber (1922–2003) designed furniture that, while unquestionably of the 20th century, drew on traditional forms, generally avoided plastics, and emphasized elegant materials and polished finishes over a more industrialized look. Vladimir Kagan (1927–) looked backward and forward, with organic forms in furniture that defined its own style. Catering to more exotic tastes, other designers produced furniture in lustrous lacquers, with applied ornament, or of parchment and other surfaces recalling the luxurious extravagance of French Art Deco design or movie-star glamour.

ABOVE: Reprising a Victorian seating form in contemporary silhouette, Edward Wormley designed the Tete-a-Tete sofa for Dunbar in 1960.

RIGHT: The undulating Mesa coffee table was designed by T. H. Robsjohn-Gibbings for Widdicomb Furniture, made of laminated birch with maple finish, c. 1950.

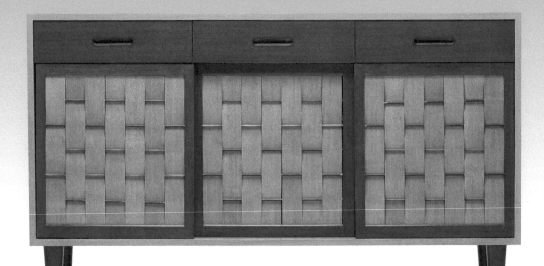

Woven-wood panels soften the straight lines of this sideboard by Edward Wormley, designed in 1956, made of bleached and unbleached mahogany with brass.

Interiors designed around this type of furniture did not necessarily reprise traditional architectural details, but they generally began with a linear modern surround, modulating its severity with warmer colors and textured surfaces. Walls might be painted, paneled, upholstered, or papered to create a rich background for the furnishings, and fabrics were likely to be lustrous velvets or silks. These and other "Moderate Modernist" interiors were generally described as Contemporary, a word with fewer off-putting connotations than the more extreme-sounding Modern.

The strain of historicism has informed the work of 20th-century interior designers from Dorothy Draper (1889–1969), William Pahlmann (1900–1987), and Billy Baldwin (1903–1983) to Angelo Donghia (1935–1985), Mark Hampton (1940–1998), and many others, and continues into the 21st century.

A modernist whose work spans generations, Vladimir Kagan designed this shapely walnut-framed lounge chair, c. 1950s, with the sculptural silhouette that characterizes his furniture.

ABOVE: Color and pattern warm up a rectilinear cabinet from 1960 by Harvey Probber, of lacquered wood, enameled copper, and brass. Probber, an exception among the prominent historicist designers of the period, was both designer and manufacturer.

BELOW: Swept-back legs and boldly curved backs in mahogany and cane armchairs by Edward Wormley, 1954, reminiscent of historic precedents.

■ Modern Made by Hand, c. 1950, Ongoing

The studio craft movement, although tracing its origins as far back as the 1930s, began to develop in America after the end of World War II. It paralleled the development of Midcentury Modernism and was a reaction to the impersonality of production furniture, initiated by individual artisans creating one-off works in small studios, and evolving into the sophisticated and highly professional practice that exists today. Incorporating a wide variety of skills, and combining elements of crafts and vernacular design, hand-made furniture and decorative objects have become an important subset of contemporary design, though remaining independent of any classification by style.

Some practitioners have adopted the philosophy of Arts and Crafts, and many draw inspiration from historic designs. Most often, however, they have pursued a gentler aesthetic than Bauhaus-inspired formalism and linearity—in works that emphasize hand-finishing, sculptural forms, and touchable materials similar to that seen in Scandinavian furniture.

After pioneers like Wharton Esherick (1887–1970) and George Nakashima (1905–1990) broke the first ground, an increasing number of young artists found creative expression in making furniture by hand. Centers for training woodworkers, like those begun by Danish-born Tage Frid (1915–2004) at Alfred University in upstate New York

Woodworker George Nakashima established his New Hope, Pennsylvania, workshop in 1943, and began producing furniture in forms derived from the natural contours of tree sections, keeping irregular edges, knotholes, and emphasizing the grain. This table is a typical example, c. 1960s. Nakashima's studio is now headed by his daughter Mira.

and the Rhode Island School of Design in Providence, helped to encourage greater professionalism in the field. Specialized schools and departments in various parts of the country have brought master craftsmen to teach traditional skills that had been largely forgotten in the pursuit of industrialization. Through associations, craft shows, and galleries, the work of artisans in wood, fabric, metal, ceramics, and glass have gained prestige commensurate with that of painters and sculptors. By the latter part of the 20th century, studio crafts were no longer a movement but an established sector of design, and they entered a new phase that began to blur the line between craft and art. Early creators like

Sam Maloof was a California craftsman who became prominent in the midcentury years. He was best known for the rocking chairs he first designed in the 1960s and continued to make throughout his lifetime. This one is of black walnut, c. 1970s.

Wendell Castle (1932–) are now regarded as artists, and contemporary craft practitioners feel free to experiment with new forms, creating objects for which function is not only secondary but often irrelevant.

Although many people collect handcrafted furniture, or Art Furniture as it is frequently called, these objects appear most often in contemporary interiors, where they coexist with machine-produced pieces and provide the contrast of emotion-generating design to counterbalance the impersonality of functionalism.

An interior designed around Art Furniture has the characteristics of any modern one, save for treating its objects with particular reverence. The furniture might take varied forms: rectilinear, abstract, biomorphic, or occasionally anthropomorphic. It may be alternatingly practical, sculptural, or humorous, and its production may rely entirely on handcraftsmanship or take advantage of modern technology in laminating or finishing

This wall-mounted Wavy Front sculpted metal
cabinet from 1964 is typical of the distinctive work of Paul
Evans, a sculptor and furniture designer based in Bucks County, Pennsylvania, who designed both studio-made and production furniture.

details. Wood is the traditional material of choice, though artisans have explored new
ways of using metal, and even plastics, in their search for new forms of expression.
Both timely and timeless, handmade furnishings can bridge the gap between past and
future in design.

Wendell Castle, who was trained as
a sculptor, devised his own method
of making furniture, stacking and
laminating layers of wood and
carving them into tables like this
walnut one, c. 1970s. He also applied
the technique to other objects of
furniture.

The pioneering work of Wharton Esherick helped spark the revival of interest in studio-made, handcrafted furniture. He made this walnut and cherry music stand in 1952.

A very early design by Wharton Esherick, this Wagon Wheel armchair of hickory and leather dates to 1933.

Style Markers

MOOD
easy living

SCALE
low and lean

COLORS
neutral or lively

ORNAMENT
simple, if any

FURNITURE
light-scaled, machine-made forms

TEXTILES
perky prints, casual textures

LOOK FOR
Eames and Saarinen chairs,
informal rooms

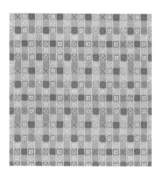

Crosspatch, a pattern by Charles and Ray Eames, was designed for a 1947 Museum of Modern Art competition.

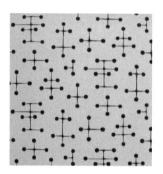

This perky 1947 pattern, Dots, is one of many small-scale abstract designs by Charles and Ray Eames.

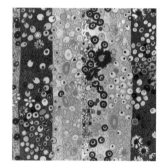

Jack Lenor Larsen, one of the most innovative textile designers of his time, designed this luxurious printed velvet, Primavera, in 1960.

CHAPTER 25
Scandinavian Modern Style, c. 1950–1970

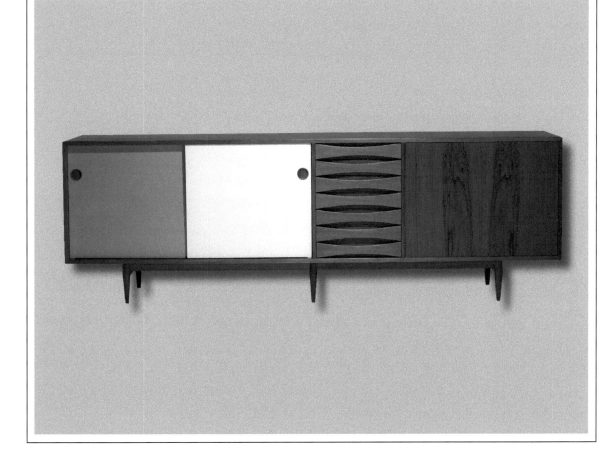

ABOUT THE PERIOD

In the years just after World War II, when the steel-and-glass design vocabulary of the International Style was making its mark, an alternative, humanistic approach to Modernism was emanating from the group of countries just north of the European continent. The style they created came to be known as Scandinavian, after the peninsula that incorporates Norway, Sweden, and the islands of Denmark, which is something of a misnomer, since the Nordic nations also include Finland and Iceland.

Until early in the 20th century, Scandinavian styles reflected those of their European neighbors, but as the last of these countries achieved independence (Norway in 1905, Finland in 1918, Iceland in 1944), they developed individual approaches to design but with shared ideals and a common aesthetic. Beginning as early as the 1930s, Alvar Aalto (1898–1976) in Finland and Bruno Mathsson (1907–1988) in Sweden, and later others like Hans Wegner (1914–2007) and Finn Juhl (1912–1989) in Denmark, were basing their designs for interiors and furniture on a love of natural materials, a respect for handcraft, and a long tradition of cabinetmaking skills.

In the Nordic countries, good design was considered a democratic right rather than an elitist privilege, following the much-quoted manifesto of Swedish critic Gregor Pahlsson: "More beautiful things for everyday use." They pursued the goal of socially responsible design, focusing on human needs as much as, and occasionally more than, aesthetics. The resulting objects, and the interiors that surrounded them, offered a less radical and more accessible option for those who were put off by severe, European-born Modernism.

Through exhibitions at international fairs, including those in Paris in 1925, New York in 1939, and the *Triennale* events in Milan in the 1950s, Scandinavian design—first Swedish glass, then Swedish Modern, and later Danish Modern furnishings—became an international success and built an important export industry for the countries that developed it. Scaled to the modest proportions of most Nordic homes, Scandinavian furniture was well suited to the apartments and suburban ranch homes of post–World War II America, which became one of its most enthusiastic markets.

After almost a century of uneasy coexistence between handmade and machine production, the Nordic designers had achieved a happy compromise, making some pieces in small craft workshops and others in medium-size factories, but even the latter retained the not-too-slick look of handcrafted objects. Others moved in new directions: architect Arne Jacobsen's (1902–1971) work shared the aesthetic of International Style designers, and in the 1960s, Nordic designers like Eero Aarnio (1932–) and Verner Panton (1926–1998) broke with tradition, introducing modern materials in molded forms and vivid colors: their experimental approach ran counter to the conservative bent of most Nordic design. Two decades after its explosive success, the focus on timelessness rather than fashion contributed to the decline of Scandinavian style, and it was eclipsed by a wave of design innovation from Italy.

In the final decades of the 20th century, Swedish home-furnishings giant Ikea translated Scandinavian style into inexpensive, cash-and-carry products for the mass market, which helped initiate a revival of interest in the genre.

ABOUT THE STYLE

The Scandinavian-style interior does not appear to be designed, but rather to have evolved naturally over the course of time and comfortable use. In these countries, where pretension is frowned upon, even the most impressive rooms are rarely grand in scale, but they have an air of openness that makes them seem larger. Reflecting the Nordic love of nature and the strains of living in a harsh climate with relatively short summers, Scandinavian interiors are typically designed to bring in the outdoors, or at least the feeling of outdoors, by using natural materials and maximizing access to natural light.

The interior architecture is simple, as in all Modernist rooms, without the cornices, moldings, or ornamental details of traditional styles. Walls, if not white, might be paneled in light wood, punctuated by expanses of windows that admit both light and landscape.

Floors are generally of light-colored wood, laid in vertical strips rather than decorative parquet. Over them, handwoven (or seeming so) wool rugs are either folk-patterned flat-weaves or shaggy *ryas*: originating in 18th-century Finland, the *rya* rug, now made by machine, has become ubiquitous in the Scandinavian design vocabulary.

In place of heavy draperies, window treatments are airy curtains, shades, or wood blinds. Upholstery fabrics, which are more often plain than patterned, tend to be simple basketweaves, tweedy textures, or natural leather.

A wood-burning fireplace is a likely feature of the Scandinavian interior—built into the wall, a traditional freestanding version in ceramic tile, or a modern shape of bright, enameled metal.

Nordic color schemes favor clear, natural hues—the blues of sky and water, the greens of foliage, the yellows of sunshine, combined with a variety of warm beiges and earth tones.

Supplementing the natural light are ceramic lamps and clean-lined lighting fixtures, adding decorative but unpretentious accents in keeping with the spare simplicity of the style. Beyond these, accessories may include ceramic bowls and vases, sculptural modern silver, and hand-blown glass—just enough to make the room look comfortable but uncluttered. Plants and flowers are reminders of nature.

ABOUT THE FURNITURE

In the design of Scandinavian furniture, comfort and function are more critical concerns than current fashion, and designers tend to focus on perfecting classics rather than innovation. A number of these classics, like Wegner's "The Chair" and Finn Juhl's "Chieftain," have become familiar, iconic objects. Scandinavian-style chairs are generally fairly simple forms in light woods like ash or birch, or deeper teak or rosewood, often with woven rather than upholstered seats, and shapely sculptural backs that add decorative interest as well as support. Sofas are linear rather than overstuffed, with squared-off or tight cushions.

Storage chests and cabinets are rectangular forms on straight legs that enhance the look of slenderness rather than bulk. In their simplicity of line, details like the dovetail joints and tambour doors become subtle decorative accent. The wall system, a clever new concept of wall-mounted shelves and cabinetry, is flexible, functional, and space-efficient. Richly grained imported rosewood and teak are most closely associated with Scandinavian Modern style, with natural matte or oiled finishes. Cabinets may have tambour doors, but hardware is minimal, with simple knobs or recessed pulls. Carving or other ornament is not so much rejected as unnecessary.

PREVIOUS PAGE: The Helsinki, Finland, home and studio of Alvar Aalto, the first Scandinavian designer to become internationally celebrated. The living room, in warm woods and natural textures, exemplifies the Scandinavian aesthetic.

ABOVE: A classic Danish Modern sideboard of rosewood, birch, and painted wood, made by cabinetmaker Arne Vodder, c. 1956.

BELOW: The Paimio armchair, an innovative form of laminated birch plywood, was designed for the Tuberculosis Sanatorium, in Paimio, Finland, c. 1932, by Alvar Aalto.

RIGHT: The Artichoke lamp, by Danish designer Poul Henningsen, has been in continuous production since its introduction in 1958. Made of copper and steel, in several sizes and variations, it diffuses light evenly throughout a space.

BELOW: A sculptured shape of teak and leather by Danish architect and designer Finn Juhl, the Chieftain armchair, from 1949, is based on an ancient Egyptian form.

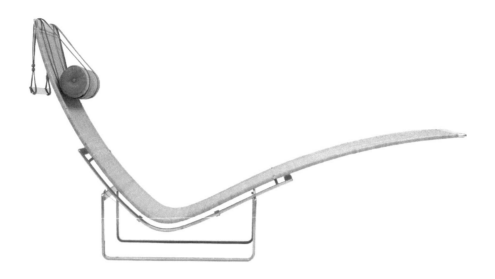

ABOVE: Danish Poul Kjaerholm designed furniture that had more in common with International Style pieces than those of most wood-loving Scandinavians. This striking chaise, in stainless steel, wicker, and leather, was designed in 1965. The body and base are held together only by gravity and friction.

RIGHT: The Egg chair (shown with matching ottoman) marked a bold departure from understated Scandinavian style, when Danish architect Arne Jacobsen designed it in 1957 for the SAS Royal Hotel in Copenhagen. The fiberglass shell, wrapped in foam and flexible fabric, is mounted on an aluminum swivel base.

Bruno Matthsson of Sweden designed this practical folding dining table, a modern adaptation of the traditional gate-leg, c. 1960; it was offered in teak, rosewood, birch, or walnut.

Austrian-born Josef Frank designed elegant furniture and colorful textiles for Swedish firm Svenskt Tenn. This walnut and glass vitrine-on-stand, from 1946, shows the influence of his early work with the *Wiener Werkstätte*.

ABOVE: The Scimitar Lounge Chair, 1962, a bold silhouette of stainless steel and leather by Preben Fabricius and Jorgen Kastholm, Danish designers who, like Kjaerholm and Jacobsen, departed from sculptural wood forms to design in a minimalist vein.

RIGHT: Possibly the single most famous Danish midcentury design, Hans Wegner's sculptural "Round Chair" became known simply as "The Chair," and was illustrated on a postage stamp in 1960. First made by Johannes Hansen, and then by PP Moøbler, it has been in continual production since it was designed in 1949.

Style Markers

MOOD calm	**SCALE** modest
COLORS mostly natural	**ORNAMENT** simple
FURNITURE clean-lined forms, oil-finished teak, rosewood, birch or ash	**TEXTILES** hand-woven fabrics, shaggy rya rugs
KEY MOTIFS plants, anything natural	**LOOK FOR** modern with a soft edge

A classic Scandinavian textile, Hallingdal was designed in Denmark by Nanna Ditzel in 1965, its subtle geometric pattern derived from the weaving process.

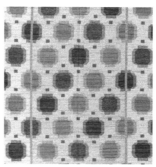

This flatweave carpet, designed in 1937 by Märta Måås-Fjetterström, Sweden, suggests the traditional folk and craft motifs that informed many midcentury Nordic designs.

CHAPTER 26

Biomorphic and Pop Art Styles, c. 1960s

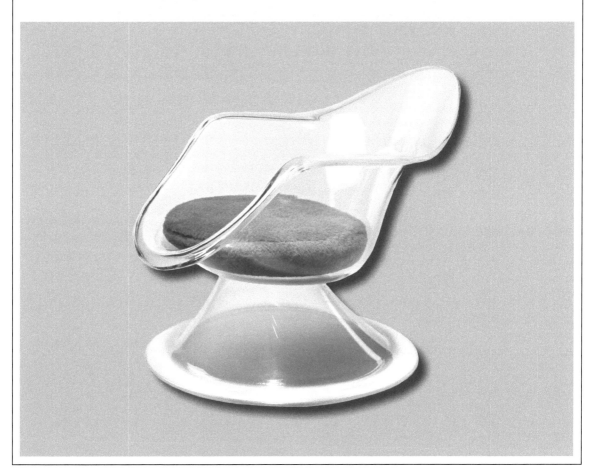

Biomorphic and Pop Art Styles, c. 1960s

About the Period

Spearheaded by a revolution in popular culture, the Swinging Sixties gave birth to a style that, while perhaps not on a par with the great design periods, paints a lively picture of the decade in which it thrived. It was a breakaway look, or series of looks, that rebelled against the constraints of serious-minded Modernism, lacking any specific design aesthetic but with more than its share of energy and visual appeal.

The "youthquake" marked the decade dominated by a generation that sought to change the world; in design, this meant rejecting anything that was too conventional. Designers of this era recycled history in a search for the new and unexpected, adapting classic forms into bold silhouettes and patterns that alternated between psychedelic and Op-Art. These eye-popping images, the beat of Beatles-generation music, and the quirky clothing styles of Carnaby Street were all reflected in extroverted interiors that sometimes seemed to be laughing at themselves—and at design.

In the postwar years, the blurring of class lines had also created a new bourgeoisie that rejected the traditional elitism of design and emphasized the point by favoring anything that was aggressively modern. Led by avant-gardists in London and New York, this design subculture emphasized offbeat colors and unconventional shapes. Designers experimented with new types of plastic, new molding technology, and new stretchy fabrics. Projects like the 1956 House of the Future in London, and one of the same name in America the following year, proposed biomorphic forms and space-age inspiration for forward-thinking design, most of which proved more eye-catching than easy to live with.

Styles in this schizoid decade took other directions as well: the jet-set interiors of Englishman David Hicks (1929–1998), who devised opulent settings with bold graphic patterns, and the unabashed ostentation of Hollywood-style rooms by California designers like William Haines (1900–1973).

The Sixties were an erratic but intriguing time, though one doomed to rapid obsolescence. As the decade waned, the fever abated, and design took a more rational, less frenetic, but sometimes less entertaining direction.

ABOUT THE STYLE

The typical interior—if this era can be said to have one—is lively, colorful, and perhaps extreme in its lack of restraint. As overdone in its way as the most exaggerated Baroque or Rococo room, its object is to create an impression—not with costliness, but with sheer flamboyance.

The basic shell of a 20th-century space—rectilinear, flat-ceilinged, free of architectural details—provides a background for furnishings in brilliant, intense, and often clashing colors. The walls might be painted white, but they are likelier to show off more intense, undiluted hues. Wallcovering made with silvery (or gold-tone) Mylar might be patterned in Pop or Op-Art geometrics, and curtains or upholstery fabrics may use similar designs, though the two are not usually combined in one room. Occasionally, three-dimensional wall treatments are assembled with large segments of molded plastic, stamped out, or injection-molded in brilliant-colored, shiny modules.

Silver or gold-tone threads might be woven into tweedy textured upholstery on curvy modular seating. Or psychedelic colors, printed in surreal swirls and coils on new stretch fabrics, are wrapped around freeform chairs and loveseats to emphasize their sinuous forms.

As in the preceding period, floors are covered with wall-to-wall carpet or smooth-surfaced vinyl, generally without patterns, but often accented with colorful area rugs.

The earth tones predominating in Midcentury Modern interiors have been abandoned in favor of undiluted brights—bubble-gum pink, zingy turquoise, and teal—paint-box colors that become the dominant element in the interior.

Lighting emanates from decorative table lamps or standing fixtures. In a decade defined by the space age, atomic and rocket motifs are frequent inspiration for patterns on wall coverings, fabrics, and laminate surfaces, and these themes often inspire accessories as well. Often witty, but sometimes crossing over into kitsch, like the mesmerizing lava lamp or multicolored plastic-bead curtains used as window dressing or room dividers, they are congenial accents for the Sixties interior.

Biomorphic and Pop Art Styles, c. 1960s

ABOUT THE FURNITURE

Much of the furniture that came out of this period is unlike anything seen before or since. The curvy forms of Aarnio or Panton, or the sensual, ribbon-like silhouettes of Pierre Paulin (1927–2009) and Olivier Mourgue (1939–) take a new view of what a chair should look like and the materials of which it can be made. The Lucite furniture introduced a decade earlier by Estelle (1915–1997) and Erwine Laverne (1909–2003) have inspired many variations in see-through seating. These biomorphic forms, evoking eggs, clouds, or amoeba shapes, are body-hugging comfortable, but they can be awkward to use in ensembles with more conventional furniture.

The seating landscape is a new application of sectional seating that offers almost limitless options for organizing the living room. Abandoning the conventional sofa frame in favor of vari-shaped and -sized modules of fabric-wrapped foam, it is a practical solution to the need for flexible furnishings in an increasingly mobile society. The often impractical step-down "conversation pit" is a variant of this idea.

Chests and tables of this period are limited to a more conventional range of geometric silhouettes, but variations in plastic surfacing, laminates, and colors make them compatible companions to the seating.

NEXT PAGE: In the staff canteen of the Spiegelverlag, in Hamburg, Germany, zingy colors and bold polka-dot patterns set the scene for an Op-Art environment.

RIGHT: The Ball chair, of shiny molded fiberglass with enameled aluminum base and upholstered foam interior, was designed by Finnish Eero Aarnio, in 1963, and has since become an iconic symbol of space-age furniture.

BELOW: The French designer Maurice Calka designed the Boomerang desk, c. 1969, of molded fiberglass.

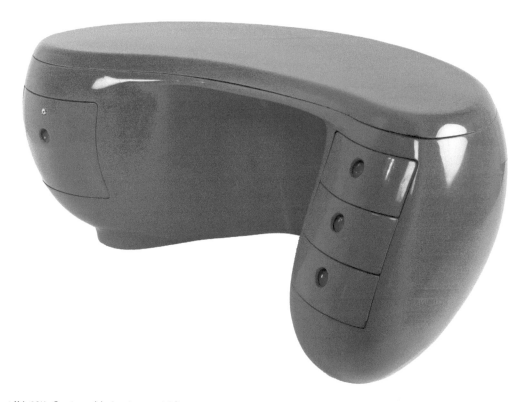

This bold cantilever chair was ahead of its time. The first one-piece, injection-molded plastic chair (of polypropylene), it was designed by Verner Panton in 1960, but technical difficulties delayed its production until 1967.

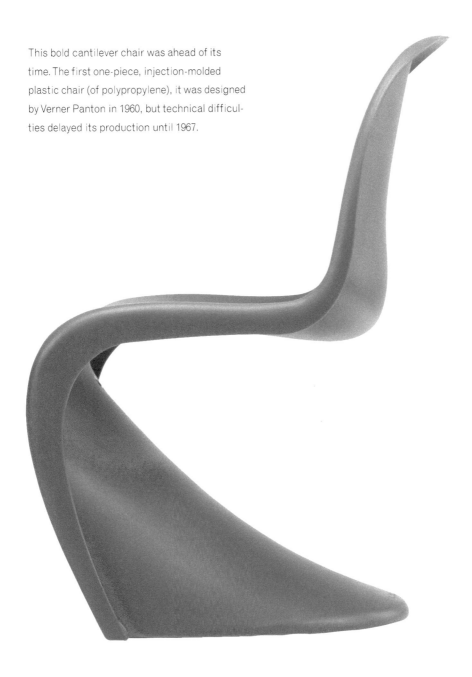

LEFT: One of the Fun series of lighting fixtures designed by Verner Panton, this version was made in 1964 of aluminum disks. All of the pieces had ball or circle forms in various configurations.

BELOW: The Invisible Chair series, by Estelle and Erwine Laverne, from 1957, resulted from an experiment in molding see-through Perspex plastic into seating pieces.

LEFT: Stainless steel, previously considered an industrial material, was translated into elegant furniture by French designer Maria Pergay. Her most famous design, the Ring Chair, dates to 1970.

BELOW: French designer Pierre Paulin devised undulating seating forms of stretch fabric over tubular-steel frames. The Ribbon chair, 1966, was the first of several designs created along these lines.

In the spirit of the times, this whimsical Golliwog planter of fiberglass on a wood base was designed by Estelle Laverne in 1961.

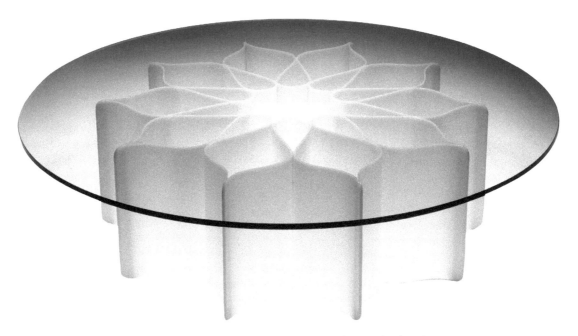

Paulin designed this coffee table, with a plastic biomorphic-form base, as a complement to his quirky seating, c. 1970.

Style Markers

MOOD upbeat	**SCALE** irrelevant
COLORS bright, saturated	**ORNAMENT** surreal and punchy
FURNITURE biomorphic forms, molded plastics	**TEXTILES** smooth or fuzzy, zingy patterns
KEY MOTIFS Op, Pop, space-age symbols	**LOOK FOR** rooms with funhouse appeal

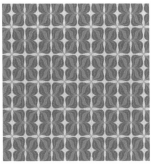

The lively colors and twisty pattern of Mind Meld wall covering create an Op-Art backdrop.

Verner Panton designed Op-Art Geometric, a bold statement for the extroverted interior from an unconventional Dane.

CHAPTER 27
Italian Modern Style, c. 1965–1980

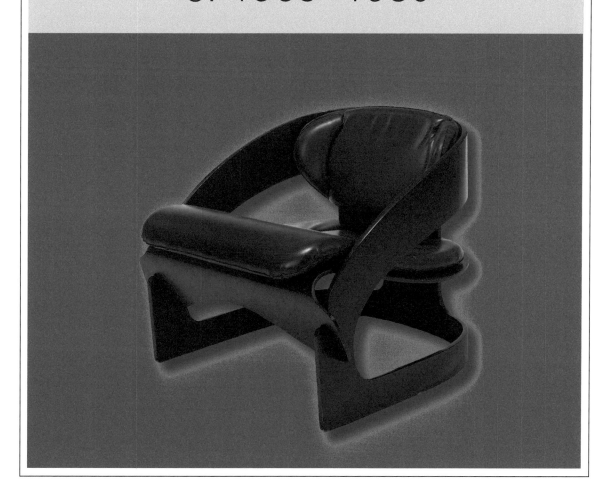

ABOUT THE PERIOD

Overlapping with and continuing after the explosion of Scandinavian Modern design, Italian Modern was nurtured in the years after World War II and became an international phenomenon in the 1970s. Its flame was fanned by the forward-thinking ideas of Giò Ponti (1891–1979), an architect and designer who encouraged and promoted Italian initiative in his role as founder (1928) and longtime editor of the design magazine *Domus* and as a leader in the establishment of the *Triennale* design exhibitions in Milan. Founded in Monza in 1923 to encourage the relationship between industry and the applied arts, the *Triennales* moved to Milan a decade later and grew to become an international showcase of innovative design.

After World War II devastated much of the country's industrial facilities, Italy faced the need to rebuild its shattered economy and revive its international image. Design proved the means of accomplishing this task. Italian designers were brilliantly resourceful, making the most of minimal resources to explore new ideas, and manufacturers were eager to cooperate. They devised witty and ingenious applications of plastics, metal, and experimental production methods, occasionally mixing in bits of social commentary. The results were a fresh take on Modernism that shifted the focus and influenced the direction of 20th-century design, particularly in furniture and lighting.

In the 1960s, Italian groups like Archizoom and Superstudio developed an approach to design that focused on the use of technology. Others followed their lead, formulating a new vocabulary that could be categorized only in terms of its diversity. Abandoning the idea that function must determine form, Italian design made form primary, teasing history with rational (and sometimes irrational) applications that challenged prior attitudes about furniture. More than the quirky shapes of Pop-influenced design, pieces by such wide-ranging talents as Joe Colombo (1930–1971), Gae Aulenti (1927–2012), Marco Zanuso (1916–2001), Gaetano Pesce (1939–), and many others conceived furniture that might stack or fold, expand or collapse; be molded of plastic or blown up like balloons; be straight-lined, overstuffed, or of indescribable shape.

Along with their contributions to interior and industrial design, Italian developments in lighting revolutionized a dormant field and represent perhaps their most groundbreaking achievements. Employing new technology that minimized bulb size and maximized illumination, designers like Achille Castiglione (1918–2002) devised lamps and fixtures that not only were the first appropriate complements to modern furniture but also treated lighting as decorative objects rather than functional equipment. Their ideas would chart a new course for the future of lighting design.

Exhibited at the *Triennale* events and widely celebrated in the press, the new Italian furniture and lighting catapulted the country to a position of style leadership that the country had not seen since the Renaissance. Italian design supplanted Scandinavian Modern in popularity and elbowed aside the avant-garde credentials of the Bauhaus aesthetic. In a now-historic 1972 exhibition, *Italy: The New Domestic Landscape*, New York's Museum of Modern Art stamped its imprimatur on Italian design as the latest fashion and the wave of the future.

Even before the explosion of Italian style in interiors and furnishings, the country's glassmaking industry had begun its own renaissance, inventing proprietary techniques for glassblowing and decoration that made their pieces as unique as the furniture and lighting designed by their compatriots. In its disregard of conventional methods and interest in provocative visual effect, Italian Modern design laid the groundwork for the movement that would be called Postmodernism.

ABOUT THE STYLE

One of the most appealing qualities of an Italian Modern interior, or any object in Italian Modern style, is its refusal to take itself too seriously. Italian design is infused with wit and humor. As extroverted as its citizens, the style is informal though elegant, colorful though unfussy, and guaranteed to elicit strong response, whether enthusiasm or aversion. The Italian Modern interior is rarely understated.

The interior itself is not so much a designed space as it is a setting for the presentation of the objects, which are the key components of Italian Modern style. White walls are the most likely background, and floors are bare, natural-tone wood. The furnishings are arranged around the room with a casualness belying the care that has been given to their selection.

Italian Modern Style, c. 1965–1980

What the objects lack in handcrafted detail—and there is rarely any—they more than make up for in panache. Stack-up seats and tables of bright molded plastic, a leather lounge shaped like a baseball glove, a compressed-foam chair that expands when unpacked, and other adventurous forms provide a repertoire of ideas to furnish an interior with style that clearly identifies with a particular time and place.

Colors are vivid, applied with abandon to any surface. Patterns, if any, are equally aggressive, and they are more likely to be drawn from modern art or the designer's imagination than from any definable source.

Furniture by the Italian Modernists is often made of plastic—this was the least expensive and most available material in the postwar years—though much of the upholstery is leather. Tables and storage pieces are crisply rectilinear or shaped with injection-molding techniques. Taking into account the space limitations of postwar housing, most pieces are relatively modest in scale; the primary exception being sofas that plumb the possibilities of modularity and flexibility with oversize elements, sometimes sinuous and sometimes square, that combine into caterpillar-like, sit-together seating groups in the center of the room.

Lighting, rather than accessories, provides the most distinctive finishing touch—standing lamps or *torchères* in pencil-slim shapes, organic forms of handblown glass, snake-like coils of plastic, tiny bulbs strung on wires—contributing to the personality and the attractions of the Italian Modern interior.

NEXT PAGE: In a white-walled modern apartment, brightly colored plastic ottomans by Zanotta suggest the light-hearted air of Italian design.

This monumental 79-inch-long cabinet, made of Italian walnut, with open display unit over plinth base on tapered legs, was designed by Giò Ponti in 1951. Architect and industrial designer Ponti was perhaps even more influential in his role as founding editor of the design magazine *Domus*.

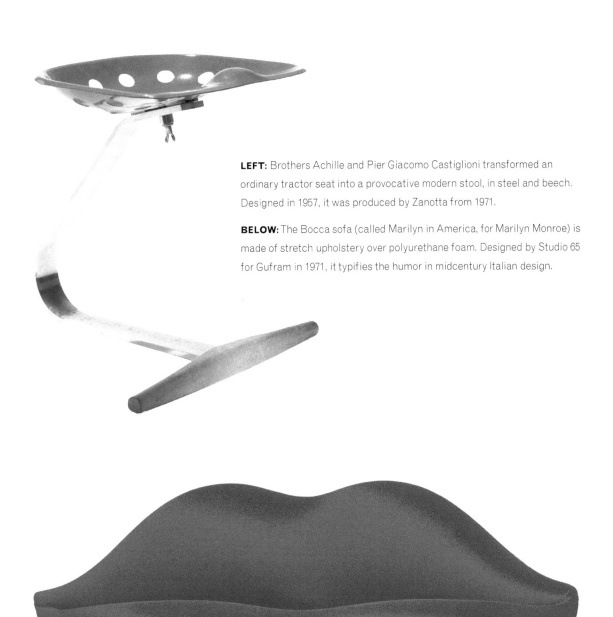

LEFT: Brothers Achille and Pier Giacomo Castiglioni transformed an ordinary tractor seat into a provocative modern stool, in steel and beech. Designed in 1957, it was produced by Zanotta from 1971.

BELOW: The Bocca sofa (called Marilyn in America, for Marilyn Monroe) is made of stretch upholstery over polyurethane foam. Designed by Studio 65 for Gufram in 1971, it typifies the humor in midcentury Italian design.

ABOVE: Provocative but practical, the Tube chair, designed by Joe Colombo in 1969, has four foam-upholstered tubular plastic sections, secured with steel rods and rubber clips. The sections can be rearranged in different seating positions, or nested for easy shipping.

BELOW: Assembled like a jigsaw puzzle from three interlocking pieces of molded, lacquered plywood, this lounge chair by Joe Colombo for Kartell, 1964, prefigures the designer's later work in plastics.

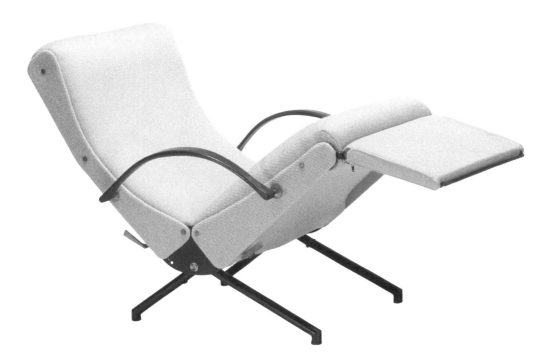

ABOVE: Adjustability is a major attraction of this articulated *chaise longue*, designed by Osvaldo Borsani for Techno, 1955, of enameled steel, foam, and upholstery.

BELOW: The Up chair and ottoman by Gaetano Pesce are aptly named: packed in a flat carton, they expand to full size when the carton is opened. Made of stretch-fabric-covered foam, designed in 1969.

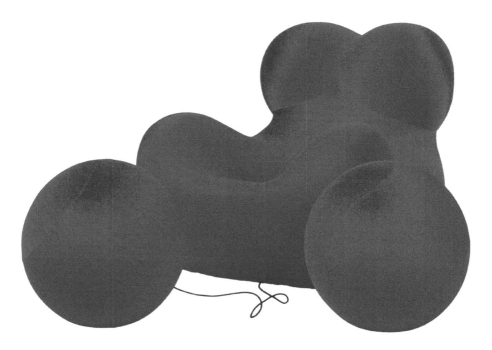

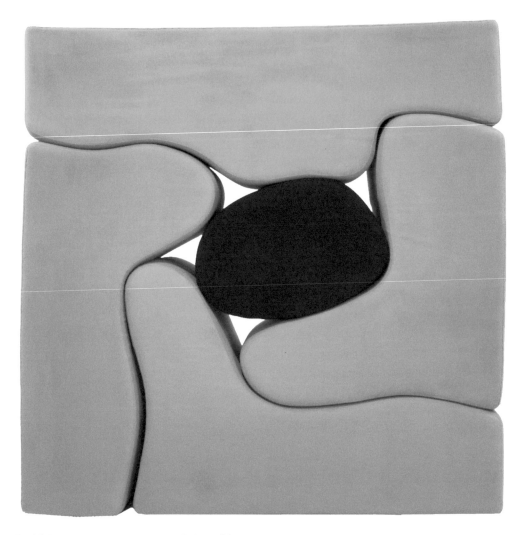

The Malitte seating system, by artist Roberto Matta, stacks several shapely units into a 64-inch square. Made of polyurethane foam and stretch wool upholstery with internal wood supports, it was designed in 1966.

One of the innovative lighting designs produced in Italy during this period, the three-arm *Triennale* floor lamp from Arredoluce, was designed by Gino Safartti, c. 1956, and has become a classic.

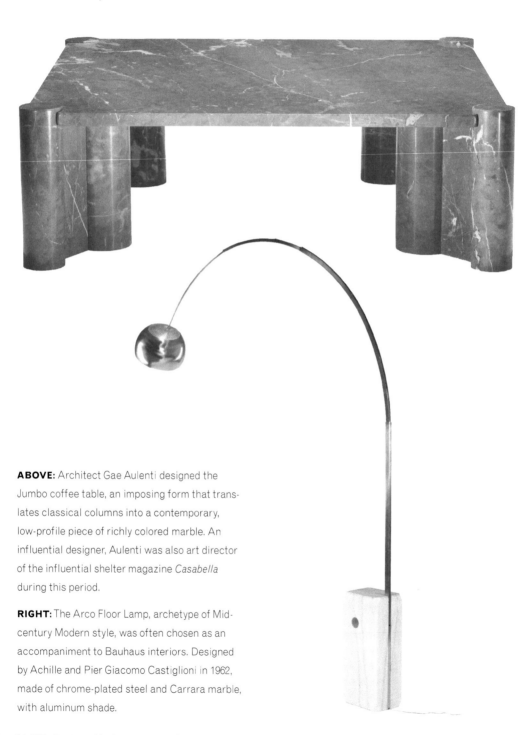

ABOVE: Architect Gae Aulenti designed the Jumbo coffee table, an imposing form that translates classical columns into a contemporary, low-profile piece of richly colored marble. An influential designer, Aulenti was also art director of the influential shelter magazine *Casabella* during this period.

RIGHT: The Arco Floor Lamp, archetype of Mid-century Modern style, was often chosen as an accompaniment to Bauhaus interiors. Designed by Achille and Pier Giacomo Castiglioni in 1962, made of chrome-plated steel and Carrara marble, with aluminum shade.

ABOVE: The Cab Armchairs, which appear to be made of unsupported saddle leather, are actually of leather wrapped and zipped over a supporting steel skeleton. Designed by Mario Bellini in 1977.

BELOW: Low-profile sofas of tufted leather were among the distinctive seating pieces introduced by Italian designers. In this example, designed by Afra and Tobia Scarpa in 1970, the cushions are supported by an external metal frame.

Italian Modern Style, c. 1965–1980

Style Markers

MOOD
serious fun

SCALE
not relevant

COLORS
lively, intense

ORNAMENT
minimal

FURNITURE
adventurous shapes and
materials

TEXTILES
leather, flat-weaves

LOOK FOR
whimsical furniture,
lighting as an art form

Alvorada Tomato,
a strong pattern in
wallpaper to stand
up to the boldest
Italian-inspired
design.

Repeat Classic, a
zingy-colored take
on houndstooth
pattern textile,
designed by Hella
Jongerius.

CHAPTER 28

Postmodernism, c. 1975–1990

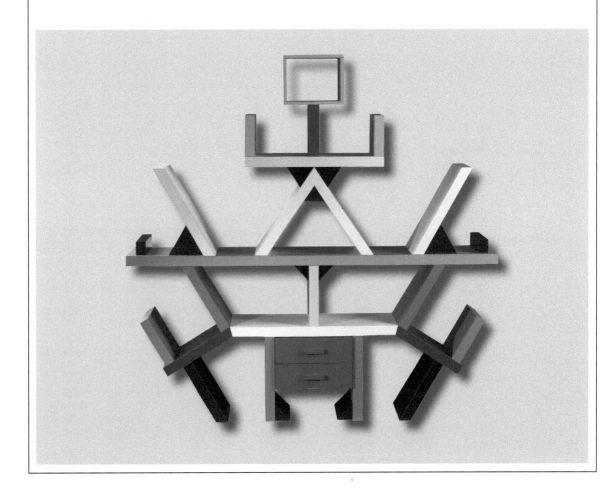

Postmodernism, c. 1975–1990

ABOUT THE PERIOD

The term Postmodernism, like Modernism, is an elusive one. It can mean anything that came after Midcentury Modern, but specifically refers to a late-20th-century philosophical concept that influenced literature, poetry, and sociology, as well as visual arts. In most areas, it sought to remove the boundaries between high art and popular culture. In architecture and design, the Postmodernist movement erupted in response to the sameness and sterility of International Style modernism. Its theories are expressed by Robert Venturi in his seminal 1966 book, *Complexity and Contradiction in Architecture*, which found the designs of the International Style to be sterile and austere. In response to Mies van der Rohe's often-quoted statement "Less is more," he countered with "Less is a bore."

Postmodernism challenged the single-minded Bauhaus rejection of historicism, believing that modern architecture ignored one of its important functions—that of communicating with the public it was intended to serve. Modernism was too elitist and intellectual and needed to project multivalent messages, to be understood and appreciated on several levels. In *Leaning from Las Vegas* (1972), Venturi proposed that vernacular materials and forms give meaning to architecture, and that design sometimes needed no deeper purpose than simply to attract or amuse. The Postmodernists introduced classical elements in designs that linked past and present; they rethought and restyled columns, pilasters, and pediments, applying them with wit and whimsy and sometimes without any functional justification, to both interiors and exteriors, though Postmodernism made its most emphatic statements in architecture.

Foreshadowed by the antiestablishment thinking of earlier Italian radicals, Postmodernism was influenced by Pop Art, Dada, and hippie culture, as well as classical design. In rejecting accepted ways of thinking about and practicing design, it engendered provocative and sometimes bizarre results: its efforts to join high art and popular culture sometimes translated into mass-market kitsch. But its challenge to those who entirely rejected the past in their search for meaningful design in the present was a wake-up call to the design community, and its use of humor and exaggeration was a refreshing reminder that design should not be taken too seriously.

Postmodernism was short-lived but very influential in the years that followed. Minimalism was the most direct response to Postmodern excess, but along with the swing to stripped-down modernism came a counterbalancing revival of traditional design and a more inclusive approach that favors combining classic and avant-garde furnishings in the same interior. Interiors toward the end of the 20th century adopted a new eclecticism.

ABOUT THE STYLE

The Postmodern interior is a striking environment and a clearly contemporary one. Its use of familiar classical motifs may seem almost a caricature, because it makes no attempt at authenticity, even seeming at times to mock it. Despite the tongue-in-cheek attitude, the Postmodern interior is intended as an homage to the timelessness of classical design. A large-scale space, it often uses abundant architectural detail, stripped-down and stylized for a strictly untraditional look. Walls may be defined with columns, arches, alcoves, and exaggerated moldings, which configure the space and avoid the linearity of steel-frame construction. Palladian elements like arches and pediments enhance windows and doorways. Lively colors and provocative furnishings are a bold and arresting decorative statement, but the Postmodern interior is designed with the intention of striking the eye more than easing it, and it may be better suited to occasional visits than long-term occupancy.

All of this architectural detail makes additional pattern unnecessary, but the absence of need is beside the point. Though walls are most often painted in solid colors, upholstery and floor coverings are frequently patterned in stylish abstract, classical, geometric, or floral motifs.

The colors of Postmodernism are drawn from color-field paintings and ice-cream vendors: vanilla, apricot, pistachio, black raspberry. Primary hues are discarded in favor of pastels and unexpected contrasts. This distinctive palette, applied to walls, carpet, and upholstery, adds liveliness that underscores the humor and irony of Postmodern style, setting it apart from anything that preceded or followed.

Postmodernism, c. 1975–1990

About the Furniture

Postmodern furniture is innovative, provocative, and often pushes the boundaries of good taste. Designed more for eye appeal than function, many of the pieces draw on architectural forms, but even more emerged entirely from their designers' imaginations. The major progenitors of the style are Italian, most notably the memorable Memphis collaborative, founded in 1981 by Ettore Sottsass (1917–2007) and a group of compatriots, who devised furniture that flew in the face of all established standards of design. Memphis soon attracted designers from other countries, who created idiosyncratic objects ranging from bowls and vases to candlesticks and even teapots. Their colorful pieces, though obviously modern in the use of metal and plastic, unconventional shapes, and lack of applied ornament, are the absolute antithesis of the austere modernist aesthetic. Zingy laminated patterns and bold combinations of colors, rather than the more traditional types of furniture ornament, enliven these exuberant works.

Though often extreme and, as noted, not always utilitarian, Postmodern designs have a winning silliness that evokes either of two emotional responses—immediate infatuation or intense dislike. Designers like Michael Graves (1934–), Frank Gehry (1929–), Philippe Starck (1949–), and many others have contributed to the reservoir of Postmodernism with a cornucopia of objects that, while uncomfortably competitive en masse, stand out as arresting accents in a contemporary setting.

Postmodern accessories also draw on architecture for both form and decoration, but their smaller size allows for witty tweaking, reassembling, and improvisation on classical themes. Colorful objects in glass, silver, ceramic, or lacquered wood, they reflect the skewed historicism that informs Postmodern design. Both decorative and functional, they avoid the criticism of impracticality to which the furniture is subject, and they are almost invariably charming.

ABOVE: American architect Robert Venturi designed the Sheraton side chair in silk-screened, laminated plywood, one of a series of tongue-in-cheek takes on period seating pieces, for Knoll, 1983.

LEFT: A provocative form accented with lively color, the First chair of varnished tubular steel and wood was designed by Italian Michele De Lucchi for Memphis, in 1983.

Another tongue-in-cheek reference to traditional forms, the Proust armchair, designed in 1978 by Alessandro Mendini for Studio Alchimia, recreates an overstuffed Baroque chair in handpainted, upholstered, and carved wood.

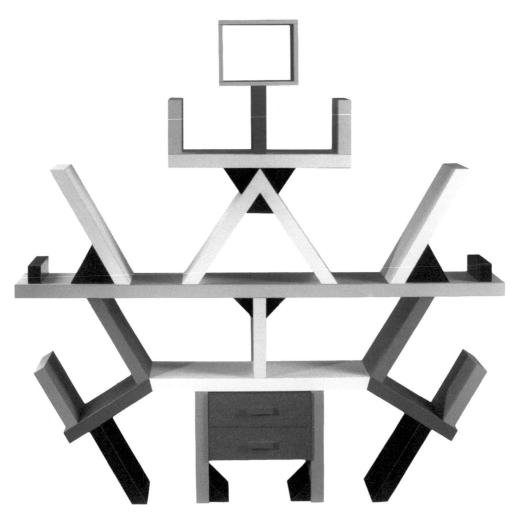

A paradigm of Postmodern design, this angular Carlton bookcase/room divider of multicolored plastic laminate was designed by Ettore Sottsass, founder of Memphis, in 1981.

RIGHT: Although Postmodern furniture did not fit easily into most interiors, accessories were more successful in combining with other modern styles; witness this whistling teakettle, with a whimsical bird at the spout, designed by American architect Michael Graves for Alessi, in 1985.

BELOW: Michael Graves designed this lounge chair, made of maple burl and lacquered wood, in 1980, a somewhat subdued iteration of postmodern elements.

Style Markers

MOOD
fun

SCALE
relatively large

COLORS
clashing pastels

ORNAMENT
stylized classical

FURNITURE
witty takes on familiar forms

TEXTILES
flat-weave, quirky patterns

LOOK FOR
columns, pediments,
quirky shapes

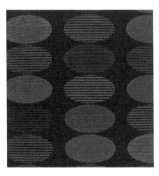

Repeating ovoid shapes on a dark ground would be complementary upholstery for postmodern seating.

A smaller-scale, single-color pattern is more subdued, but still in the right mood.

CHAPTER 29
High-Tech and Minimalism, c. 1980s–1990s

ABOUT THE PERIOD

More elusive to pinpoint than most 20th-century styles, Minimalism grew out of the 1960s art movement exemplified by such practitioners as Donald Judd, Robert Ryman, Dan Flavin, and others whose ascetic, academic approach treated artworks as objects rather than as artistic expressions. The experience of art became physical and spatial, rather than emotional.

The theories spawned by Minimalist art crystallized into a design aesthetic that took Mies's "Less is more" dictum to its most literal extreme. Interiors were stripped of nonessentials, creating spartan spaces furnished with the fewest possible objects. Critics of the style, as well as its supporters, attested to its effectiveness in translating the anomie of modern life.

In the 1970s, the strikingly simple designs of American Ward Bennett (1917–2003) and the industrial chic of "High-Tech" (from the 1978 book of the same name) were precursors of the style, which became prominent decades later in the work of American Joe D'Urso (1943–) and London architect John Pawson (1949–). Their striking, astringent interiors presented a refreshing, although radical, alternative to the highly decorative interiors popularized by shelter magazines and showhouse presentations. Minimalism was embraced by the media, but only the most adventurous home dwellers were comfortable in its unforgiving starkness.

Another direction in late Modernist architecture was Deconstructivism, a literary criticism term adopted in the 1990s to describe structures with jagged, irregular configurations that were uniquely arresting, though often impractical to build. Architects like Frank Gehry, Zaha Hadid, Rem Koolhaas, and Daniel Libeskind were among those associated with the style.

More intellectual than aesthetic, Minimalism had a limited audience and a relatively short life. It became one of many options in a decade of inclusive design, and it was overshadowed by styles that offered greater creature comforts, although it attracted a committed constituency of purists.

ABOUT THE STYLE

The Minimalist interior is striking, though sometimes intimidatingly severe. It evokes an air of enveloping space, in surroundings sculpted with geometric precision. In its utter lack of decoration, it appears unplanned, or even unfinished, but the illusion is deceptive; every element of the composition has been meticulously designed and placed. Minimalism can be viewed as an extension of the International Style, pared down to its barest essentials. Closer to artwork than interior design, it serves as a background that uses the occupants as decoration.

Walls are ruler-straight, or sharply angled, and they might be simply painted white or finished in high-gloss lacquer, polished steel, or even concrete. Though texture is acceptable, any pattern is avoided. Ceilings, whether high or low, appear to recede into space.

Expanses of windows may be included, but only if the landscape is equally pristine. Floors may be smooth concrete, or are covered with flat industrial carpeting, sisal, or jute. Other surfaces add subtle contrast—with polished or patinated steel, clear or frosted glass, textured slate, translucent plastic, or lacquered wood. Lighting is most often concealed, becoming part of the background rather than the furnishings.

Except for a precisely placed object or two, decorative accents are banished, as is anything that might soften the linearity of the composition; no clutter or pattern is permitted to break the mood of the astringent, but seductive surround. Color is also avoided: white, black, and grey are the chosen palette, which can be varied with textures, tonalities, and applications of light.

Minimalist furniture fuses into its surroundings, punctuating the space like sculpture. Rectilinear or sharply angular, it is likely to include sectional seating that seems rooted to the floor, glass or slate-top tables, and low, built-in cabinetry. Horizontal lines are emphasized rather than verticals, to enhance the feeling of openness.

NEXT PAGE: In a loft interior with a high-tech look, an open-plan kitchen area features exposed beams and a modern spiral staircase outlined in bright-red metal tubing.

PREVIOUS PAGE: This striking all-white room is the ultimate expression of a minimalist aesthetic. Avoiding color, pattern, and almost all objects, it is only for the most disciplined occupants.

BELOW: This overscaled steel-mesh armchair, How High the Moon, is the outline of a chair without a structure. Its see-through quality evokes an air of weightlessness. Created by Japanese designer Shiro Kuramata, in 1986.

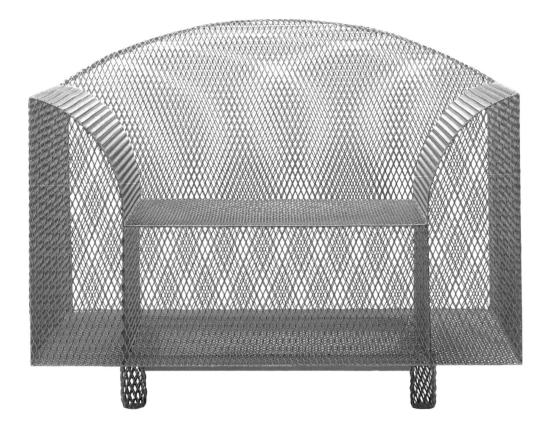

Very much in the minimalist style, the Low Rolling Table, designed by Joseph Paul D'Urso in 1980, is a stripped-down form of stainless steel and glass.

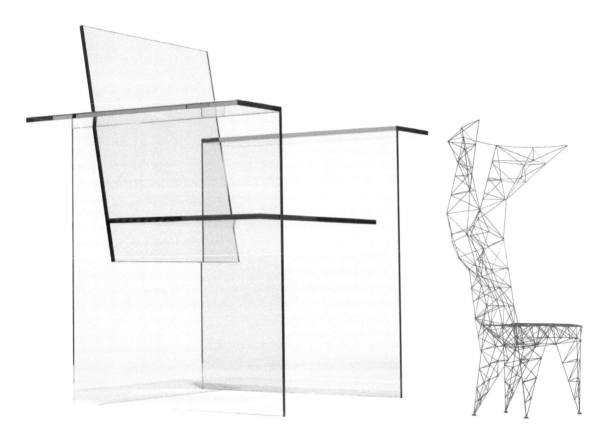

ABOVE LEFT: Another Shiro Kuramata design takes minimalism to the point of transparency. The Glass chair, of laminated glass and less fragile than it appears, dates to 1976.

ABOVE RIGHT: The Pylon Chair, looking like a pen-and-ink drawing, is made of hand-welded steel rods, by British designer Tom Dixon for Capellini, 1992.

ABOVE: Several artists have designed furniture, particularly in minimalist mode; this pine bed by Donald Judd, in 1993, resembles the artist's sculptural work.

RIGHT: American artist and director Robert Wilson's stainless steel Pierre Curie Chair was designed in 1996.

High-Tech and Minimalism, c. 1980s–1990s

Style Markers

MOOD
unemotional

SCALE
may vary, feels grand

COLORS
white, black, and grey

ORNAMENT
banished

FURNITURE
strictly linear

TEXTILES
flat-pile upholstery, high-tech sheers

LOOK FOR
industrial finishes, Zen-like space

Minimalist interiors call for the least possible pattern; this muted grey herringbone is just enough.

The merest bit of pebbly texture relieves the dark tones of densely woven Balance upholstery fabric.

CHAPTER 30

Late Modernism: Design in Transition, c. 1985–2000

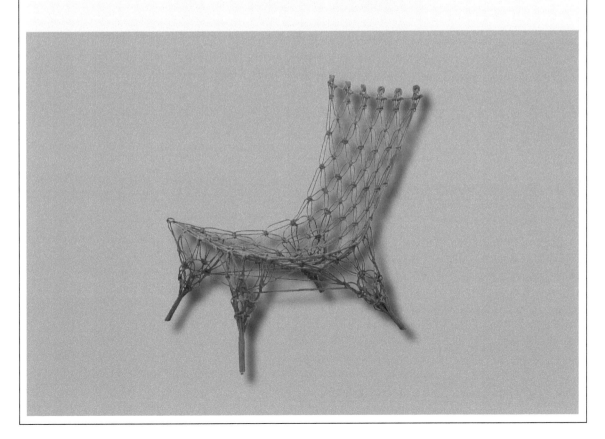

ABOUT THE PERIOD

The 1990s were a time of exhilarating highs and tragic lows. The end of the Cold War and the explosive growth of the Internet signaled the start of a global community, but financial crises and genocide showed that civilization still had a long way to go. As the 20th century drew to a close, the design pendulum did not so much swing back as remain in stasis, uncertain which direction would suit the approaching millennium. Pulled with equal force toward moving forward and looking backward, designs were either cautiously avant-garde or wistfully nostalgic. Despite the equivocation, however, this was the first decade in which modernism became entirely accepted—if not universally revered—by the general public.

Designers retreated from the iconoclasm of postmodernism and the severity of minimalism, taking a more conservative and often conventional approach to interiors and furnishings. As casual dress prevailed in fashion, living rooms were supplanted by the family room or—in suburban areas—the "great room," a high-ceilinged, open space, incorporating entertaining, dining, and kitchen areas to become the main gathering place for family and guests. In a corollary move, loft apartments proliferated even in otherwise conventional buildings, where they became a key selling point for new construction as well as renovations. Interiors with few walls and open areas instead of closed-off rooms were more flexible, but they also helped to conceal the reduced square footage made necessary by rising construction costs and limited building space in increasingly congested cities.

Technological developments brought new design tools; the computer supplanted the compass to create increasingly complex curves, some of which could have been made only with painstaking handwork, but many that had not previously been possible. The wherewithal for experimentation opened countless new territories for designers to explore.

Another by-product of technology's advances was an interest in kitchen design. The super-equipped, super-modern, touch-button kitchen became every homeowner's dream, and industrial equipment like Viking stoves and Sub-Zero refrigerators were the must-have prestige acquisitions, whether or not the occupants had much interest in cooking. A few years later, the bathroom would receive a spotlight of its own, both rooms among the status symbols of a free-spending economy.

As environmentalists became more outspoken, public awareness of the dangers of global warming grew more widespread, awakening interest in products and buildings that minimize environmental damage. As the "green design" movement took hold, designers learned to choose sustainable materials and to find ways to conserve energy.

At the same time, designers began to take into account several sectors of the population that had been underserved: the aged or aging, the disabled, and the otherwise disadvantaged. Design took on a new role as a discipline that could not only create beautiful things but could also improve people's lives.

In these key years, when modern communication was bringing countries closer together, a new generation of designers came to maturity, respecting the legacy of mid-century masters while introducing fresh approaches that were unrestricted by national borders or traditional ways of working. Scandinavians, Italians, Americans as well as Japanese, French, British, and others began to exchange ideas and often to collaborate.

Perhaps the freshest source of inspiration in this decade was in the Netherlands, at the Design Academy Eindhoven, whose interdisciplinary approach emphasized innovation and encouraged students to let their imaginations, rather than practical considerations, generate design ideas. The Academy and its graduates came to international attention with the work of the collective Droog Design and others, including Marcel Wanders (1963–), co-founder of Mooi; Jurgen Bey (1965–); Hella Jongerius (1963–); and Tord Boontje (1968–), whose work invigorated the design scene as had the Memphis Collective more than a decade earlier. The Dutch designers, however, were not rebelling against existing styles but seeking new ideas, which meant that their products, though still provocative, were generally more adaptable to "real" interiors than were those of the Italian rebels.

About the Style

Late Modernism might be described as modernist style in a holding pattern. Eclectic was the catch-all word to describe an increasingly inclusive design climate, one that could accept both old and new with equal enthusiasm. This was in many ways a positive development: there was less pressure to produce new styles, allowing time for designers (and consumers) to absorb and respond to developments that would lead to unprecedented changes in the way buildings were constructed, interiors designed, and furnishings conceived and produced.

The typical late-20th-century interior—if such a thing can be said to exist—is inviting and somewhat middle-of-the-road, with comfortable seating on plump-pillowed sofas, in a style that is clearly contemporary without being severe. Walls are painted, sometimes textured, probably in white or soft neutral tones, and polished wood floors are accented with textured rugs or carpet, either beige toned or classically patterned. Faux painting or textured wall coverings might be used in the entry foyer, hallway, or on an accent wall.

Furniture in the room is clearly contemporary, but there might be an occasional object from earlier decades. The idea of mixing styles has begun to take hold, with more interest in expressing individuality and personal taste than in sticking strictly to the rules.

Window treatments are likely to be simple: vertical blinds, shades, or simple curtains. If draperies are used, they hang straight, without elaborate swags, trim, or cornices.

The room is graced with a pleasant color palette: stark black-and-white has given way to warm neutral tones, upholstery is soft and sittable, and a congenial mix of accessories and artwork helps the interiors look lived in and livable.

Reflecting the interest in looking back, recent museum exhibitions (at the Philadelphia Museum of Art, the Montreal Museum of Decorative Arts, and the Museum of Modern Art among them) have featured objects from the midcentury decades, and an increasing number of design galleries are offering what has become designated as vintage furnishings, leading to a healthy secondary market that would thrive in the decades to come. By the early years of the 21st century, many of the original producers, such as Knoll, Herman Miller, and others, were promoting and reissuing postwar furniture classics by Charles and Ray Eames, George Nelson, and others. Midcentury textiles followed a similar path, as did Scandinavian design classics. Reaching back even further, the inclusive design climate meant that traditional interiors remained a constant, despite the dominance of Modernism.

ABOUT THE FURNITURE

Most of the furniture found in the Late Modern period looks much like that of the preceding decade, modifying forms like sectional seating and clean-lined cabinetry in pieces of practical scale that adapted well to an eclectic mix of furnishings.

There have been, however, some furniture designers who struck out in new directions. Some are working with objects reclaimed from industrial roots, using rough materials with a factory-fresh look; Ron Arad's "Rover" chair is an icon of this genre. Others have explored the potential of newly acceptable plastics, and the first limited-edition works from designers like Israeli-born Arad (1951–) and Australian Mark Newson (1963–) are beginning to blur the lines that once separated design from either craft at one end of the spectrum or art at the other.

PREVIOUS PAGE: As the 20th century drew to a close, interiors began to mix modern with accents from other periods, like the curvy chandelier that modulates the linear furniture in this London living room.

ABOVE: Blurring the barriers between furniture, craft, and art, You Can't Lay Down Your Memories, a limited-edition cabinet by Tejo Remy for Dutch collaborative Droog Design, is assembled from recycled drawers, bound with canvas belting. Designed in 1991.

LEFT: Australian designer Mark Newson shaped the Embryo chair, made of neoprene and tubular steel in 1988, prefiguring a new interest by modernists in biomorphic shapes, an aesthetic that would inform most of his designs.

RIGHT: Designers began to explore the use of unexpected material, as in the Knotted Chair by Dutch designer Marcel Wanders for Droog. More comfortable than it appears, it suggests macramé handcraft with carbon fibers, coated with epoxy, designed in 1995.

BELOW: Moving from deconstructivist forms to biomorphic ones, Iraq-born architect Zaha Hadid designed the Woosh Sofa in 1986.

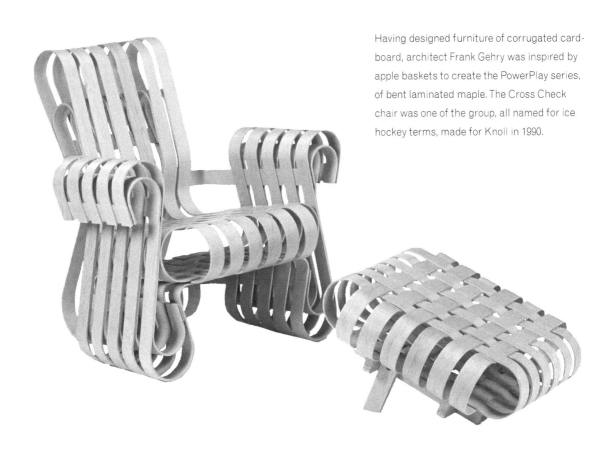

Having designed furniture of corrugated cardboard, architect Frank Gehry was inspired by apple baskets to create the PowerPlay series, of bent laminated maple. The Cross Check chair was one of the group, all named for ice hockey terms, made for Knoll in 1990.

LEFT: Made of lacquered metal and woven straw, the S Chair recalls the form of Verner Panton's injestion-molded plastic chair. Tom Dixon designed this one in 1991.

BELOW: Rody Graumans, a member of the Droog collective, designed the 85 Lamps Chandelier in 1993. It makes much of little, with a cluster of ordinary bulbs and plastic-coated wire.

The Feltri chair, designed in 1987 by Italian Gaetano Pesce, impregnated felt with resin for the supporting structure of this armchair, whose flexible sides adjust for seating comfort.

Style Markers

MOOD comfortable	**SCALE** largish, without being grand
COLORS beiges and neutral tones	**ORNAMENT** limited
FURNITURE soft-edge contemporary	**TEXTILES** texture, restrained pattern

LOOK FOR
conservative eclecticism

This irregular pattern of vari-colored and vari-sized squares are a bright change of pace from conventional modern textiles.

Understated enough to go anywhere, this simple textured fabric works with any period or style.

Part V

21ST CENTURY:
The Future Is Here

CHAPTER 31
Styles of the 21st Century: The New World of Design

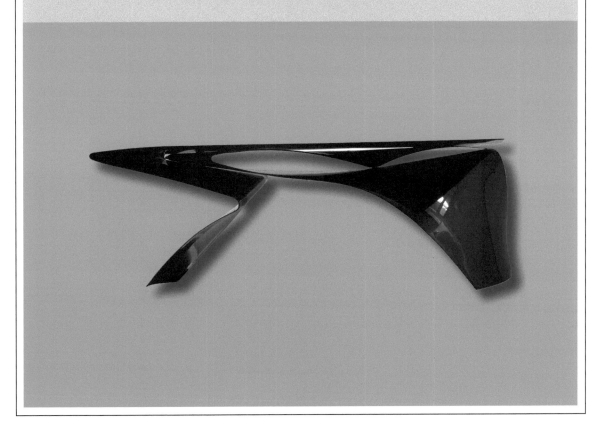

ABOUT THE PERIOD

As Modernism defined the styles of the 20th century, so it promises to dominate the 21st, but the definition of the term remains in flux. Current design is certainly modern, in not being based on traditional designs, but it is a more diverse form of Modernism, split in several directions, with no predominating strain. Several influences have changed the parameters and the objectives of new design.

The innovative forms of the new century were heralded by the tradition-smashing architecture of Frank Gehry's 1997 Guggenheim Bilbao Museum in Spain and the provocative furniture conceived by graduates of Eindhoven Academy in the Netherlands. Design by computer, design that prioritized concept and technique before function, and design with sociological concerns all signaled broader and more significant parameters for the discipline, beyond aesthetics—and occasionally beyond functionality.

The world-shaking events of the century's first decade—the cataclysm of 9/11, the collapse of the Soviet Union, the explosive growth of China, and the conflicts of the Middle East—made design an issue of less importance than considerations of survival, and aesthetic issues often took a back seat to more humanistic ones.

Sustainability is the dominant concern of any current conversation about design, whether in materials used, energy expended, or recyclability, and it has given rise to buildings, interiors, and objects guided by these considerations. Designers have accepted responsibility for choosing materials and planning interiors with minimal impact on the environment.

Sociological issues such as universal design and aging in place have made planning and furnishing interiors important elements of a much broader picture, taking into consideration both a growing senior citizen population and the increased diversity of modern families and living arrangements.

Design is also broader in another sense; travel and communications have created a global community, in which ideas are exchanged in moments rather than weeks. National differences and cultural barriers have been almost entirely erased as designers from countries far removed geographically are exploring similar aesthetics. It is no longer possible, or even desirable, to place national labels on design styles. The Netherlands, Germany, Japan, England, France, Spain, and others are contributing as much to cutting-edge design as Italy and America did in the late 20th century. Cultural pluralism dominates today's design world.

In what can be regarded as a second industrial revolution, technology continues its inexorable and invigorating advance, reinventing the vocabulary of design at a faster pace than anytime in the past and making the earlier industrial age seem a mere blip on the timeline of history. As the pace of change has quickened, the possibility of early obsolescence threatens each new idea and each new object, accelerating the pressure for continual innovation—or at least the perception of newness.

Developments in architecture include buildings wrapped in coils of metal, shaped like soaring wings or jagged shards, formed with paper tubes or organic materials, embellished with LED (light-emitting diode) lighting, or surfaced with space-age textiles or reclaimed scrap. Wind-tunnel technology has enabled the construction of ever-taller slivers of buildings that appear fragile but are structurally stable. Architects like Frank Gehry (1929–), Santiago Calatrava (1951–), Rem Koolhaas (1944–), Zaha Hadid (1950–), Jean Nouvel (1945–), and others have changed our expectations of how a modern building should—and can—look.

So-called smart houses, with preprogrammed lighting and appliances and touch-activated electronics, are only the beginning of what will be possible in the next few years: walls can already change colors or patterns according to climate or choice, lighting can be modulated to accommodate changing moods, and furniture can take shape to suit different occupants. These and other developments will change the way interiors are planned, as information becomes a tool in the designer's workbox.

Like any language, design will continue to evolve, responding to society, culture, politics, and scientific development. It is thus far impossible to identify a single defining style in this century; it may never again be possible to do so.

ABOUT THE STYLES

The 21st-century interior has kept pace with changes in environment, materials, and technology. There is, however, no single emerging aesthetic except the debate between two opposing views; one that builds on history in expressing modernism and the other that rejects it, continuing the controversy that began in the century just past. A room in today's contemporary style may be a starkly minimalist space whose structural surround almost disappears with the use of transparent walls and translucent curtains. It may be sculpted with biomorphic forms inspired by nature, reflecting the search for humanistic elements that deny the rigors of strict modernity. Or it may be an idiosyncratic mixture of new ideas and those reclaimed from history.

Walls may be light or dark, plain or patterned, textured, smooth or layered, for an effect that is both soigné and a bit eccentric. Spaces might be divided with resin, extruded aluminum, digitally printed glass, honeycombed paper, or woven polypropylene.

Textile design is as much scientific as it is creative. New fabrics are woven, extruded, or pressed out with plastics and thermoplastics, metallic or wire mesh, carbon fiber and resin, or fiber-optics that allow them to emit light. They may be intricately woven, pleated, pressed, cut, crushed, or otherwise manipulated, or digitally printed with unique and customized designs.

The other side of the coin is a counter-trend, a return to natural materials: lighting fixtures and fabrics of paper, unfinished wood, or veneers woven into forms that revert back to those in nature. Recyclable materials are being used for furnishings—such likely ones as bamboo and concrete, and such unlikely ones as seeds, spider webs, and even garbage bags.

Parallelling the use of natural materials is a new interest in craft and a new respect for those artisans engaged in making things by hand—an understandable response to the predominance of machine-made objects. The most striking accessories in today's interiors are often expressive handcrafted objects, valued for their aesthetic appeal rather than their function, and treated as works of art.

A new generation of lighting technology enables designers to exploit the possibilities of miniaturization in sophisticated applications unlike any fixtures previously available. High-intensity and LED lighting have opened new horizons, enabling entire walls to be illuminated, colors to change, and illumination to be either a decorative tour de force or entirely invisible. Along with this—or instead of it—the interior may have bare-bulb lighting, chandeliers of crystal, paper, foil-like chips, feathers, or holographic images as varied as the imagination can conceive.

Furniture design has gone in several directions. Designers are exploring new possibilities in existing materials or devising applications using new materials and technologies, including some borrowed from the automotive or aerospace industries. The results may be novel variations on familiar forms or intriguing new creations heretofore not possible. Partnerships with engineering and science have produced objects made with injected polypropylene, laser-cut polystyrene, flexible polycarbonate, and injection-molded foam, or alternatively with string, rope, or cutout aluminum. Sustainability concerns have led to inventive applications of materials like sand, silica, cement, and paper, materials not traditionally used for furniture, as well as scrap materials that were once discarded in landfills.

Most of these new designs avoid conventional ornament, instead finding decorative potential in texture, transparency, or other characteristics of the particular materials. In some cases, the urge to experiment trumps the need for user-friendly design; in others, comfort takes priority over appearance. Conditioned by design-savvy media and increasingly high-profile architecture and design stars, there is a general acceptance and appreciation of design that departs from expected types and even subverts them.

A new category of objects, design/art, designates works that are still recognizable as furniture, but for which function is secondary. Some are intended simply to explore processes, but most are expressions of ideas or concepts that must be understood in order to be appreciated; in this, they demand intellectual or emotional responses that are not customarily associated with furniture. Designers like Ron Arad, Zaha Hadid, and Mark Newson create objects that invite tactile experiences, whereas others like Patrick Jouin (1967–), Joris Laarman (1979–), and Studio Job (Job Smeets, 1971–, and Nynke Tynagel, 1977–) challenge the viewer to understand the concepts behind the visual expressions.

OPPOSITE: An interior that could not have been designed in any other era; the MAXXI National Museum of XXI Century Arts in Rome, Italy, by architect Zaha Hadid, 2010.

ARCHITECTURE-DRIVEN DESIGN

Some modern buildings set the parameters for the spaces they enclose, either by expanses of glass that integrate interior, exterior, and landscape, or by spatial configurations so demanding that the interior designer has few options. In these environments, there is no separation between the disciplines.

OPPOSITE: In this double-height living room in Malibu, California, designed in 2003, American architect Stephen Kanner's dramatic enclosure dictates the design of the interior space.

ABOVE: German Konstantin Gric designed this limited-edition Chaise Longue, an architectonic sweep of carbon fiber, in 2008.

BELOW: Using polished stainless steel, Israeli designer Arik Levy created this minimalist table of glazed bronze, in 2007.

RIGHT: Swedish design firm Claesson Koivisto Rune, conceived this angular desk lamp of a new paper and plastic composite, weighted with cast iron, in 2010.

BELOW: Italian Piero Lissoni designed this sofa with a sleek contemporary form that suits the century's eclectic modern taste.

ECLECTIC DESIGN

Today's interiors may be modern, but they are rarely planned along a single trajectory. It is increasingly the practice to mix periods, to punctuate one style with accents of another, and to use contrast and counterpoint to bring individuality to a space. This quality of eclecticism is what distinguishes the 21st-century interior from those preceding it.

OPPOSITE: In the parlor of New York's landmark Villard Houses, interior designer Juan Montoya devised this arresting showhouse interior with a virtuoso mix of styles, from fine crystal chandelier to undulating custom sofa and craft objects.

LEFT: A play on children's toys, and an ingenious use of existing objects, the Mixed Banquete Chair, by Brazilian designers Fernando and Humberto Campana, c. 2002, is one of several versions clustering stuffed animals on a tubular steel frame.

BELOW: Marcel Wanders' Crochet Chair, a limited edition designed in 2006, combines hand-crocheted flowers, molded and stiffened with resin, into a curvy low lounge chair.

BELOW: The Polder sofa, by Dutch designer Hella Jongerius, 2005, made of polyurethane form on a wood frame, is more unconventional than it appears; the armrest cushions are filled with sand, making them easy to push into irregular forms.

ABOVE: A serpentine-back sofa with sleek modern lines, the Orgy was designed by Egyptian-born designer Karim Rashid in 2009.

BELOW: The Confluences sofa is designed to look like a random cluster of sections, by French designer Philippe Nigro, 2009.

SUSTAINABLE DESIGN

Designers now consider the ecological aspects of the harvesting, use, and disposal of the products they use, planning interiors that are energy-efficient and choosing materials that are renewable, recyclable, biodegradable, or otherwise making the best possible use of natural resources without depleting them.

OPPOSITE: American architects Bromley Caldari Associates designed this vacation house with sustainability requirements in mind. It has maximum light, good air circulation, and natural materials that are artfully deployed for eye appeal.

ABOVE: The Cahhage Chair, by Japanese designer Nendo (Oki Sato), 2008, uses recycled pleated paper from fabric production, wraps it into a roll, which the user peels back to create the seating space.

RIGHT: Spanish designer Patricia Urquiola's Crinoline Chair, 2008, wraps natural and bronze rope around a painted aluminum frame, for an indoor-outdoor piece that's both pretty and practical.

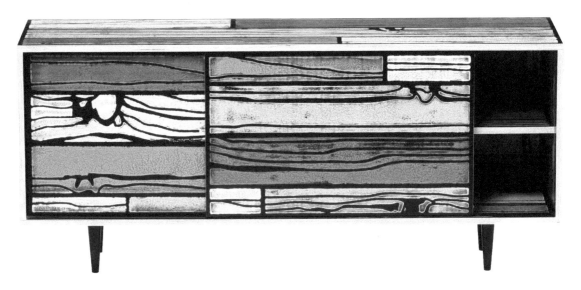

ABOVE: Wrongwoods (Richard Wood and Sebastian Wrong) designed this cabinet with variegated lengths of plywood and finished it with paint, lacquer, and glass, 2007.

BELOW: Jurgen Bey, a Dutch designer, made the Pixélisée Armchair in 2008 of wood fragments that give the illusion of something randomly put together.

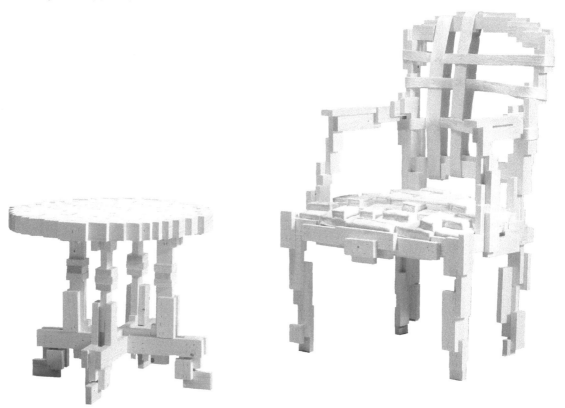

COMPUTER-ENABLED DESIGN

Designs that cannot be drawn or sculpted can be created on the computer, making possible enclosures, interiors, and objects with intricate, once-impossible forms. Walls can be angular or undulating, hallways can coil or meander like sculpture. Laser-cutting machinery, guided by computer, can turn out paper-thin slices that assemble into intriguing new silhouettes. Motion-capture allows the designer to draw images in the air, which are captured on computer and can be printed with three-dimensional (3D) printing. Additive or reductive fabrication will change the way objects are made, allowing designs to be customized at will.

OPPOSITE: The undulating walls of this illuminated kitchen in a modern studio were rendered on a computer, which made possible forms that couldn't have been designed with a ruler and T-square. Designed by Milk-Studio Architects in 2004.

ABOVE: The Cloud bookcase unit, made of polyethylene with rotational technology, assembles in varying configurations by means of simple clips. By French designers Ronan and Erwan Bouroullac for Cappelini, 2004.

BELOW: Laser-cut sheets of aluminum are assembled by hand to form this sculptural Slice Chair by Danish designer Mathias Bengtsson, a limited edition from 2000.

BELOW: The Cinderella Table begins with a composite drawing of 17th-century tables fed into a computer, creating a virtual design that is computer-sliced; the multiple layers are then assembled and hand-finished. A limited edition in birch and plywood from Dutch designer Jeroen Verhoeven, 2005.

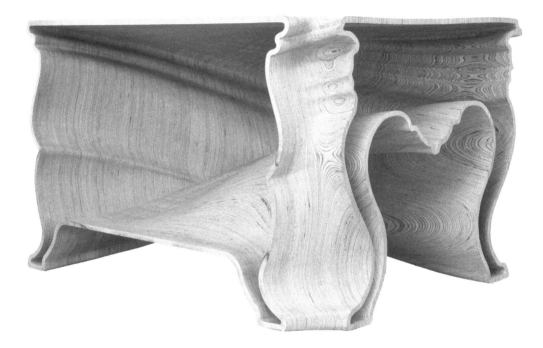

COMMERCIAL DESIGN

The 21st-century office has its own character. It is a collaborative environment, as much playground as workspace, where private and communal areas intersect. The typical office is a multilevel space, configured around a light-filled atrium joined by spiral staircases, ramps, or slides, and energized with vibrant color—a dynamic environment that stimulates creativity, although sometimes at the expanse of repose.

Work and play can coexist comfortably in the 21st-century office, as in this lighthearted environment designed by Rosan Busch for Lego. Photograph by Anders Suneberg.

ABOVE: The atrium has become almost ubiquitous in the modern office building, allowing maximum natural light and a feeling of openness that facilitates interaction.

LEFT: The archetype ergonomic office chair, the Aeron, by Bill Stumpf and Don Chadwick for Herman Miller, was designed in 1994. Made largely of recycled material, the chair itself is mostly recyclable, and it has spawned countless copies.

RIGHT: Conceived in Norway by Peter Opsvik in the 1980s, Balans introduced a new seating posture. It is now implemented in many forms, from task seating to executive chairs. Here, a compact stool.

FURNITURE FOR A NEW WORLD

Although no single style of furniture dominates the century to date, several directions can be identified in the cornucopia of distinctive contemporary designs.

Techno-Centric

These objects would not have been possible a few years in the past. They employ technologies that have only recently been developed, or those that have been borrowed from other industries to be newly applied to the fabrication of furniture. They may take the form of conventional furniture, but they are otherwise without precedent.

ABOVE: The Go chair, by Welsh designer Ross Lovegrove for Bernhardt in 2001, is a one-piece swoop of powder-coated magnesium, one of the first such objects made for mass production.

RIGHT: French designer Patrick Jouin's C2 Chair, designed in 2004, is a skeletal form made with rapid prototyping and stereo-lithography. Its complex structure is built up with many layers of a digitally-sliced 3D drawing.

ABOVE: Formed with software used in automotive production, and mimicking the natural growth of bone, the Bridge Table is cast in aluminum. Joris Laarman designed it in 2010.

RIGHT: First designed by recording freehand sketching on a computer, the epoxy resin Sketch Chair is then fabricated by means of rapid prototyping. From the Swedish group Front Design, 2005.

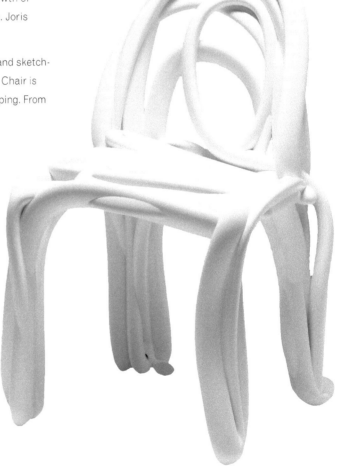

Conceptual

Objects like these cannot be appreciated if they are not fully understood; they are political, social, or cultural statements by the artist, and the aesthetic elements of the design are not the primary consideration. They may be attractive, and even useful, but that may be, in the designer's judgment, beside the point.

As much concept as design, this macassar ebony bench from the 2006 Perished collection by Studio Job has laser-cut marquetry motifs of fossils, commemorating species that are now extinct.

LEFT: Secondhand chairs, stacked, glued, and hand-painted, make the Second-Hand Bookcase by Netherlands designer Maarten Baas, 2006. Because different chairs are used, each finished piece is unique.

BELOW: Sebastian Brajkovic, another Dutch designer, made the Lathe Chair VIII in 2008, a play on Victorian-era design extruded in bronze and stretched into an exaggerated form that echoes the originals.

Design/Art

These designs eradicate the boundaries between design and art, and they can be placed in either category. Some are made entirely by machine, some entirely by hand, some combining both techniques. They may be one-of-a-kind or limited editions; sold in galleries and priced as artworks, they have spawned a new category of collectible furniture.

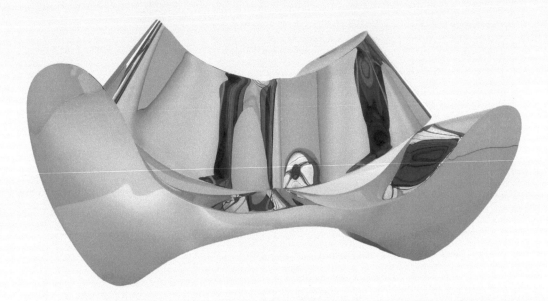

ABOVE: Israeli-born Ron Arad designed the D Sofa in 1994, one of his ongoing explorations of seating in stainless steel in limited-edition seating-as-artwork. His latest designs are of inflated aluminum.

BELOW: Zaha Hadid designed the liquid-looking Aqua Table, of glass-reinforced polyester, in 2005. The top sits on three curvy supports, and recesses in the top create the illusion of melting.

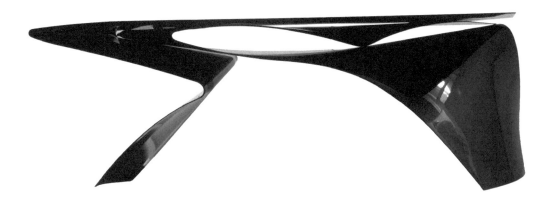

ABOVE: The Side Line Table is an arresting shape of carbon fiber, by London-based American Philip Michael Wolfson, designed in 2009.

BELOW: British designer Amanda Levete created this fluid silhouette of cement and crushed limestone, called Drift Concrete, in 2006.

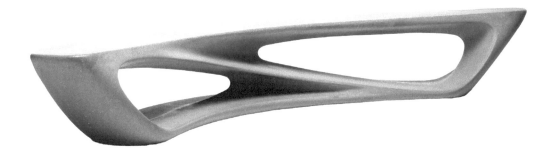

Craft-Conscious

The new respect for handmade, a reaction to the impersonality of modern machine-made designs, echoes the ideals of the Arts and Crafts movement, but contemporary hand-crafted furniture straddles the line between craft and fine art, making it clear that traditional classifications may no longer be meaningful.

David Ebner designed this graceful lacewood Desk Chair in 2006, in a hand-crafted form that recalls the lines of the Grecian *klismos* chair.

LEFT: Evoking a bouquet of flowers, folded petals of felt are sewn onto a shell of polyurethane foam over a steel frame. From Japanese designer Tokujin Yoshioka, 2008.

BELOW: Evoking traditional French craftsmanship, Claude Lalanne's Bureau Croc is a skillfully handworked table of bronze, in a limited edition designed in 2007.

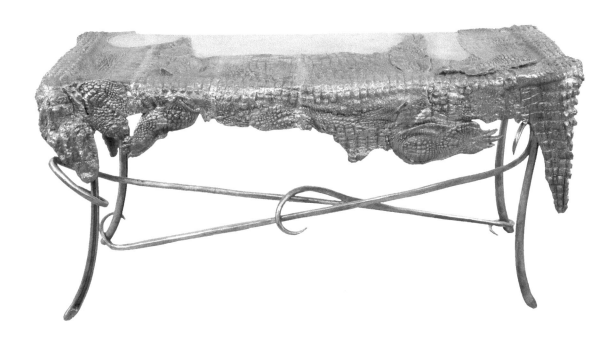

Historicist

In one sense a continuum, in another a response to the abundance of innovation, a contrary strain of design persists—the retention of traditional styles and the revival of 20th-century classics, many midcentury, others even later. In the wake of revivalist fever, vintage designs have been rediscovered, and many furniture objects several decades old are being returned to production. Flat-packed furniture, conceived by Scandinavians in the 1940s, is in comeback mode.

Vladimir Kagan's sectional sofa, designed in 2005, carries the designer's signature curving silhouettes into a new century.

LEFT: Proving that good designs can flourish in more than one period, the Ox Chair, by Danish master Hans Wegner, was designed in 1960 and reissued in 2012.

BELOW: French iconoclast Phillipe Starck's Louis Ghost, translating a classic 18th-century French arm-chair into injection-molded poly-carbonate, became a best-seller after its introduction in 2002.

RIGHT: Though designed in 1986, Marc Newson's Lockheed Lounge is an apt symbol of 21st-century innovation, since the riveted sheet-aluminum over fiberglass-reinforced resin piece (one of three made) set a record for contemporary furniture when it sold for more than £1.1 million in 2009.

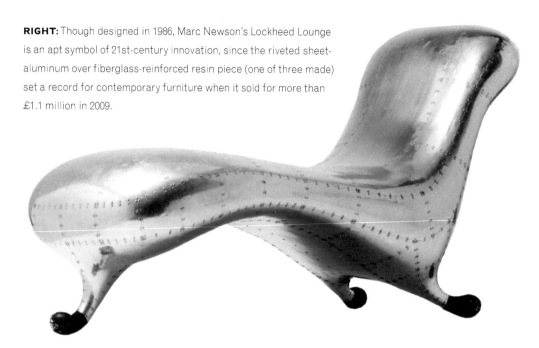

BELOW LEFT: Designed in 1940, the Pelican Chair by Danish architect Finn Juhl was reintroduced in 2008, looking just as avant-garde as it did when it was first made. Leather over foam on a steel frame.

BELOW RIGHT: The classic Navy chair, first made by Emeco in 1944 for use on submarines, has been reissued in an appropriately 21st-century version, made entirely of recycled Coca-Cola bottles.

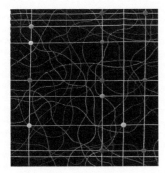

Independent of any particular style, the Rabari rug was designed by Doshi Levien for Nanimarquina in 2014.

Park by Hella Jongerius, a pattern that renders familiar motifs in an untraditional modernist manner.

Aftermath by Studio Job is a striking textile design and a commentary on the destruction of cities.

CONCLUSION

In a world that is increasingly disrupted by economic uncertainty, political controversy, and military conflicts, it may seem superficial to even think about fluctuations in style. But style is inextricably bound to our everyday lives, be they stressful or placid, and the study of style helps chart the course of history.

The landscape of 21st-century design is as intriguing as in any period in the past. What will distinguish its styles from those that came before? It is too soon to tell, but one thing is certain: the lines will not be as clearly drawn as they were in the past. It is likely that no single fashion will predominate, although design will continue to shape the world, ensuring both a stimulating experience and an ongoing challenge for those who follow its development.

What style is that? Whatever its appearance, it will be an expression of its time.

Chronology of Design Periods and Styles

17TH AND 18TH CENTURIES

FRANCE

PERIOD: c. 1643–1715, Reign of Louis XIV

STYLE: Baroque/Louis XIV (Versailles; Louis Le Vau, Charles Le Brun, André Le Notre, André-Charles Boulle)

PERIOD: c. 1710–1730, Regency of Louis XV

STYLE: Régence: Transitional between LXIV and LXV (Charles Cressent)

PERIOD: c. 1730–1750, Reign of Louis XV

STYLE: Rocaille/Rococo/Louis XV: First domestic, not court, style (Hôtels particuliers)

PERIOD: c. 1774–1792, Reign of Louis XVI (1789, French Revolution)

STYLE: Neoclassical/Louis XVI (Jean-Henri Riesener)

PERIOD: c. 1790–1804, Directoire, Consulat

STYLE: Directoire (Transitional to Empire)

PERIOD: c. 1804–1814, Napoleonic Era (Napoleon as Emperor)

STYLE: Empire: Late Neoclassical (Percier and Fontaine, Malmaison)

ENGLAND

PERIOD: c. 1688–1702, William and Mary (joint monarchy)

STYLE: Baroque/William and Mary (Christopher Wren, Daniel Marot), Age of Walnut

PERIOD: c. 1700–1720, Reign of Queen Anne

STYLE: Queen Anne: Manifestation of Rococo influence in England

PERIOD: c. 1720–1810, Georgian: Reigns of George I, II, and III, Age of Mahogany

1. c. 1720–1760, Early Georgian: Reigns of George I and II

STYLES: Early Georgian: More elaborately decorated Queen Anne forms

PALLADIAN (1730–1760, WILLIAM KENT)

2. c. 1760–1810, Late Georgian: Reign of George III

STYLES: Rococo and Neoclassical

> *Robert Adam*: 1760–1800, Architecture and interiors, Neoclassical

> *Thomas Chippendale: The Gentleman and Cabinet Maker's Director,* 1754, 1755, 1762–1763, French/Rococo, Gothic, Chinese, Neoclassical style influences

> *George Hepplewhite: Cabinet-Maker and Upholsterer's Guide,* 1788, Neoclassical

> *Thomas Sheraton: Cabinet-Maker and Upholsterer's Drawing-Book,* 1791, 1794. Neoclassical

PERIOD: c. 1810–1830, Regency of George IV

STYLE: Late Neoclassical (John Soane, John Nash, Thomas Hope), also called Regency

AMERICA

1600–1790: Colonial (early settlers to post-Revolution and new government)

PERIOD: c. 1620–1720, Early Colonial

STYLES: Pilgrim: vernacular, "Medieval" styles

> Jacobean: from English Renaissance style

> William and Mary: from English Baroque style

PERIOD: c. 1720–1790, Late Colonial (1776–1781, American Revolution)

STYLES: Queen Anne: from English, more fluid and sculptural

> *Chippendale:* based on Chippendale's *Director*

PERIOD: 1785–1820: Federal American colonies become a nation

STYLE: Federal/Neoclassical (Thomas Jefferson's Monticello)

PERIOD: 1810–1830, American Empire (overlaps with Federal and sometimes considered part of it)

STYLE: Late Neoclassical (Duncan Phyfe, Charles-Honoré Lannuier, Greek Revival architecture)

19TH AND 20TH CENTURIES
19TH-CENTURY ENGLAND

Regency (Neoclassical), 1810–1820

(Biedermeier in Germany and Austria, 1820s–1840s)

Greek Revival, 1825–1840

Gothic Revival, 1830–1870

Reign of Queen Victoria, Victorian era, 1837–1901

Arts and Crafts Movement, 1860–1880

Aesthetic Movement, latter part of century (c. 1880 peak)

Eclectic–Exotics, Asian Influence, 1870s on

19TH-CENTURY AMERICA

Empire (Late Federal, Neoclassical), 1815–1840

Greek Revival (Pillar and Scroll furniture), 1830–1855

Gothic Revival, 1840–1870

Rococo Revival, 1840–1870

Renaissance Revival (also Neo-Grecian and Egyptian Revivals), 1860–1890

Aesthetic Movement, c. 1870–1890 (era of The Gilded Age)

Arts and Crafts, c. 1880–1915

PREMODERN AND EARLY MODERN MOVEMENTS AND GROUPS

Art Nouveau, 1890–1910 (Belgium, France, variants in European countries, *Stile Liberté* in Italy, *Jugendstil* in Germany, Tiffany in U.S.

Glasgow School (Charles Rennie Mackintosh), 1890–1910

Deutsche Werkbund, founded 1907

Wiener Werkstätte (under Vienna Secession), 1903–1933

De Stijl (Netherlands), 1917–1928

Russian Constructivism, 1917–1922

Futurists (Italy), c. 1910–1930s

MODERN ERA

Bauhaus, 1919–1933

Art Deco, 1920–1940 (*Le Style Moderne* in France)

Moderne, Streamline Style, Skyscraper Style in America

Machine Age/birth of Industrial Design, began 1920s, key decade 1930–1940

Modern Movement (International Style, Mid-century Modern), 1930s–1960s

Scandinavian Modern, 1950–1960s = key years

Italian Modern, 1965–1970s = key years

Postmodern, 1980s

Deconstructivism, 1980s

Minimalism, 1980s–1990s

21ST CENTURY

2000s, still to be determined

Glossary of Furniture and Decorative Arts Terms

3D PRINTING / Refers to any means of printing a three-dimensional object, of which additive process is the most common, where successive layers of material are laid down under computer control based on a 3D model or other electronic data source. Also referred to as *additive manufacturing* (AM) or *additive layered fabrication*.

ACAJOU / French term for mahogany.

ACANTHUS / Representation of the *Acanthus spinosus* leaf in classical ornament.

ANILINE DYES / Chemical dyes made from coal tar derivatives, enabling more varied colorations than are possible with only natural dyes.

ANTHEMION / Classic Greek decoration, a conventionalized honeysuckle or leaf ornament radiating from a single point.

APPLIQUÉ / Ornament affixed to a surface.

APRON / Panel below the seat of a chair that connects its legs, or below the underframing of cabinets, desks, and so forth.

ARABESQUE / Decorative scroll pattern derived from vegetation and arranged into a symmetrical design.

ARCH / A curved structural form that spans an opening, between walls or columns.

ARCHITRAVE / The lowest horizontal member of the **entablature**.

ARCUATED / Architectural composition based on a system of arches, rather than a columnar or trabeated system.

ARMOIRE / A large cupboard or wardrobe intended for clothes, with one or two doors, that was originally used for the storage of armor.

AUBUSSON / French carpet and tapestry producer in the 17th and 18th centuries.

AXMINSTER / Flat-weave carpet developed in England in mid-18th century, inspired by Turkish models, used in royal residences and grand country houses.

BALL-AND-CLAW FOOT / Furniture foot in imitation of a claw grasping a sphere. Believed to be Chinese in origin, inspired by a dragon holding a pearl.

BALUSTER / The upright support in a balustrade; it is a short, usually turned, square, or circular, post or column. Often used for furniture legs or to form part of a chair back. Also termed a banister.

BANQUETTE / A small bench that is usually upholstered.

BARREL CHAIR / Easy chair with a completely rounded back. Originally developed in England.

BASE / Lowest part of a column or a piece of furniture, one or a series of moldings.

BENTWOOD / A technique of forming strips of wood into curves by applying steam heat and placing the softened wood on molds.

BERGÈRE / Upholstered armchair with closed upholstered sides and an exposed wood frame.

BLOCKFRONT / Chest or cabinet with a three-part front, projecting on either side and recessed in the center; popular with 18th-century American (especially New England) cabinetmakers.

BOISERIE / French term for wood lining, associated with the elaborate paneling of 17th- and 18th-century French interiors.

BOMBÉ / An exaggerated swelling or flowing curve typical to commodes and chests of the Rococo.

BONHEUR DE JOUR / A small ladies' desk with drawers in a cabinet top, and usually a drop-down front.

BONNET TOP / Arched topmost section of a case piece, formed by a broken pediment shaped into opposing curves. Also called a hooded top.

BOSS / A projecting ornamental knob or sphere, Gothic in origin, located at the intersection of ribs in a vault or ceiling. Also, knob-like projections on cabinetry or metalwork.

BRACKET FOOT / Simple foot for case furniture, formed of two pieces of wood and joined at the corner.

BREAKFRONT / Large, three-section storage piece with shelves above and drawers below, whose central section projects slightly forward from either end.

BREWSTER CHAIR / An elaborate form of stick furniture with a framework of heavy turned posts and vertically turned spindles.

BROCADE / A rich fabric, usually silk, woven with a raised pattern, typically with gold or silver thread.

BROKEN PEDIMENT / A *pediment* with a break in its crown.

BRONZE DORÉ / French term for **gilded** bronze. See **ormolu**.

BUFFET / A cupboard or sideboard, used in the dining room.

BUN FOOT / Furniture foot, of Flemish origin, resembling a somewhat flattened sphere.

BUREAU / Desk or writing table that was originally covered with fabric for use as a writing surface.

BUREAU À CYLINDRE / Rolltop desk that closes to cover both the interior and writing surface.

BUREAU PLAT / Flat writing table or desk, usually with a leather-covered top surface.

BURL / Growth in the bole or root of a tree, producing highly figured decorative veneer.

BUTTERFLY TABLE / Small drop-leaf table with leaves supported by a swinging bracket.

CABINETMAKER / A skilled artisan who makes fine furniture.

CABOCHON / A round or oval smooth-surfaced polished stone.

CABRIOLE LEG / Furniture leg or support shaped in a double curve, composed of a regularized animal's leg, including knee, ankle, and foot.

CAD / Acronym for computer-aided design.

CAMELBACK / A double-curved sofa back (also serpentine back).

CAMEO GLASS / Two layers of glass, each of a different color, with the top layer carved away to reveal a pattern, which then projects from the surface in relief.

CANAPÉ / A 17th-century two-seater couch covered with a canopy. The term continued to be applied to small sofas without canopies.

CANOPY / Fabric covering over a bed or throne and suspended from a wall or ceiling.

CANTERBURY / A small music stand partitioned to hold sheets of music; also used to hold plates and cutlery.

CANTILEVER / A horizontal projection supported only at one end: in a chair, one without legs, supported by a single bent element.

CARYATID / Sculpted female figure used in classical architecture instead of a column for support. Male figures are termed atlantes.

CASE PIECE / Item of furniture to store or hold objects.

CASEMENT / Window hinged at the side to open like a door; also a plain, sheer fabric used as for curtains.

CASTING / Process of metalworking that involves melting the raw materials and pouring them into a mold to achieve a specific shape. The finished object is a casting.

CASSAPANCA / Italian wooden bench or settee formed by adding arms and back to a chest.

CASSONE / Italian chest, typically richly adorned with paint, carvings, or inlaid decoration.

CHAISE LONGUE / A long chair for reclining that is upholstered and supported by additional legs.

CHANDELIER / Hanging light fixture suspended from the ceiling, derived from the French term for candlestick.

CHEST OF DRAWERS / A case piece completely fitted with drawers.

CHEST ON CHEST / A chest of drawers in two sections, one placed on top of the other.

CHESTERFIELD / Overstuffed couch with no exposed woodwork.

CHINOISERIE / European adaptation of Chinese ornamental motifs.

CHINTZ / A fine cloth with designs printed by blocks, copper plates, screens, or rollers, and usually calendered or glazed.

CHIP CARVING / Carving in low relief, using chisels and gouges to create simple, mostly geometric motifs. Associated with early American Colonial furniture, also 17th-century English.

CLUB FOOT / Foot in the shape of the head of a club.

COCKFIGHT CHAIR / Chair with a narrow back with wings. During the 18th century, gentlemen at cockfights straddled the seat, facing the narrow back, and kept score on an adjustable easel.

COFFER / An ornamental panel sunk into a ceiling or soffit, usually square but sometimes polygonal.

COLONNADE / A row of columns, supporting a horizontal lintel.

COLONETTE / A miniature column, often used in clusters as a table support.

COMB BACK / Windsor chair back where several spindles extend above the main back in imitation of old-fashioned high combs.

COMMODE / A chest of drawers or cabinet, typically low with two or three drawers.

COMPASS SEAT / A round chair seat.

CONNECTICUT CHEST / New England chest ornamented with three carved panels and split spindles. Used extensively throughout the northern colonies as a dower chest and for storage.

CONSOLE TABLE / A side table affixed to the wall, supported by scroll-shaped legs that bracket together at their base.

CORNICE / Projecting element on top of an entablature; also used directly below the ceiling as wall ornament. On windows, a decorative element over curtains or draperies, wood or fabric-covered, similar to **lambrequin**, **pelmet**, or **valance**.

CORINTHIAN / The slimmest and most elaborate of the Greek classical **orders**, consisting of **base** on a **plinth**, fluted **shaft**, and **capital** distinguished by two rows of **acanthus** leaves, and four small volutes. The height of the column is ten times the diameter of the shaft.

COURT CUPBOARD / A low cupboard or a double cupboard, usually on legs, used for display and service.

COVE MOLDING / Molding from ceiling to wall in a concave downward curve.

CREDENZA / Serving table with a cupboard below the surface. Originally an Italian term for a credence, a Gothic sideboard or side table.

CREST RAIL / The top rail of a piece of furniture, generally referring to a chair.

CREWEL / Type of crochet embroidery using wool and varied stitches to form a design, usually on a linen or cotton fabric.

CURULE LEG / An X-shaped leg derived from a classic Roman chair design.

DADO / Lower portion of a wall, usually separated by a strip of molding.

DAMASK / A firm, lustrous, patterned fabric of silk, wool, linen, cotton, or synthetic fibers formed with a jacquard weave.

DELFT / Tin-glazed ceramics first produced in Delft, Holland, emulating Chinese porcelain. Generally blue and white, but also in other colors. Similar to faience and majolica.

DEMILUNE / A table top or chest that is half-round in plan.

DORIC / The oldest and simplest classical **order** distinguished by its lack of **base**, thick and broadly fluted **shaft**, and undecorated **capital**. The height of the column is eight times the diameter of the shaft.

DRESSER / Low chest of drawers of cupboard, with a mirror above, for the storage of clothing. Also a sideboard or buffet for the storage and display of eating utensils.

DROP-LEAF / Hinged flap or leaf on a table that enlarges the table when raised.

DUCHESSE BRISÉ / French, an upholstered chaise with separate footrest element.

ÉBENISTE / French term, originally for cabinet workers of the French Renaissance who specialized in furniture made of ebony glued onto blackened pearwood. Later used to refer to those cabinetmakers who specialized in working with fine veneers.

EGG-AND-DART / A decorative molding composed of an alternating pattern of round and downward-pointing elements.

EMBOSSING / Technique of working metal by hammering from the reverse side to produce a relief pattern.

ENAMEL / Glaze bonded to a metal or ceramic surface by heat. After firing, the glaze forms an opaque or translucent substance, which is fixed to the ground. Also refers to paint with a similarly glossy finish.

ENFILADE / A series of rooms whose doorways align, providing an uninterrupted vista.

ENTABLATURE / The entire horizontal section of material carried on columns consisting of the **architrave**, **frieze**, and **cornice**.

ESCUTCHEON / A shield with a heraldic device. In furniture, the decorative metal plate around a keyhole, pull, or doorknob.

ÉTAGÉRE / Open shelf unit, hanging or standing.

FANBACK CHAIR / Radiating design of a fan with flaring spindles and curved top rail.

FARTHINGDALE / An armless chair with an especially large seat that allows the large farthingdale skirts of Elizabethan fashion to completely spread out.

FAUTEUIL / French upholstered armchair with open sides.

FESTOON / A design imitating a loop of drapery, usually depicting fruit and flowers. See **garland** and **swag**.

FIDDLE-BACK CHAIR / Chair back with a splat that resembles a violin.

FILIGREE / Delicate, lace-like ornamental work, usually in metal.

FINIAL / The terminating element projecting from a pediment, post, or downward from the apron of a case piece, often in the shape of an urn, spiral, flame, or knob.

FLAP TABLE / English term for a drop-leaf table.

FLUTING / Shallow, vertical grooves set parallel to each other, especially on the shaft of a column and furniture supports.

FRET / A band of horizontal and vertical lines that form a geometric pattern or border motif.

FRIEZE / The central horizontal member of an **entablature**. Also the decorative band or strip beneath the **cornice** of an interior wall. It may be carved, painted, fabric, or wallpaper.

GADROONING / A decorative pattern formed with a series of convex ridges. Seen on silver hollowware and edges of furniture.

GATE-LEG TABLE / A table with hinged leaves supported by swinging its leg(s) out.

GESSO / Plaster mixture for molded relief decoration, often applied to wood or other surfaces and painting or **gilding**.

GILDING / The application of gold-leaf or gold pigment to an object of a different medium.

GIRANDÔLE / A wall sconce with multi-branched candleholders whose back-plate is fixed to the wall.

GOBELINS / French workshops established to supply tapestries, furniture, and decorative objects to the court of Louis XIV.

GROTESQUE / Classical ornament incorporating animals, figures, fruits, and plants that are all intertwined. Named after ancient Roman decorations discovered during the Renaissance.

GUÉRIDON / A small ornamental stand or **pedestal**.

GUILLOCHE / A continuous decorative band composed of interlacing circles.

HADLEY CHEST (ALSO CALLED CONNECTICUT CHEST) / Rectangular chest with a hinged top standing on short legs formed by a continuation of the stiles. The front has three sunken panels with one or more drawers below.

HIGHBOY / American variant on the English tallboy. Chest of drawers supported by a stand or a table-like base fitted with drawers.

HISTORICISM / The practice of using historic forms in design.

HOOPBACK CHAIR / Uprights and top rail formed a continuous rail curve.

HUTCH / Chest for the storage of food or clothes, from the French *huche*.

INCISED / Decoration that is deeply cut or carved, as differentiated from relief decoration.

INGLENOOK / A recessed seating area by a fire or hearth, with benches on either side. Associated with Arts and Crafts interiors.

INJECTION MOLDING / A manufacturing process for producing parts by injecting a material into a mold. A variety of materials can be used, including metals, glasses, and thermoplastic polymers.

INTARSIA / Elaborate decoration created with inlay using different types of wood set into wood, a process developed in the Renaissance.

IONIC / The Classical **order** distinguished by tapering, **fluted** columns, and bold **volutes** on the **capital**. The height of the column is nine times the diameter of the shaft.

JACQUARD WEAVE / A textile woven on a type of loom created by Joseph-Marie Jacquard in the early 19th century. The textiles are often constructed with intricate, multicolored patterns. Examples include damasks, tapestries, and brocades.

JAPANNING / A finishing process popular in the 18th century in imitation of Japanese lacquerwork. Furniture and metalwork were enameled with colored shellac, and the decoration was in relief, colored with paint, and gilded.

JOINER / Artisan who builds by simple joining of pieces of wood; less skilled than a carpenter or cabinetmaker.

KLISMOS / An ancient Greek chair with a deep top **rail** curving forward from the back and curved, splayed-out legs. Often imitated in 19th-century classical revivals, particularly Empire, Regency, and American Empire.

KNEE / The upper, convex curve or bulge of a cabriole leg.

KNEEHOLE DESK / A desk with a central, open space for leg room that is located under the writing surface and on either side of drawers.

LACQUER / An Asian varnish made from a tree sap indigenous to China and Japan.

LADDER-BACK / A tall-backed chair with several horizontal slats between the posts.

LAMBREQUIN / Stiff, flat **valances** with decoratively shaped lower edges often descending at either side. Also **pelmet**.

LAMINATION / A technique for manufacturing a material in multiple layers with the use of heat, pressure, welding, or adhesives. The final composite material will have improved strength and stability because of the use of different materials.

LED / Acronym for light-emitting diode, an electronic device that emits light when an electric current passes through it.

LOVESEAT / Double chair or small sofa.

LOWBOY / Double chest or table with drawers; companion piece to a highboy.

MANTELPIECE / The framework surrounding a fireplace, generally in wood or stone, often treated as a decorative statement in an interior.

MARCHAND-MERCIER / Both a merchant and design-director who commissioned and sold furniture within the parisian guild system in the 18th century.

MARLBOROUGH LEG / A straight-grooved furniture leg with a block as a foot. Used in English and American furniture, but most associated with late Chippendale designs.

MARQUETRY / A decorative pattern formed from different pieces of thin wood veneer, or occasionally other materials, and applied as a single sheet to the surface of furniture. The process replaced **intarsia** by the 18th century.

MARQUISE / French term for a small **canapé** or large chair for two people; a type of **settee**.

MENUSIER / French term for a craftsperson who made furniture, mostly chairs, sofas, benches, tables, or other furniture from solid pieces of wood. The menusier practiced joinery and carving, as differentiated from the veneer work of the **ébeniste**.

MOIRÉ / Fabric with a waved or watered effect created by pressing the fabric between engraved cylinders, which emboss grained designs onto the material.

MOTION CAPTURE / The process of recording the movement of objects or people for validation of computer vision and robotics. It is used to translate the movement of objects and people in the real world to information that can be rendered by a computer.

MULLION / An upright bar that vertically divides a window or other opening.

OGEE ARCH / A pointed arch formed by two reversed curves.

ORDER / The basis of classical architecture, the orders are composed of a column, with or without **base** or **capital**, supporting an **entablature**. The Greek orders are the **Doric**, **Ionic**, and **Corinthian**. The Romans added the Tuscan and Composite.

ORMOLU / French term for **gilt bronze**. See also **bronze doré**.

OTTOMAN / Upholstered bench or seat with neither arms nor back.

PAD FOOT / A club foot that rests on a disc.

PALLADIAN WINDOW / Window in three sections, divided by pilasters, with the center section an arched semicircular cornice and the sides straight-topped.

PARCEL GILT / A partially **gilded** portion of a surface, often done with stencils.

PARQUETRY / Small pieces of colored hardwood assembled into a geometric pattern for flooring.

PEDIMENT / The triangular gable conforming to the slope of the roof. Term also used to describe similar ornamental motif applied above windows, doors, and on furniture. Variations on the standard form include the broken and scrolled pediments.

PELMET / See **lambrequin**.

PEMBROKE / Small rectangular drop-leaf table with a drawer.

PIECRUST TABLE / A round **pedestal** table with the raised edge of the top surface carved in scallops resembling the crimped edge of a pie. See in English and American furniture.

PIER GLASS / Tall mirror originally designed to hang on a pier, between two windows. Now any wall mirror used over a console table.

PIER TABLE / Side table designed to stand against a pier, a column-like section of masonry, in the space between two windows. Now refers to a console-type table used beneath a pier glass.

PIETRA DURA / An Italian Renaissance mosaic inlay of marbles and assorted semiprecious stones.

PILASTER / Vertical cross-section of a column, flat-faced and projecting from a wall, or carved as ornament on furniture, usually depicting the characteristics and elements of a classic column.

PLASTIC / A material made from any of a wide range of synthetic or semisynthetic organic solids that are moldable. They are usually synthetic, most commonly derived from petrochemicals, but many are partially derived from naturally occurring polymers.

PLINTH / Square portion at the **base** of a column. Also the platform-like, solid base section used in place of legs on case furniture.

POLYCHROMY / Surface design of many colors.

POLYESTER / A synthetic resin, mainly used to make synthetic textile fibers.

PORCELAIN / Vitrified, white, translucent **ceramic** made with kaolin clay, fired at an extremely high temperature. Desirable for its lustrous glaze and imperviousness to moisture. Made in China from the 9th century; first European version developed in Germany in the early 18th century.

PORTIERES / Curtains or draperies used in a doorway or arch, in place of a door.

POTTERY / General term for objects made of clay hardened by firing in a kiln. See **ceramics**.

PRESS / A cupboard or armoire for the storage of linens or clothing.

RAIL / Structural horizontal band of a piece of furniture, such as a top rail.

REEDING / Narrow, convex molding in parallel strips divided by grooves.

RELIEF / Carved or applied ornament, projecting above the level of a surface.

RINCEAU / Decorative scroll and leaf ornament, usually horizontal and symmetrical, used on walls or paneling. Similar to **arabesque**.

ROTUNDA / A round hall, topped by a dome, usually in the center of a building.

SABOT / French term for the decorative metal covering used for the feet of wood furniture.

SAVONNERIE / Prestigious French manufactory of wool and silk knotted-pile carpet, established in the 17th century in a former soap factory in Paris.

SCAGLIOLA / Material composed of plaster and marble chips, used since antiquity to imitate marble.

SCONCE / A wall bracket for mounting a light source.

SCREEN PRINTING / A technique for printing text, images, or patterns that uses a woven mesh to support an ink-blocking stencil to apply ink onto a substrate, such as a textile.

SCROLL FOOT / Flattened scroll at the base of a cabriole leg.

SCROLL PEDIMENT / A **broken pediment** with each end shaped in the form of a reverse curve and terminating in an ornamental scroll.

SEAWEED MARQUETRY / Veneering in pattern of leaves and botanical forms, popular in English William and Mary furniture.

SÉCRETAIRE À ABATTANT / French term for a desk with a vertical fall front enclosing drawers and pigeonholes. It will generally have doors above the fall front, and drawers below.

SECRETARY / Desk with shelves located below the writing surface and shelves above.

SELECTIVE LASER SINTERING (SLS) / An additive manufacturing technique using a laser as power source, working from a 3D model, to sinter powdered material (usually metal), making it coalesce into a solid mass.

SEMAINIER / Tall bedroom chest with seven drawers, which were originally used for each day of the week.

SERPENTINE / The juxtaposition of concave and convex forms to create a sinuous line.

SETTEE / Derived from the settle, it is composed of two or more engaged armchairs.

SETTLE / Wood bench with arms and flat back for two or more people.

SHAFT / The body or trunk of a column extending from the top of the **base** to the bottom of the **capital**.

SHAGREEN / Sharkskin, untanned with granular surface and greenish in color.

SHIELD BACK CHAIR / Open chair back that resembles the shape of a shield.

SIDEBOARD / A table with wide central drawers flanked by additional drawers or cupboards intended for dining room service.

SPINDLE / Long, slim length of **turned** wood, varied with swellings or turned moldings.

SPLAT / The central, vertical panel of a chair back that reaches from the chair's seat to the top rail.

STAINLESS STEEL / A steel alloy with a minimum of 10.5 percent chromium content by mass, which prevents the steel from rust, stain, or corrosion to which ordinary steel is subject.

STILE / Structural, vertical bands in the framework of a piece of furniture.

STRETCHER / Horizontal crosspiece that links furniture legs to provide support.

SWAG / Fabric draped between two supports.

TABOURET / A low, upholstered stool for sitting.

TALLBOY / Tall case piece, generally with seven or more drawers, divided by a cornice into two sections, with the lower section supported on raised legs. Composite of a chest set on a larger chest on legs. See **highboy**.

TALL CASE CLOCK / A pendulum floor clock with a tall case developed in England in the mid-17th century. Also called **grandfather clock**, popular in Colonial America.

TAMBOUR / French term for a flexible roll-over top, rolltop desk, or table. Also thin strips of wood adhered to canvas backing to form a flexible sheet to conceal storage areas.

TAPER LEG / A straight, rectangular furniture leg that narrows down evenly toward the foot.

TAPESTRY / A thick textile fabric with a ribbed surface and pictures or designs woven in during the manufacturing process, used as upholstery or wall hangings.

TILT-TOP / Table top attached to the base with a hinge that allows for the top to swing into a vertical position.

TOILE / Linen or cotton canvas-like fabric, usually white or off-white, printed with scenic designs in one color. Toile de Jouy is the best-known of this type, made in Jouy-en-Josas, France.

TORCHÈRE / A stand for a candle or lamp that casts light upward.

TRABEATED / Architecture based on a post-and-lintel, rather than an arcuated, system.

TRIPOD / A three-legged pedestal table.

TURNING / Decorative or structural member produced by rotating wood on a lathe and shaping it into forms with cutting tools.

VALANCE / A horizontal element of fabric or other materials, hung across the top of windows, doors, or bed hangings, generally to conceal the top of curtains or draperies. See **lambrequin** or **pelmet**.

VAULT / Roof constructed using the arch as its basis. Variants are barrel vault, groin vault, and ribbed vault.

VELOUR / A plush, closely woven fabric resembling velvet. It is usually made from cotton but can also be made of synthetic materials such as polyester.

VENEER / A very thin layer of decorative wood, or occasionally other material, applied to the surface of a lesser material. Wood veneers are obtained by slicing the vertical section of a log to produce a series of sheets with identical, figured grain, which may then be used to create ornamental patterns on case furniture or table tops.

VITRINE / A display cabinet with a glass front or door.

VOLUTE / A scroll or spiral, shaped like a ram's horn, found on an **ionic** column, or used as a decorative motif on furniture.

WAINSCOT / Wood paneling that covers the dado level of the wall.

WAINSCOT CHAIR / Named for its similarity to a wainscot wall, its panel splat is typically carved or inlaid. With an especially high seat, a footstool is a usual accompaniment.

WARP / The threads that run lengthwise on a loom; the vertical threads of a fabric.

WEFT / The threads that run crosswise from selvage to selvage, and are woven in and out of the **warp** threads by a shuttle or bobbin. Also called filler threads.

WICKER / Woven fibers of rattan, bamboo, or other materials used to form furniture.

WHEEL-BACK CHAIR / Chair back composed of spokes radiating from the center in imitation of a wheel.

WINDSOR CHAIR / Chair developed in 18th-century England with **spindle** back, shaped seat, and turned, canted legs. Popular in 18th- and 19th-century America, where variations include fan-back, bow-back, comb-back, and hoop-back designs.

WING CHAIR / A high-backed, upholstered easy chair with wings or ears on either side of the chair back.

WOODBLOCK/WOODCUT PRINTING / A technique for printing text, images, or patterns using a carved woodblock.

WROUGHT IRON / A tough, malleable form of iron alloy (containing very little carbon) that is suitable for forging or rolling rather than casting.

YOKE BACK / A cross-bar in the form of two S-curves, resembling an oxen yoke, used for the top rail of a chair back.

Further Reading

General and Reference

Aaronson, Joseph. *Encyclopedia of Furniture*, 3rd ed. New York: Potter Style, 1961.

Abercrombie, Stanley, et al. *Interior Design and Decoration*, 6th ed. Upper Saddle River, NJ: Prentice Hall, 2008.

Banham, Joanna, ed. *Encyclopedia of Interior Design*, 2 vols. Chicago and London: Fitzroy Dearborn, 1997.

Blakemore, Robbie. *A History of Interior Design and Furniture from Ancient Egypt to Nineteenth-Century Europe*. New York: Wiley, 1997.

Boger, Louise Ade. *The Complete Guide to Furniture Styles*, revised ed. Prospect Heights, IL: Waveland Press, 1997.

Boyce, Charles. *Dictionary of Furniture*, 3rd ed. New York: Skyhorse Publishing, 2014.

Byers, Mel. *The Design Encyclopedia*. London: Laurence King, 2004.

Calloway, Stephen, et al. *Elements of Style: An Encyclopedia of Domestic Architectural Detail*. Richmond Hill, Ontario: Firefly Books, 2012.

Campbell, Gordon. *The Grove Encyclopedia of Decorative Arts*. New York: Oxford University Press, 2006.

Crochet, Treena. *Designer's Guide to Furniture Styles*, 2nd ed. Upper Saddle River, NJ: Prentice Hall, 2003.

Fazio, Michael, et al. *World History of Architecture*. London: Laurence King, 2008.

Ferebee, Ann, et al. *A History of Design from the Victorian Era to the Present: A Survey of the Modern Style in Architecture, Interior Design, Industrial Design, Graphic Design, and Photography*, 2nd ed. New York: W. W. Norton, 2011.

Gottfried, Herbert, et al. *American Vernacular Buildings and Interiors, 1870–1960*. New York: W.W. Norton, 2009.

Gympel, Jan. *The Story of Architecture: From Antiquity to the Present.* Berlin: H. F. Ullmann, 2013.

Harwood, Buie, et al. *Architecture and Interior Design: An Integrated History to the Present*. Upper Saddle River, NJ: Prentice Hall, 2012.

Hinchman, Mark. *The Fairchild Books Dictionary of Interior Design*, 3rd ed. New York: Fairchild Books, 2014.

Hinchman, Mark. *History of Furniture: A Global View.* New York: Fairchild Books, 2009.

Jones, Owen. *The Grammar of Ornament: Illustrated by Examples from Various Styles of Ornament*. New York: DK Publishing, 2001.

Ireland, Jeannie. *History of Interior Design*. New York: Fairchild Books, 2009.

Kirkham, Pat, and Susan Weber. *History of Design: Decorative Arts & Material Culture, 1400–2000*. New York: Bard Graduate Center for Studies in the Decorative Arts, Design & Culture.

Morley, John. *The History of Furniture: Twenty-Five Centuries of Style and Design in the Western Tradition*. Boston: Little, Brown and Co., 1999.

Peck, Amelia, ed. *Period Rooms in The Metropolitan Museum of Art*. New York: The Metropolitan Museum of Art, 1996.

Pile, John F., and Judith Gura. *A History of Interior Design*, 4th ed. Hoboken, NJ: Wiley, 2014.

Praz, Mario. *An Illustrated History of Interior Decoration from Pompeii to Art Nouveau*. London: Thames and Hudson, 1987.

Raizman, David. *History of Modern Design*, 2nd ed. Upper Saddle River, NJ: Prentice Hall, 2011.

Riley, Noel, and Patricia Bayer. *The Elements of Design: A Practical Encyclopedia of the Decorative Arts from the Renaissance to the Present*. New York: Free Press, 2003.

Sossons, Adrianna Boidi. *Furniture: From Rococo to Art Deco*. Köln, Germany: Evergreen, 2000.

Thornton, Peter. *Authentic Decor: The Domestic Interior 1620–1920*, revised ed. London: Seven Dials, 2001.

Wilk, Christopher, ed. *Western Furniture: 1350 to the Present Day, in the Victoria and Albert Museum London*. London: Cross River Press, 1996.

Theory

Frank, Isabelle, ed. *The Theory of Decorative Art: An Anthology of European and American Writings*. New Haven, CT: Yale University Press, 2000.

Giedeon, Siegfried. *Mechanization Takes Command: A Contribution to Anonymous History*. Minneapolis: University of Minnesota Press, 2014.

Pevsner, Nikolaus. *Pioneers of Modern Design: From William Morris to Walter Gropius*. Bath, England: Palazzo, 2011.

French Design, General

Bremer-David, Clarissa, ed. *Paris: Life & Luxury in the 18th Century.* Los Angeles, CA: Getty Trust Publications, 2011.

Brunhammer, Yvonne. *L' Art De Vivre: Decorative Arts and Design in France 1789–1989*. New York: Thames and Hudson, 1989.

Friedman, Joe. *Inside Paris: Discovering the Period Interiors of Paris*. New York: Rizzoli, 1990.

Kisluk-Grosheide, Danielle. *The Wrightsman Galleries for French Decorative Arts.* New York: The Metropolitan Museum of Art, 2010.

Peck, Amelia. *Period Rooms in the Metropolitan Museum of Art.* New York: The Metropolitan Museum of Art, 1996.

Pradere, Alexandre. *French Furniture Makers: The Art of the Ebeniste from Louis XIV to the Revolution*, Perran Wood, trans. Los Angeles: J. Paul Getty Museum, 1991.

Raymond, Pierre. *Masterpieces of Marquetry*, Brian Considine, trans. Los Angeles: J. Paul Getty Museum, 2001.

Verlet, Pierre. *French Furniture of the Eighteenth Century*. Charlottesville: University of Virginia Press, 1991.

Whitehead, John. *The French Interior in the Eighteenth Century*. New York: Dutton Studio Books, 1992.

Wilson, Gillian, et al. *French Furniture & Gilt Bronzes: Baroque & Regence*. Los Angeles: Getty Trust, 2008.

English Design, General

Beard, Geoffrey. *Upholsterers and Interior Furnishings in England, 1530–1840*. New Haven, CT: Yale University Press, 1997.

Bowett, Adam. *English Furniture 1680–1714: From Charles II to Queen Anne*. London: Antique Collectors' Club, 2002.

Gilbert, Christopher. *English Vernacular Furniture, 1750–1900*. New Haven, CT: Yale University Press, 1991.

Girouard, Mark. *The Victorian Country House*, revised ed. New Haven, CT: Yale University Press, 1979.

Gore, Allan. *The History of English Interiors*. London: Phaidon Press, 1995.

Musson, Jeremy. *The Drawing Room: English Country House Decoration*. New York: Rizzoli, 2014.

American Design, General

Axelrod, Alex, ed. *The Colonial Revival in America*. New York: W.W. Norton, 1985.

Fairbanks, Jonathan, and Elizabeth Bates. *American Furniture, 1620 to the Present*. New York: Marek, 1981.

Fitzgerald, Oscar P. *Four Centuries of American Furniture*, revised ed. Iola, WI: Krause Publications, 1995.

Greene, Jeffrey. *American Furniture of the Eighteenth Century: History, Technique, Structure*. Newton, CT: Taunton Press, 1996.

Montgomery, Charles F. *American Furniture: The Federal Period in the Henry Francis Du Pont Winterthur Museum*. Atglen, PA: Schiffer, 2001.

de Noailles Mahey, Edgar. *A Documentary History of American Interiors: From the Colonial Era to 1915*. New York: Simon & Schuster, 1986.

Peirce, Donald C., and Hope Alswang. *American Interiors, New England & the South: Period Rooms at the Brooklyn Museum*. Brooklyn, NY: Brooklyn Museum, 1983.

Sack, Albert. *The New Fine Points of Furniture: Early American*. New York: Crown, 1993.

Baroque Styles

Augard, Jean-Dominique, et al. *Andre-Charles Boulle: A New Style for Europe*. Paris: Somogy, 2013.

Baarsen, Reiner, et al. *Courts and Colonies: The William and Mary Style in Holland, England, and America*. Seattle: University of Washington Press, 1989.

Cooper, Nicholas. *Houses of the Gentry, 1480–1680*. New Haven, CT: Yale University Press, 2000.

Garrett, Wendell. *American Colonial: Puritan Simplicity to Georgian Grace*. New York: Monacelli Press, 1998.

Gruber, Alan, ed. *The History of Decorative Arts: Classicism and the Baroque in Europe*, John Goodman, trans. New York: Abbeville Press, 1996.

Mowl, Timothy. *Elizabethan and Jacobean Style*. London: Phaidon Press, 1993.

Rococo Styles

Boyer, Marie-France. *Really Rural: Authentic French Country Interiors*, Veronique Wood and John Wood, trans. London: Thames & Hudson, 1997.

Chippendale, Thomas. *The Gentleman and Cabinet-Maker's Director*. New York: Dover Publications, 1966.

Coleridge, Anthony. *Chippendale Furniture: The Work of Thomas Chippendale and His Contemporaries in the Rococo Taste: Vile, Cobb, Langlois, Channon, Hallett, Ince and Mayhew, Lock, Johnson and Others, circa 1745–1765*. London: Faber and Faber, 1968.

Downs, Joseph. *American Furniture: Queen Anne and Chippendale Periods in the Henry Francis Du Pont Winterthur Museum*. Atglen, PA: Schiffer, 2001.

Girouard, Mark. *Life in the French Country House*. London: Cassell & Co., 2000.

Heckscher, Morrison H. *American Furniture in the Metropolitan Museum of Art, Late Colonial Period: The Queen Anne and Chippendale Styles*. New York: The Metropolitan Museum of Art, 1986.

Parissien, Steven. *Palladian Style*. London: Phaidon Press, 1999.

Scott, Katie. *The Rococo Interior: Decoration and Social Spaces in Early Eighteenth-Century Paris*. New Haven, CT: Yale University Press, 1995.

Vandal, Norman L. *Queen Anne Furniture: History, Design, and Construction*. Newton, CT: Taunton Press, 1990.

Neoclassical Styles

Chase, Linda, and Karl Kemp. *The World of Biedermeier*. London: Thames and Hudson, 2001.

Deschamps, Madeleine. *Empire*. New York: Abbeville Press, 1994.

Fontaine, Pierre-Françoise-Léonard, and Charles Percier. *Receuil de décorations interieurs*. Paris, 1801. Reprinted, New York: Dover Publications, 1981.

Garrett, Wendell. *Classic America: The Federal Style and Beyond*. New York: Rizzoli, 1992.

Geck, Francis. *French Interiors and Furniture, Vol. 9: The Period of Louis XVI*. Roseville, MI: Stureck Educational Services, 1996.

Gere, Charlotte. *Nineteenth-Century Decoration: The Art of the Interior*. New York: Harry N. Abrams, 1989.

Harris, Eileen. *The Genius of Robert Adam: His Interiors*. New Haven, CT: Yale University Press, 2001.

Heckscher, Morrison H. *American Furniture in the Metropolitan Museum of Art, Late Colonial Period*. New York: The Metropolitan Museum of Art, 1986.

Hepplewhite, George. *The Cabinet-Maker and Upholsterer's Guide*. London, 1786. Reprinted, New York: Dover Publications, 1969.

Kenny, Peter. *Duncan Phyfe: Master Cabinet-maker in New York*. New York: The Metropolitan Museum of Art, 2011.

Montgomery, Charles F., and Gilbert Ask. *American Furniture, the Federal Period in the Henry Francis Du Pont Winterthur Museum*. Atglen, PA: Schiffer, 2001.

Morley, John. *Regency Design, 1790–1840*. New York: Harry N. Abrams, 1993.

Parissien, Steven. *Regency Style*. London: Phaidon Press, 1992.

Roberts, Hugh. *For the King's Pleasure: The Furnishings and Decoration of George IV's Apartments at Windsor Castle*. London: Thames and Hudson, 2002.

Sheraton, Thomas. *The Cabinet-Maker and Upholsterer's Drawing Book*. London, 1783. Reprinted, New York: Dover Publications, 1972.

Vincent, Nancy. *Duncan Phyfe and the English Regency, 1795–1830*. New York: Dover Publications, 1980.

Voorsanger, Catherine Hoover, ed. *Art and the Empire City: New York, 1825–1861*. New Haven, CT: Yale University Press, 2000.

Watkin, David, and Philip Hewat-Jaboor. *Thomas Hope: Regency Designer*. New Haven, CT: Yale University Press, 2008.

Wilkie, Angus. *Biedermeier*. New York: Abbeville Press, 1987.

19th-Century Revivals, the Aesthetic Movement

Aldrich, Megan. *Gothic Revival*. London: Phaidon, 1997.

Banham, Joanna, et al. *Victorian Interior Design*. London: Cassell, 1991.

Burke, Doreen Bolger, et al., eds. *In Pursuit of Beauty: Americans and the Aesthetic Movement*. New York: Rizzoli, 1986.

Cook, Clarence. *The House Beautiful: An Unabridged Reprint of the Classic Victorian Stylebook*. New York: Dover Publications, 1995.

Cooper, Jeremy. *Victorian and Edwardian Décor: From Gothic Revival to Art Nouveau*. New York: Abbeville Press, 1987.

Cooper, Wendy A. *Classical Taste in America, 1800–1840*. New York: Abbeville Press, 1993.

Eastlake, Charles L. *Hints on Household Taste: The Classic Handbook of Victorian Interior Decoration*. New York: Dover Publications, 1986.

Edwards, Clive D. *Victorian Furniture: Technology and Design*. New York: St. Martin's Press, 1993.

Frankel, Lory. *Herter Brothers: Furniture and Interiors for a Gilded Age*. New York: Harry N. Abrams, 1994.

Gere, Charlotte, et al. *Nineteenth-Century Design: From Pugin to Mackintosh*. New York: Harry N. Abrams, 2000.

Heckscher, Morrison H. *American Rococo, 1750–1775: Elegance in Ornament*. New York: Harry N. Abrams, 1992.

Kirk, John T. *The Shaker World: Art, Life, Belief*. New York: Harry N. Abrams, 1997.

Lambourne, Lionel. *The Aesthetic Movement*. London: Phaidon Press, 1996.

Mahoney, Kathleen. *Gothic Style: Architecture and Interiors from the Eighteenth Century to the Present*. New York: Harry N. Abrams, 1995.

Pugin, Augustus Welby Northmore, et al., eds. *A.W.N. Pugin: Master of Gothic Revival*. New Haven, CT: Yale University Press, 1996.

Rieman, Timothy D., and Jean M. Burks. *The Complete Book of Shaker Furniture*. New York: Harry N. Abrams, 1993.

Smith, Alison, et al., ed. *Pre-Raphaelites: Victorian Art and Design.* New Haven, CT: Yale University Press, 2013.

Wilson, Richard Guy, et al. *The American Renaissance, 1876–1917*. Brooklyn, NY: Brooklyn Museum, 1979.

The Mysterious East

Handler, Sarah. *Austere Luminosity of Chinese Classical Furniture.* Berkeley: University of California Press, 2001.

Hattstein, Markus, and Peter Delius. *Islam: Art & Architecture.* Berlin: H.F. Ullmann, 2012.

Nishikawa, Takeshi. *Katsura: A Princely Retreat*. Tokyo: Kodansha International, 1977.

Arts & Crafts, Art Nouveau, Glasgow Style

Anscombe, Isabelle. *Arts and Crafts Style*. London: Phaidon Press, 1996.

Arwas, Victor. *Art Nouveau: The French Aesthetic*. London: Andreas Papadakis, 2002.

Cathers, David. *Gustav Stickley*. London: Phaidon Press, 2003.

Duncan, Alastair. *Art Nouveau*. London: Thames and Hudson, 1994.

Duncan, Alastair, Martin Eidelberg, and Neil Harris. *Masterworks of Louis Comfort Tiffany*. New York: Harry N. Abrams, 1998.

Greenhalgh, Paul, ed. *Art Nouveau, 1890–1914*. New York: Harry N. Abrams, 2000.

Heinz, Thomas A. *Frank Lloyd Wright Interiors and Furniture*. London: Academy Editions, 1994.

Kaplan, Wendy, ed. *Charles Rennie Mackintosh*. New York: Abbeville Press, 1996.

Kaplan, Wendy, et al. *The Art That is Life: The Arts and Crafts Movement in America, 1875–1920*. Boston: Bulfinch Press, 1987.

Komanecky, Michael, ed. *The Shakers: From Mount Lebanon to the World.* New York: Skira Rizzoli, 2014.

Macaulay, James. *Charles Rennie Mackintosh: Life and Work*. New York: W. W. Norton, 2010.

Makinson, Randell L. *Greene and Greene: Architecture as a Fine Art, Furniture, and Related Designs*. Layton, UT: Gibbs Smith, 2001.

McCarthy, Fiona. *Anarchy and Beauty: William Morris and His Legacy.* New Haven, CT: Yale University Press, 2014.

McKean, John. *Charles Rennie Mackintosh: Architect, Artist, Icon*. Stillwater, MN: Voyageur Press, 2000.

Parray, Linda. *William Morris*. New York: Harry N. Abrams, 1996.

Sembach, Klaus-Jürgen. *Art Nouveau*. Köln, Germany: Taschen, 2007.

Volpe, Tod M., et al. *Treasures of the American Arts and Crafts Movement, 1890–1920*. New York: Harry N. Abrams, 1991.

20th-Century Design, General

Curtis, William J. R. *Modern Architecture Since 1990*, 3rd ed. London: Phaidon, 1996.

Duncan, Alastair. *Modernism: Modernist Design 1880–1940: The Norwest Collection, Norwest Corporation, Minneapolis*. Woodbridge, Suffolk, England: Antique Collectors' Club, 1998.

Eidelberg, Martin, ed. *Design 1935–1965: What Modern Was: Selections from the Lilian and David M. Stewart Collection*. New York: Harry N. Abrams, 2001.

Glancey, Jonathan. *Modern: Masters of the Twentieth-Century Interior*. New York: Rizzoli, 1999.

Fiell, Charlotte, and Peter Fiell. *Design of the Twentieth Century.* New York: Taschen, 1999.

Heisinger, Kathryn, and George Marcus. *Landmarks of Twentieth-Century Design: An Illustrated Handbook*. New York: Abbeville Press, 1993.

Massey, Anne. *Interior Design Since 1900*, 3rd ed. London: Thames and Hudson, 2008.

Sparke, Penny. *A Century of Design: Design Pioneers of the 20th Century*. Woodbury, NY: Barrons, 1998.

Woodham, Jonathan M. *Twentieth-Century Design*. Oxford, England: Oxford University Press, 1997.

Early Modernism, the International Style, the Bauhaus

Bergdoll, Barry, and Leah Dickerman. *Bauhaus 1919–1933.* New York: The Museum of Modern Art, 2009.

Brandstätte, Christian. *Wiener Werkstätte: Design in Vienna 1903–1932*. New York: Harry N. Abrams, 2000.

Cohen, Jean-Louis. *Ludwig Mies Van Der Rohe*. Basel, Switzerland: Birkhäuser, 2011.

Droste, Magdalena. *Bauhaus, 1919–1933*. Köln, Germany: Taschen, 2006.

Le Corbusier. *The Decorative Art of Today*, James I. Dunnell, trans. Cambridge, MA: MIT Press, 1987. First published as *L'Art décoratif d'aujourd'hui*. Paris: Editions G. Crès, 1925.

Macel, Otakar, Alexander Von Vegesack, and Marhias Remmele. *Marcel Breuer: Design and Architecture.* Weil am Rhein, Germany: Vitra Design Museum, 2013.

Marcus, George H. *Le Corbusier: Inside the Machine for Living*. New York: The Monacelli Press, 2000.

McLeod, Mary, ed. *Charlotte Perriand: An Art of Living*. New York: Harry N. Abrams, 2003.

Art Deco, Modernistic, Streamline Style, French Modernists

Arwas, Victor. *Art Deco*, revised ed. New York: Abradale Books, 2000.

Bayer, Patricia. *Art Deco Interiors: Decoration and Design Classics of the 1920s and 1930s.* London: Thames and Hudson, 1998.

Benton, Charlotte, and Tim Benton, eds. *Art Deco 1910–1939.* London: Victoria and Albert Publications, 2003.

Bony, Anne. *Furniture and Interiors of the 1940s.* Paris: Flammarion, 2003.

Bréon, Emmanuel, and Rosalind Pepall, eds. *Ruhlmann: Genius of Art Deco.* New York: The Metropolitan Museum of Art, 2004.

Brunhammer, Yvonne, and Suzanne Tise. *The Decorative Arts in France: Le Societé des Artistes Décorateurs, 1900–1942.* New York: Rizzoli, 1990.

Camard, Florence. *Ruhlmann.* New York: Rizzoli, 2011.

Clark, Robert J. *Design in America: The Cranbrook Vision, 1925–1950.* New York: Harry N. Abrams, 1984.

Cohen, Jean-Louis, ed. *Le Corbusier: An Atlas of Modern Landscapes.* New York: The Museum of Modern Art, 2013.

Constant, Caroline. *Eileen Gray.* London: Phaidon Press, 2000.

Duncan, Alastair. *Art Deco Complete: The Definitive Guide to the Decorative Arts of the 1920s and 1930s.* New York: Harry N. Abrams, 2009.

Goss, Jared. *French Art Deco.* New York: The Metropolitan Museum of Art, 2014.

Hillier, Bevis, and Stephen Escritt. *Art Deco Style.* London: Phaidon Press, 1997.

Pinchon, Jean-François. *Robert Mallet-Stevens: Architecture, Furniture, Interior Design.* Cambridge, MA: MIT Press, 1990.

Taylor, Brian B. *Pierre Chareau: Designer and Architect.* Köln, Germany: Taschen, 1998.

Troy, Nancy J. *Modernism and the Decorative Arts in France: Art Nouveau to Le Corbusier.* New Haven, CT: Yale University Press, 1991.

Wilk, Christopher, ed. *Modernism: Designing a New World.* London: V&A Publications, 2006.

Wilson, Richard Guy, et al. *The Machine Age in America, 1918–1941.* New York: Harry N. Abrams, 1987.

Wood, Ghislaine, ed. *Essential Art Deco.* Boston: Bulfinch Press, 2003.

Midcentury, Scandinavian, Italian Modern

Aav, Marianne, and Nina Stritzler-Levine. *Finnish Modern Design.* New Haven, CT: Yale University Press, 1998.

Albrecht, Donald, et al. *The Work of Charles and Ray Eames: A Legacy of Invention.* New York: Harry N. Abrams, 1997.

Bony, Anne. *Furniture and Interiors of the 1960s.* Paris: Flammarion, 2004.

Bosoni, Giampiero, and Paola Antonelli. *Italian Design.* New York: The Museum of Modern Art, 2008.

Bradbury, Dominic. *Midcentury Modern Complete.* London: Thames & Hudson, 2014.

Fiell, Charlotte, and Peter Fiell. *Scandinavian Design.* Köln, Germany: Taschen, 2003.

Fiell, Charlotte, and Peter Fiell. *Design of the 20th Century*. Köln, Germany: Taschen, 2012.

Fremdkörper Studio and Andrea Mehlhose. *Modern Furniture: 150 Years of Design*. Berlin: H. F. Ullmann, 2013.

Gura, Judith. *Sourcebook of Scandinavian Furniture*. New York: W. W. Norton, 2007.

Habegger, JerryIII, and Joseph H. Osman. *Sourcebook of Modern Furniture*, 3rd ed. New York: W. W. Norton, 2005.

Hanks, David, Anne Hoy, and Martin Eidelberg. *Design for Living: Furniture and Lighting, 1950–2000*. Paris/New York: Flammarion, 2000.

Heisinger, Kathryn B., and George H. Marcus. *Design Since 1945*. Philadelphia, PA: Philadelphia Museum of Art, 1983.

Jackson, Lesley. *Contemporary: Architecture and Interiors of the 1950s*. London: Phaidon Press, 1994.

Jackson, Lesley. *The Sixties*. London: Phaidon Press, 2000.

Labaco, Ronald T. *Sottsass: Architect and Designer*. New York: Merrill, 2006.

Lees-Maffei, Grace, and Kjetil Fallan, eds. *Made in Italy: Rethinking a Century of Italian Design*. London: Bloomsbury Academic, 2014.

Lutz, Brian. *Knoll, A Modernist Universe*. New York: Rizzoli, 2010.

Merkel, Jane. *Eero Saarinen*. New York: Phaidon, 2014.

Polano, Sergio. *Achille Castiglioni: Complete Works, 1938–2000*. Milan, Italy: Electa, 2001.

Smith, Elizabeth. *Case Study Houses*. Köln, Germany: Taschen, 2009.

Sparke, Penny. *Design in Italy: 1870 to the Present*. New York: Abbeville Press, 1990.

Postmodernism, Minimalism

Bangert, Albrecht, et al. *80s Style: Design of the Decade*. New York: Abbeville Press, 1990.

Collins, Michael, and Andreas Papadakis. *Post-modern Design*. London: Academy Editions, 1989.

Jencks, Charles. *The New Paradigm in Architecture: The Language of Postmodernism*, 7th ed. New Haven, CT: Yale University Press, 2002.

Miller, R. Craig, et al. *US Design: 1975–2000*. New York: Prestel, 2002.

Pawson, John. *Minimum*. London: Phaidon Press, 1998.

Radice, Barbara. *Memphis: Research, Experience, Results, Failure, and Successes of New Design*. New York: Rizzoli, 1985.

Sudjic, Dejan. *Shiro Kuramata*. New York: Phaidon, 2013.

Tasma-Anargyros, Sophie. *Andrée Putman*. Woodstock, NY: The Overlook Press, 1997.

Venturi, Robert. *Complexity and Contradiction in Architecture*. New York: The Museum of Modern Art, 2011.

Modern Made by Hand

Adamson, Jeremy. *The Furniture of Sam Maloof*. New York: W. W. Norton, 2001.

Nakashima, Mira. *Nature, Form, and Spirit: The Life and Legacy of George Nakashima*. New York: Harry N. Abrams, 2003.

Smith, Paul. *Objects for Use: Handmade by Design*. New York: Harry N. Abrams, 2001.

Williams, Gareth. *The Furniture Machine, Furniture Since 1990*. London: V&A Publications, 2006.

Contemporary Design

Antonelli, Paola, and Judith Benhamou-Huet. *Ron Arad.* New York: The Museum of Modern Art, 2009.

Bell, Jonathan. *21st Century House*. London: Laurence King Publishing, 2006.

Celant, Germano. *Zaha Hadid*. New York: Guggenheim Museum Publications, 2006.

Fiell, Charlotte, and Peter Fiell. *Designing the 21st Century*. Köln, Germany: Taschen, 2005.

Gura, Judith. *Design After Modernism: Furniture and Interiors 1970–2010*, New York: W. W. Norton, 2012.

Klanten, Robert, Sophie Lovell, and Birga Meyer, eds. *Furnish: Furniture and Interior Design for the 21st Century.* Berlin, Germany: Gestalten, 2007.

Koolhaas, Rem, and Veronique Patteeuw. *Considering Rem Koolhaas and the Office for Metropolitan Architecture*. Rotterdam, The Netherlands: NA Publishers, 2003.

Miller, R. Craig, et al. *European Design Since 1985: Shaping the New Century*. New York: Merrell, 2009.

Moxon, Siân. *Sustainability in Interior Design*. London: Laurence King Publishers, 2012.

Ragheb, J. Fiona, ed. *Frank Gehry, Architect*. New York: Guggenheim Museum Publications, 2001.

Rawsthorn, Alice. *Marc Newson*. London: Booth-Clibborn Editions, 2000.

Ross, Philip, and Jeremy Myerson. *21st Century Office*. New York: Rizzoli, 2003.

Shibata, Naomi. *Herzog & de Meuron, 2002–2006*. Tokyo: A+U Publishing, 2006.

Credits

7 © Andreas von Einsiedel / Alamy

8 Courtesy of Sotheby's, Inc. ©

9 Courtesy of Sotheby's, Inc. ©

9 Courtesy of Sotheby's, Inc. ©

10 Courtesy of Sotheby's, Inc. ©

10 Courtesy of Sotheby's, Inc. ©

11 © RMN-Grand Palais / Art Resource, NY

12 Courtesy of Prelle Et Cie S.A.

12 Courtesy of Prelle Et Cie S.A.

17 © The National Trust Photolibrary / Alamy

18 Courtesy of Hyde Park Antiques

18 Courtesy of Hyde Park Antiques

19 Courtesy of Hyde Park Antiques

19 Courtesy of Sotheby's, Inc. ©

19 Courtesy of Sotheby's, Inc. ©

20 Courtesy of Ronald Phillips Antiques

20 Courtesy of RubelliSpA

26 © Brenda Kean / Alamy

27 Courtesy of Sotheby's, Inc. ©

27 Courtesy of Bernard & S. Dean Levy, Inc./Ed Freeman

28 Courtesy of Pook and Pook Antiques

28 Courtesy of Sotheby's, Inc. ©

29 Courtesy of Box House Antiques

29 Courtesy of Bernard & S. Dean Levy, Inc./Ed Freeman

29 Courtesy of Sotheby's, Inc. ©

30 Courtesy of Prelle Et Cie S.A.

30 Courtesy of Brunschwig & Fils ®

37 Gianni DagliOrti / The Art Archive at Art Resource, NY

38 Gianni DagliOrti / The Art Archive at Art Resource, NY

39 Courtesy of Sotheby's, Inc. ©

39 Courtesy of Sotheby's, Inc. ©

40 Courtesy of Sotheby's, Inc. ©

40 Courtesy of Sotheby's, Inc. ©

41 Courtesy of Partridge Fine Arts

41 Courtesy of Partridge Fine Arts

41 Courtesy of Sotheby's, Inc. ©

42 Courtesy of Prelle Et Cie S.A.

42 Courtesy of Prelle Et Cie S.A.

42 Courtesy of Kravet®

47 National Trust Photo Library / Art Resource, NY

48 Courtesy of Hyde Park Antiques

49 Courtesy of Sotheby's, Inc. ©

49 Courtesy of Sotheby's, Inc. ©

50 Photo by DeAgostini/Getty Images

50 Courtesy of Sotheby's, Inc. ©

51 Art Resource, NY

52 Courtesy of Scalamandré

52 Courtesy of Courtesy of Rubelli Spa Spa Fabrics

57 Erich Lessing / Art Resource, NY

58 Courtesy of Hyde Park Antiques

58 Courtesy of Sotheby's, Inc. ©

59 Courtesy of Partridge Fine Arts

60 Courtesy of Hyde Park Antiques

60 Courtesy of Sotheby's, Inc. ©

61 Courtesy of Hyde Park Antiques

61 Courtesy of Partridge Fine Arts

62 © Arcaid Images / Alamy

65 © Arcaid Images / Alamy

66 Photo by: Universal History Archive / UIG via Getty Images

68 Courtesy of Scalamandré

68 Courtesy of Brunschwig & Fils ®

76 © Nathan Benn / Alamy

76 © Mira / Alamy

77 Courtesy of Bernard & S. Dean Levy, Inc./Ed Freeman

78 Art Resource, NY

79 Courtesy of Sotheby's, Inc. ©

79 Courtesy of Bernard & S. Dean Levy, Inc./Ed Freeman

80 Courtesy of Bernard & S. Dean Levy, Inc./Ed Freeman

80 Courtesy of Sotheby's, Inc. ©

81 Art Resource, NY

82 Courtesy of Pook and Pook Antiques

82 Courtesy of Sotheby's, Inc. ©

83 Courtesy of Bernard & S. Dean Levy, Inc./Ed Freeman

83 Courtesy of Bernard & S. Dean Levy, Inc./Ed Freeman

84 Courtesy of Prelle Et Cie S.A.

84 Courtesy of Scalamandré

89 © The Metropolitan Museum of Art. Image source: Art Resource, NY

90 Courtesy of Sotheby's, Inc. ©

90 Courtesy of Sotheby's, Inc. ©

91 Courtesy of Partridge Fine Arts

91 Courtesy of Partridge Fine Arts

92 Courtesy of Sotheby's, Inc. ©

93 Courtesy of Sotheby's, Inc. ©

94 Courtesy of Sotheby's, Inc. ©

95 Courtesy of Partridge Fine Arts

96 Courtesy of Prelle Et Cie S.A.

96 Courtesy of Prelle Et Cie S.A.

101 © BildarchivMonheim GmbH / Alamy

102 © Andreas von Einsiedel/ Corbis

115 Courtesy of Dover Publications

115 Courtesy of Dover Publications

105 © The National Trust Photolibrary / Alamy

106 Courtesy of Hyde Park Antiques

106 Courtesy of Hyde Park Antiques

107 Courtesy of Sotheby's, Inc. ©

108 Courtesy of Sotheby's, Inc. ©

109 Courtesy of Sotheby's, Inc. ©

109 Courtesy of Ronald Phillips Antiques

110 Courtesy of Ronald Phillips Antiques

110 Courtesy of Hyde Park Antiques

111 Courtesy of Sotheby's, Inc. ©

112 Courtesy of Hyde Park Antiques

113 Courtesy of Ronald Phillips Antiques

116 Courtesy of Rubelli Spa Spa Fabrics

116 Courtesy of Rubelli Spa Spa Fabrics

121 ridgeman-Giraudon / Art Resource, NY

122 Courtesy of Mallet

122 Courtesy of Sotheby's, Inc. ©

123 Courtesy of Sotheby's, Inc. ©

123 Courtesy of Sotheby's, Inc. ©

123 Courtesy of Sotheby's, Inc. ©

124 Courtesy of Sotheby's, Inc. ©

124 Erich Lessing / Art Resource, NY

125 Courtesy of Sotheby's, Inc. ©

126 Courtesy of Prelle Et Cie S.A.

126 Courtesy of Brunschwig & Fils®

131 © Arcaid Images / Alamy

132 Courtesy of Sotheby's, Inc. ©

133 Courtesy of Bernard & S. Dean Levy, Inc./Ed Freeman

133 Courtesy of Bernard & S. Dean Levy, Inc./Ed Freeman

134 Courtesy of Bernard & S. Dean Levy, Inc./Ed Freeman

134 Courtesy of Bernard & S. Dean Levy, Inc./Ed Freeman

135 Courtesy of Bernard & S. Dean Levy, Inc./Ed Freeman

135 Courtesy of Bernard & S. Dean Levy, Inc./Ed Freeman

136 Courtesy of Prelle Et Cie S.A.

141 © Heritage Image Partnership Ltd / Alamy

142 Courtesy of Hyde Park Antiques

142 Courtesy of Hyde Park Antiques

143 Courtesy of Sotheby's, Inc. ©

144 Courtesy of Ronald Phillips Antiques

145 Courtesy of Hyde Park Antiques

145 Courtesy of Box House Antiques

147 Erich Lessing / Art Resource, NY

148 Courtesy of Prelle Et Cie S.A.

153 Photo by Frank Moscati; Courtesy of Boscobel House and Gardens, Garrison, NY

154 Courtesy of Hirschl And Adler Antiques

154 Courtesy of Hirschl And Adler Antiques

155 Courtesy of Hirschl And Adler Antiques

155 Courtesy of Hirschl And Adler Antiques

155 Courtesy of Hirschl And Adler Antiques

156 Courtesy of Bernard & S. Dean Levy, Inc./Ed Freeman

156 Courtesy of Sotheby's, Inc. ©

157 Courtesy of Prelle Et Cie S.A.

164 © Andrew Holt / Alamy

167 © Blaine Harrington III / Alamy

168 Courtesy of Hirschl And Adler Antiques

169 Courtesy of Hirschl And Adler Antiques

169 Courtesy of Sotheby's, Inc. ©

172© BildarchivMonheim GmbH / Alamy

173 Courtesy of Associated Artists, LLC

174 Courtesy of Associated Artists, LLC

175 Courtesy of H. Blairman And Sons Ltd

176 Courtesy of H. Blairman And Sons Ltd

179 Art Resource

180 Courtesy of Sotheby's, Inc. ©

180 Courtesy of Associated Artists, LLC

181 Courtesy of Butchoff Antiques

181 Courtesy of Pook and Pook Antiques

184 © Arcaid Images / Alamy

185 Courtesy of Pook and Pook Antiques

186 Courtesy of Associated Artists, LLC

187 Courtesy of Sotheby's, Inc. ©

187 Courtesy of Sotheby's, Inc. ©

188 Courtesy of Prelle Et Cie S.A.

188 Courtesy of Flavor Paper

190 © Robert Harding Picture Library Ltd / Alamy

195 © Arcaid Images / Alamy

196 © PrismaBildagentur AG / Alamy

197 Courtesy of H. Blairman And Sons Ltd

197 Courtesy of Phillips Auctioneers Llc

198 Courtesy of Phillips Auctioneers Llc

199 Courtesy of Sotheby's, Inc. ©

200 Courtesy of Associated Artists, LLC

201 Courtesy of Associated Artists, LLC

202 Courtesy of Associated Artists, LLC

204 Courtesy of Associated Artists, LLC

204 Courtesy of Associated Artists, LLC

207 © Dennis Cox / Alamy

208 ©TiborBognar / Alamy

209 © Michel Setboun / Corbis

210 Courtesy of Prelle Et Cie S.A.

210 Courtesy of Brunschwig & Fils®

215 © Arcaid Images / Alamy

Index